THE
BOOK OF
GARDEN
DESIGN

THE
BOOK OF
GARDEN
DESIGN

JOHN BROOKES

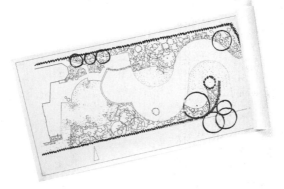

Macmillan • USA

A DORLING KINDERSLEY BOOK

Editor for the American edition Pam Hoenig
Location photographer Steven Wooster
Senior art editor Carole Ash
Project editor Sarah Pearce
Art editor Sarah Ponder
Designer Tracey Clarke
DTP designer Dawn Ryddner
Editors Laura Harper, Mark Ronan
Production manager Maryann Rogers
Managing editor Daphne Razazan
Managing art editor Anne-Marie Bulat

First published in Great Britain in 1991
by Dorling Kindersley Limited,
9 Henrietta Street, London WC2E 8PS

MACMILLAN
A Simon & Schuster Macmillan Company
1633 Broadway
New York, NY   10019 – 6785
MACMILLAN is a registered trademark of Macmillan, Inc.

Library of Congress Cataloging-in-Publication Data
Brookes. John. 1933-
    The book of garden design/John Brookes.
        p.   cm.
    "A Dorling Kindersley book."
    Includes index.
    ISBN 0-02-516695-6
    1. Gardens—Design. 2. Landscape architecture. 3. Landscape
gardening. I. Title.
SB473B723 1991
712'6—dc20   91-6843
                                                           CIP

10 9 8 7 6 5 4 3

Printed and bound in Singapore by Imago

CONTENTS

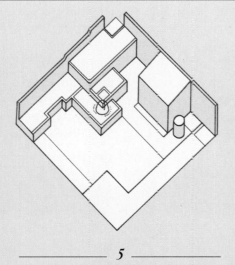

INTRODUCTION

In preparing a book such as this, based very much on practical experience and the lectures that I give, I am all too conscious how much easier it is to explain certain principles standing up than it is to write about them sitting down.

However, since both my editor, Sarah Pearce, and Carole Ash, my art editor, virtually had to do my five-week course which is the basis of this book (although in reality it took much longer in book preparation terms), I did feel that if they understood what I was saying, perhaps my readers would also. Incidentally, both graduated with distinction.

In order to get some rationale into such a book, the theoretical how's have to be accompanied by the philosophical why's, and also the practical do's, although I have kept these to a minimum; so if it takes time to get to the nuts and bolts of what specifically interests you, please bear with me. The other sections, believe me, *are* relevant; even if not directly to your immediate problem, they will, I hope, give food for thought for the alternatives to a future one.

To illustrate many of the points I make throughout the book, I have used gardens that I have built recently – some you will notice are very raw. To illustrate garden designs in climates where I have not worked, or techniques that are not my own, I have used other designers' work that I admire (listed on page 352). Now, all designers, including myself, get very edgy when their work is not credited, but because photographers do not always credit designers, it has not been possible to identify some. Budding landscape designers should note this and try to ensure that their work is always credited, for without this exposure who is to know of their excellence?

I hope that this book may go some way towards healing the breach between the horticulturalist and the garden designer; both, I believe, have much to say to the other, yet each, I suspect, does not comprehend what the other is about, all of which breeds suspicion. It is an understanding of the other's problems and viewpoint – not a coup of one over the other – that I would wish.

Finally, I would like to give credit to all my staff who run Denmans, with its increasing demands. For their long sufferance during my absences, mentally if not physically, during the preparation of this book, and for tolerating my petulances brought about by its added workload, I am indebted to them.

1
WHAT IS A GARDEN?

The influences that affect our ideas of a garden are diverse – they may be romantic or historical, they will certainly be geographical, and are dependent upon climate and altitude; hopefully they will be horticultural, even practical too! But where do design concepts fit in, and socioenvironmental movements? Whether we know it or not, aspects of contemporary life temper the ultimate look of the garden, and its place within a broader spectrum than that contained by the garden wall.

THE GARDEN IN ITS SETTING

Designing a garden, on one level, is the solving of various logistical problems — where to route a path, should the terrace be in sun or shade, how to integrate an area for children's play — to suit those who use it. As important and satisfying as this operation is, it will never provide the character that is the essence of a good garden, the secret ingredient to which we respond. This comes from what I call styling. But where does the feel of a garden come from? I believe that it should develop from the site in which the house sits. It is the relationship of the garden to its setting, both physically and intellectually, that ought to pervade every aspect of the design.

The Traditional Way

National and regional styles of garden were traditionally born out of their site; their shape and the materials that formed them were of the region, since transporting materials over any distance was unthinkable. It was difficult to make a garden that was not an expression of the physical geology of an area. Nowadays it is worth thinking through the link between your garden and its setting.

The shape of the landscape above ground level as well as the character of rock, subsoil, and topsoil is the result of geological formations and of the weather. These factors affect drainage, soil texture, and ultimately an area's streams and rivers.

Flora, from herbs to forest trees, and fauna are both expressions of the physical characteristics of a region. In rural areas, the look of the land will have been further influenced by farming and other forms of land management to reveal field patterns, hedges, walls, gates, and fences. As a result, there will be a tradition of vernacular building styles and materials to inspire you when it comes to creating your own garden style.

View to fields, left
A mature country garden in its Sussex setting. Loose arrangements of mixed decorative planting lead past a native whitebeam to the view of fields beyond.

Informal planting, above
Here planting in the form of fox-gloves in gravel has fused with surfacing to create, if not a wild look, certainty one more relaxed than the traditional border-flanked path.

Urban setting, right
The ambience of this urban rooftop garden seems the antithesis of the country garden opposite, yet it too is thoroughly of its setting. From this sanctuary the roofscape of New York City can be contemplated.

Garden in a landscape, right
Landscape has been fused with garden in this Oxfordshire design – the artificial reach of water providing the dividing line. The lake (which is clay lined) has provided a reason for opening out the garden and allowing the view to come in.

You might think that in a city or suburban setting the physical character of a place does not apply, but it is a salutary exercise to consider that if you were to lift a paving slab from the pavement in the center of any city, under it there is soil – in fact "dirt" is a more relevant term since this soil has been so manipulated that any organic quality is probably missing. Nevertheless, research into a site's soil and drainage and an awareness of its potential flora and fauna are always relevant, though the visual value of an urban site is not so obvious as in the country. While you will not be looking at field patterns and horizons, you will become conscious of views in and out of the site, and of exciting vegetation in the gardens nearby.

New Directions

There is now, without a doubt, a concern for making gardens that merge with their settings, a concern linked with today's heightened ecological awareness. The wildflower garden in Great Britain and the prairie garden look of the United States are good examples of this. These garden styles merge beautifully with their surroundings, particularly where shaped land forms help to integrate the garden into its landscape.

It is the use and styling of native plants that give a garden its local flavor. The natural look for a garden was proposed early in this century in the work of Jens Jensen (an associate of the architect Frank Lloyd Wright), who was interested in the native plant material of Illinois at a time when landscape designers generally were oriented towards the beaux-arts school of garden architecture. At about the same time and at the other end of the world, an Australian woman, Edna Walling, was beginning to encourage the gardeners of western Victoria to look at their natural landscapes, for, bizarre though it might seem, the English tradition did, and still does, pervade the country gardens of that part of the world.

Other designers have manipulated the landscape through shaping, planting, and architecture to bond the environmental relationship. Ian Hamilton Finlay has used stark Scottish backdrops, opened up woodlands, and composed with reeds and rushes to site his carved classical pieces of sculpture to spectacular effect. Luis Barragan, a Mexican architect/designer, has built some glorious complexes whose form and coloring lift the heart whenever one sees them illustrated, and in Brazil some of the larger compositions of Roberto Burle Marx integrate themselves into their landscape with supreme mastery. In South Africa the landscape architect Patrick Watson has introduced modernity into his gardens, while maintaining a truly African styling in flora.

There are many others working in this field, the content of their work being far stronger than the word *styling* suggests. They successfully combine tradition with the modernist's eye to produce a look and a feeling that interpret the mood of the period in their particular location.

Plant Material and Design

With the planting design comes the stage that many garden designers find most inspiring. We all have our own chief interests. For myself it is design with line, and the shapes described that make a pattern, that never fails to attract and to stimulate. For others it is plants – their arrangement sometimes, but mostly the *growing* of plants themselves. Surely this is an expression of a very basic attachment to nature which we all share to some degree. But while plants affect us as the strongest element in a landscape or garden, in the evolution of a garden plan they are introduced towards the end of the process. First must come the layout, which provides the vessel for them.

There is a chronology in the introduction of plant material which the astute plantsman may consult to match period buildings, and indeed there are now conservation societies that seek out plants of a period, researching and preserving their particular characteristics. Some are trying to breed back the many Victorian flowering garden plants that have disappeared, for example. Most of us, however, are happy to work with the available range of plants, only loosely classifying them by period.

"Real" Gardens

Whereas British and American period styles of gardening have developed at different times to reflect newly available foreign plant material, some national garden styles have remained pure in terms of the selection of plants used. Good gardens from these traditions are hugely inspiring for those of us keen to make gardens right for their setting. The Italian garden, for instance, has many forms according to period but broadly its plant range is the same. The same may be said of styles of the north of France, and those using the Mediterranean palette of plant material in the south. California gardens have always been planted with what will grow naturally and therefore survive in the climatic conditions. The success of such "real" gardens now makes the concept of the native garden – desert, tropical, water, scrub, alpine, or just wild – the desirable norm rather than the exception.

The horticulturalist seeks to grow as much material as possible, whatever the location. The peppering of different plant forms and colors does not disturb, nor does the juxtapositioning of, say, a yucca from Mexico against a bergenia from Siberia. At the other extreme the conservationist has a rightful concern for native vegetation. But selecting only native species for urban situations might look just as bizarre. English natives, for example, generally lack visual strength and appear weak when planted next to buildings.

We must steer a middle course between selecting from plants that are easy to obtain, and our own developing instinct as to the utility and look of more native species. It is an interesting path to tread, but not an impossible one, as I hope you will see through the pages of this book.

Mediterranean context, left
A garden that is truly of its setting, and proclaims it in its styling details and its planting. The cypress and olive trees woven into the design feature strongly, as they do in the natural landscape.

South American context, left
Another approach to designing for a setting: here native plant material is grouped in broad, patterned, brightly colored masses, the masses in scale with the surrounding land forms and the wild vegetation.

A HISTORY OF THE GARDEN

I t seems almost obligatory to begin a book on garden design with an historical analysis, for the past must be a major source and a basis for informed thought on the subject. But no historical review can see garden design in isolation. Each style is the product of its social environment; each shift in approach reflects a change in man's concerns and ideals. What particularly fascinates me is the way the pendulum has swung back and forth between the desire to push nature out, and the need to include her as an integral part of the design.

THE ISLAMIC GARDEN

Enclosure, water, sanctuary, and shade – these are the elements and the legacy of the Islamic style. The garden was perceived as a world deliberately set apart, removed from the daily concerns of nomadic desert life; it was a place where the sight and sound of water played an important role.

Given the harshness of the desert environment it is no surprise that the ideal – the paradise garden of the Koran – was rarely achieved. Its form, a quartered garden dissected by a cruciform canal, was comparatively easy to realize where there was water. Abundant planting must have presented a larger problem, requiring trees for both shade and fruit, with pavilions for pleasure set, at least in contemporary illustrations, among carpets of flowers. Coolness was brought into the heart of a building by enclosing the garden within colonnades. Inner and outer space came together in a way that appealed to the Islamic sense of volume, and which enhanced the ever-changing perception of space with decoration, brought about by the interplay of light and shade.

Mogul miniature, above
The pavilion is surrounded by
a squared pattern of irrigation channels which water a
flower garden.

The cruciform pattern, left
and far left
The quartered garden, divided
by water channels, is represented repeatedly in Islamic
art forms – to the left in a
Persian carpet pattern. The
paradise concept was realized
in the garden of the Generalife
above the Alhambra in
Granada. The view is from a
three-story tower from which
one can experience cool
summer breezes above the
heady scent of citrus and the
murmur of fountains in the
garden below.

THE FORMAL GARDEN

Man is center stage in the formal garden tradition, his perception of space being ordered according to the classic principles of geometry, proportion, and symmetry. This is garden design's ultimate construct, a vision of order stamped firmly upon the landscape, which became a universal style adopted and imitated in all the courts of Europe. Its origins are in the vibrant society of renaissance Italy.

The style evolved slowly. Geometrical designs with symmetrical planting came first, advocated by

Boboli gardens
Characteristic of the late Italian Renaissance, the Boboli gardens behind the Pitti Palace in Florence has grand statuary and balustrades creating focal points and vistas, fountains, and exquisitely contrived spaces.

early Florentines, although based on the written descriptions of the gardens of ancient Rome. By the mid-sixteenth century patterned planting was common, with whole gardens planned around circles, squares, triangles, pentagons, or hexagons; plantings of short-lived herbs gave way to parterres of box. One highly influential work as far as layout was concerned was Bramante's plan, commissioned in 1503, for Pope Julius II's garden in Rome, linking the Villa Belvedere to the Papal palace. Building into the hillside, Bramante chose to heighten the drama of the site by creating a dominant central perspective with steps constructed across the run of the ground. The garden had moved from a static gridiron pattern on flat ground to a directional flow through an axis across a slope.

The two centuries that followed saw many variations on these themes in Italy and later in France, where water and tree cover played a larger role. Supreme among all the gardens are the creations of André Le Nôtre for Louis XIV. Le Nôtre's feel for unity, balance, and proportion, his insistence on sunlit spaces and unimpeded vistas, brought the French garden to a peak of classical perfection.

The grand formal tradition, left
The grand scale upon which the garden at Versailles was conceived is suggested in this engraving. The design deliberately sets the garden apart from nature to demonstrate the status of its owner.

Complex geometry
The plan of the gardens around this pavilion shows the geometry of the formal layout.

THE LANDSCAPE GARDEN

Nature was the model for the eighteenth-century garden park in England, although it was nature idealized; to borrow Horace Walpole's words on William Kent, the first practitioner of the landscape style, designers "leaped the fence and saw all nature was a garden." Such a sentiment reflected a philosophical change, for man now saw himself as a part of the universe and not superior to it.

Britain's great garden designers of the period, William Kent, "Capability" Brown, and later Humphrey Repton, sought to clear the area around the house of its post-medieval knots and pleasure gardens leading to views, and so run meadow right up to the house to enable it to sit proud in an open, lawned space. Around this lay an idealized landscape of woodland, water, and statuary under a play of light and shade. A concealed ditch, or ha-ha, dissuaded deer and cattle from too close an association with the new class of landowner, but without interrupting views from the house. With clumps of largely native trees grouped to conceal boundaries and repeated in the farmland beyond, and with the odd inconvenient village resited and rivers dammed to create artificial lakes, the park seemed to roll on forever in one glorious, unimpeded sweep.

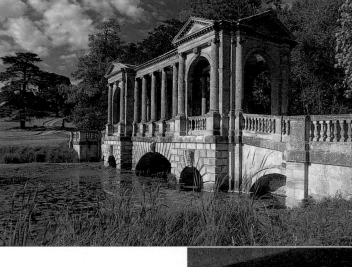

Nature improved
The setting of Harewood House in Yorkshire, painted by J. M. W. Turner (far right), *is typical of a late eighteenth-century layout. The house sits proud above its meadow, which descends to a stretch of water; trees and plantings are grouped and massed to increase the apparent area of grazed land. At Stowe in Buckinghamshire a Palladian bridge* (right) *provides an equally typical eye-catcher, or amusing incident, within the overall* pastorale.

COUNTRY STYLE

A country mood
*The characteristic herbaceous border
of the Edwardian country garden.*

Although the eighteenth century sought to tame the landscape, it was not until the end of the next century that the new breed of horticulturalist sought to work with it. This transition came after a period of hectic artificiality, of novelty in new exotic species, and hybridization techniques.

A key figure was Gertrude Jekyll, following the lead of William Robinson. Jekyll wrote of what she saw as the vanishing style of the rural cottage garden, and its place within the countryside. Later, in association with the architect Sir Edwin Lutyens, she created plantings within his classic garden layouts using groupings of perennials and non-exotic trees and shrubs; and in classic literature on planting design, she described these natural harmonies of color and shape in foliage and flower. Her thinking was incorporated into many of the essentially inward-looking gardens of the early twentieth century, such as Sissinghurst in Kent.

The style has been attempted worldwide, although with time the labor-intensive plantings emphasized horticultural expertise at the expense of design. Jekyll herself had a true sense of location, but her work now seems interpreted through a deadening veil of nostalgia.

A MODERN LOOK

While in Britain the country garden style became the overriding influence on a generation of garden designers at the turn of the century, in North America a wholly new concept was emerging. In lieu of herbaceous borders and intricate plant groupings, the new ethic was public spaces designed for maximum use and enjoyment. It was more a dialogue between architectural shape and landscape form than a look for the horticulturalist, although eventually it came together with domestic garden themes and modern movement ideas to create a new vocabulary for garden designers to explore.

Frederick Law Olmsted's design for Central Park in New York began the process in the second half of the nineteenth century with an asymmetrical, fluid plan encompassing a range of different public areas. With Olmsted's work came the new discipline of landscape architecture.

By the late 1930s the tenets of modernism had been absorbed into landscape thinking in Britain with, among other events, the publication of *Gardens in a Modern Landscape* (1938) by the landscape architect Christopher Tunnard. His ideas were later adopted by H.F. Clark and synthesized with a theory for Britain's new postwar landscape: it was to be based upon function and utility, provide for activity and relaxation, and avoid axial planning and monumental construction. Such principles have been a potent force in modern garden design.

It was in 1930s' America where the truly innovative thinking took place. The theater of garden

Rus in urbe
*Central Park, New York, was a
visionary landscape within the city.*

Modernism in a landscape
The work of Thomas Church has been one of my great influences. The simplicity and fluidity of line of his designs synthesize the natural forms that surround the garden with a dynamic new approach. This garden is in Sonoma County outside San Francisco.

design had decamped there, following the Bauhaus and the leading modernist thinkers. There evolved, via the silver screen and the garden settings of Hollywood, a new interpretation of the Spanish patio as an outside stage for affluent entertaining and general socializing. One key figure was Thomas Church, who crystallized a new garden look of modernist principles in conjunction with the California ranch house. His country garden layouts were often of abstract shapes molded within a landscape view, some exhibiting the timeless simplicity of an eighteenth-century landscape park. Other leaders in the American field were — and still are — Dan Kiley, James Rose, Garret Eckbo, and Lawrence Halprin, while the Brazilian Roberto Burle Marx has produced extraordinary fluid landscapes realized with massed groupings of tropical plants.

Postwar Europe saw affluence coupled with huge programs of social and urban renewal; with this came a new awareness of the town house, its adjoining small garden an extension of the space within. The garden as "outside room" was conceived — not the gracious horticultural space of the Edwardian garden, but rather more along the California lines of usable space — and this presented garden designers with a new set of imperatives. It was with this shift towards the acceptance of smaller garden spaces that I began designing. Other social changes influenced my work too: the loss of a domestic labor force and the expansion of leisure pursuits have created a need for low-maintenance gardening — and hence garden designs to match.

Today, I see the garden starting to look outwards again, seeking to establish its own identity within its location. It is an ecological, environmental approach, visible in the wilder look of many gardens: a desire to manage a property rather than enclose it with alien plants, a use of bolder groupings of native trees and shrubs in scale with the countryside that backs them, and an enthusiasm for the wildflower meadow and the informal plantings of gravel gardens. The garden is still, as it ever was, a retreat, but it is no longer a retreat from the "awefulness" of nature; rather, it is a retreat from the awfulness of the twentieth-century manifestations of man himself.

A new look, above
Much current thinking on garden design is evident in this modern Dutch garden; the strong ground plan, related to the building, contrasts with the semi-wild plant forms.

My terrace in Sussex, left
It is into this space that I look whenever I am at home. It is used for summer entertaining, and in winter I just enjoy its shapes, which constantly change, for surrounding the paved terrace are gravel areas in which I allow plants to romp and self-seed. Contrasted with a philosophy of wildness is a love of architectural plantings when used with structural shapes. The combination of the two is the essence of my "look."

CLIMATIC VARIATIONS

C limate is a major determining factor in any design philosophy, for plants and gardens look best when they have an affinity with the area in which they lie. Plants that are native to their area obviously have the greatest sympathy with their surroundings, and could therefore be said to be in style with them.

Most plants can tolerate conditions on either side of their optimum, so their use in other climates is certainly possible, but has to be practical as well.

Within the overall picture there are variations, and every garden will have its own microclimate. Location, exposure, wind, altitude, and topography all contribute, as do local factors such as exposure to salt spray. In cities, the temperature is higher than in the surrounding countryside, and rainfall could be reduced since buildings can block it.

TEMPERATE CLIMATE

The temperate climate is typified by a lack of extremes, making growing conditions favorable for an immense range of plants, including many successful alien imports. The climate is typically damp, with mild winters and cool summers. Seasonal variations are marked, with a long spring and autumn.

Regions enjoying an oceanic temperate climate include Britain and northern Europe, parts of Scandinavia, parts of the west coast of Canada and eastern United States, the Pacific Northwest, New Zealand (South Island), Tasmania, and, in Australia, eastern Victoria and New South Wales. Within large land masses the influence of the ocean is much reduced. Rainfall is generally lower, winters colder, often with prolonged periods of snow, and summers hotter and drier; this type of climate is found in a broad belt across the northern and central United States, and in continental Asia.

Spring bulbs
Strong seasonal differences are a feature of the temperate climate. This wild carpet of color has daisies, bluebells, and rough grass, with some civilizing lily-flowered tulips pushing through.

Summer verdure
The typical soft, lush, overwhelmingly green look of the temperate climate. Alchemilla mollis, ferns, deciduous trees and shrubs, trimmed lawn, and grazing meadows make up this summer scene. To the left is a cedar of Lebanon (Cedrus libani).

TYPICAL PLANTS

Acer
Aconitum
Carpinus
Carya
Cytisus
Erythronium
Fagus
Fraxinus
Geranium
Hypericum
Liquidambar
Pinus
Primula
Quercus
Ranunculus
Sorbus

Late summer, Maryland
Late summer and autumn in temperate climates have great visual strength. Ornamental grasses are at their best – here Calamagrostis x acutiflora 'Karl Foerster' *in the background, and* Pennisetum orientale. *Both these and the* Sedum 'Autumn Joy' *will retain dramatic dead seed heads and stems through the winter months.*

Within such a widely spread climatic type, variations are many, yet temperate vegetation has a typical appearance. Many trees and shrubs are deciduous, with many bulbs flowering in spring before the leaf canopy develops. In summer the vegetation is green and soft-looking with few emphatic statements. There is an enormous range of wildflowers, making a typical meadow tapestry, although this aspect is probably even more characteristic of both continental and subalpine areas. Grass is a valuable and dominant feature.

The type of soil influences the vegetation. In Europe, for example, oak and sycamore make up much of the woodland on heavy clay soils, while on sandy acid soils pine trees grow with brooms and heathers beneath. On chalky uplands yew, box, and juniper form a low evergreen covering, with beech often the dominant tree. Ash woodland is typical of harder limestone areas.

Since the temperate climate is so favorable, it follows that the land has been intensively farmed in Europe for generations. Natural stands of vegetation are now rare without conservation initiatives to allow them to reestablish.

The temperate regions in the United States have a richer palette than those of Europe, with many more species of oak, maple, and other genera such as *Liquidambar* and *Carya*. The forests of temperate parts of the Far East are also rich in species and are sources of a wide range of garden plants.

Autumn color
The conifer here is temporarily eclipsed by the dramatic colors of the maple and sedum, but will soon come into its own as a winter form.

SUBALPINE CLIMATE

My concern here is the climate found at the highest altitudes and latitudes at which trees will grow. Such regions include the alpine areas of southern Europe (Switzerland, Austria, and northern Italy), parts of western North America (the Sierra Nevada in California and the Canadian Rockies), and the mountainous areas of New Zealand. All these areas have extreme winter conditions and brief summer growing seasons. Climatic and temperature variations are enormous, with cold winters and hot, bright summers; at the beginning and end of the growing season, temperatures can vary widely even within a single day, making this an extremely taxing climate in which to garden. This is principally a zone of summer gardens.

The plants found in colder parts of the world are usually deciduous, and small-leaved or needle-leaved. The birch and alder are common, as they can withstand both great cold and great heat. Acid soil prevails. Where the land becomes waterlogged, mosses — and very little else — grow in abundance. Peat bogs occur in these areas of extremes.

Away from boggy or tree-covered areas, heaths, heathers, gorse, and brambles are among the few plants able to survive the extreme conditions.

The true alpine in horticultural terms grows in well-drained ground probably at a higher altitude still, above the tree line. All are specially adapted for the climatic and soil conditions, and similarly their cultivated forms require excellent drainage and bright light to thrive. Many alpines, such as saxifrage, gentian, and spring crocus, have evolved brightly colored flowers, large in relation to the rest of the plant, to attract early insects and so achieve swift pollination — essential in such a truncated growing season.

Garden of alpines
The dense, low, flower-specked mats of alpine plants are a fascination for gardeners in alpine and temperate climates. Generous slabs provide the necessary drainage and make this an unusually stylish rock garden.

Alpine meadow
A speckled, richly colored matrix of spring flowers is characteristic of the alpine meadow. Here poppies, ox eye daisies, buttercups, and geraniums grow at 6,000ft (2,000m) in a European alpine region.

TYPICAL PLANTS

Alnus
Androsace
Arabis
Betula
Crocus
Gentiana
Linnaea
Pedicularis
Picea
Pinus
Populus
Pulsatilla
Salix
Saxifraga
Sorbus
Vaccinium

MEDITERRANEAN CLIMATE

It is the timing of rainfall that really conditions what will grow in this climatic zone. Most rain falls in winter and autumn; summer rainfall is very low, and summer temperatures rise to 98.6°F (37°C). Most plants are, therefore, dormant in summer, and spring and early autumn, when the weather is still warm but rain more plentiful, are the main growing seasons.

The southern Soviet Union and the Balkans both have a Mediterranean climate, as does, of course, the Mediterranean region itself, including the Middle East. Other areas with a similar climate are California, parts of Chile, the southwest Cape in South Africa and parts of southern Australia, particularly the southwest.

Around the Mediterranean, typical plants are evergreen oaks, the spirelike Mediterranean cypress, the stone pine with its umbrella-shaped canopy, and the olive tree. In some areas, maquis is a strong feature – low evergreen thicket or bush made up of various shrubs, including strawberry tree, juniper, *Quercus coccifera*, santolina, and rock rose. Many of the common culinary herbs originate in this climatic zone and artichokes, sunflowers, and vines overhead are all strongly characteristic crops.

In a Mediterranean climate, lawns grow only with irrigation for they cannot withstand the summer drought; where irrigated they look incongruous and are, therefore, best avoided.

Classic forms
The Mediterranean cypress has to be one characteristic symbol of this climate. In the hotter regions the date palm begins to make an appearance.

TYPICAL PLANTS

Arbutus
Asphodelus
Bougainvillea
Cistus
Crocus
Cupressus
Juniperus
Muscari
Olea
Ophrys
Pinus pinea
Plumbago
Quercus coccifera
Quercus ilex
Santolina
Spartium
Tulipa
Viburnum

Color splashes
The bright sunlight of the Mediterranean summer produces profuse quantities of color-saturated flowers. Plumbago auriculata *and* Nerium oleander *feature here.*

33

DESERT CLIMATE

A desert is not necessarily hot all the year — but it is dry, usually with an annual rainfall of less than 10in (250mm). Central Australia is desert, and deserts occupy vast tracts of land in northern and southwestern Africa, the Middle East, central Asia, western coastal South America, and southwestern United States. Some of these regions also have average summer temperatures above 95°F (35°C).

Pure desert is not an area in which to garden, nor is it indeed a place where many people would choose to live. Yet where water is introduced by man and the desert harshness is alleviated by vegetation, the dry air and crystal-clear light are very attractive. Large areas of desert in the southwestern United States are now being increasingly colonized, often to make second homes as a refuge from the winter tedium of the northern states. It is not appropriate, though, merely to import the horticultural norms of suburbia: making the desert grow decoratively with bright green grass and bougainvillea only serves to reduce the visual vigor of the landscape.

True desert planting has enormous visual strength. The plants have a range of characteristics to reduce transpiration, including a waxy leaf surface that reduces water loss, leaves that roll up tightly in the heat, or even no leaves at all, and hairy leaves and stems to provide insulation. Many are succulent and are able to store large quantities of water. The result of these adaptations is a range of sometimes extraordinary plants, often of attractive or architectural form. They include mesquite, prickly pear, yucca, artemisia, and tamarisk.

Rainfall in a desert region is unpredictable in timing and quantity but after it comes the desert often blooms with a myriad of wildflowers.

Architectural forms
In desert regions with no native architecture to echo, modernist buildings can make play with strong lines softened by exuberant desert plantings. This garden design in Arizona features prickly pear, ocotillo, and yucca.

California style
Prickly pear, well adapted as a water storage unit, in a planting composed of strong forms and bright colors; both these features are typical of hotter desert regions.

TROPICAL CLIMATE

I have to confess to never having gardened in this hot climate, which can be broadly divided into humid and dry zones. Within the humid tropics, rainfall is frequent and heavy, sometimes daily and sometimes seasonal, and temperatures remain high throughout the year.

Subtropical regions of the world include the southeastern states of the United States and parts of Mexico, South America, Japan, China, the Pacific Islands, and Australia. They experience exceptionally mild winters and hot summers.

What is common throughout the tropics and subtropics is that the combination of moisture and heat encourages a tremendous rate of growth, with plants characterized by their lush appearance. Many have exaggerated leaf forms, and flowers tend to be highly colored.

The tropical rain forests are the source of many stunning horticultural plants of all sizes and forms. Ferns, orchids, and bromeliads (members of the pineapple family) perch in the branches of the canopy; these are all epiphytes, adapted to living on other plants. Climbers, including passion flowers and clerodendrum, stretch from ground level to the treetops. Among the brightly colored flowering shrubs, some of the more well-known are hibiscus and frangipani, while the herbaceous plants include aechmea and heliconia.

The subtropical garden
Large, lush leaves and the feeling of active growth among all plant life is a feature of subtropical regions. Plants and foliage seem to burst from any crevice where they can get a hold in this Florida garden.

Vibrant color

Bromeliads make up a large proportion of subtropical plants; top right is Guzmania lingulata, *below*, Aechmea fasciata. *On the left is flaming sword* (Vriesea splencens).

TYPICAL PLANTS

Aechmea
Allemanda
Anthurium
Billbergia
Cattleya
Chamaedorea
Clerodendrum
Hedychium
Hibiscus
Monstera
Passiflora
Platycerium
Plumeria

2
LEARNING TO DESIGN

Nothing is ever designed in isolation; things do not just happen, there has to be a set of rules governing the patterns we evolve for a garden plan, in order that the ultimate layout will be pleasing as well as workable. This chapter is both a discipline and a release, teaching you how to build a framework and then to appreciate the variety you can create within it.

DESIGN PRINCIPLES

An understanding of the ways shapes relate to each other is at the very heart of garden design, for it is the underlying abstract shapes that give a garden its visual strength. The first essential step is to take off your horticultural blinders and begin to conceive the design as a series of abstract shapes. Only later do you decide what practical form the shapes will take, and start to bring together the organic and inorganic garden elements: soil, plants, water, brick, and stone.

Both natural and man-made objects influence my thinking – not that I ever translate them literally into a design, but they do constantly refresh my awareness of the relationship of shape, line, and proportion. Some of the objects and works of art that have inspired me are shown on the right.

Compositions Outside

Proportion is as important in garden design as in any other type of design. Most people have an eye for putting together shapes in the home: whether you are arranging a group of pictures, or furniture, you can instantly see if the arrangement is pleasing or if the furniture looks uncomfortably crowded. Yet somehow when it comes to the garden that visual capacity tends to vanish, even though the process is more or less the same – moving elements – albeit on a larger scale.

You may not be aware of it, but when arranging objects you are seeking a balance between the masses (a sofa or picture, for example) and the spaces (the wall or the floor). The harmony between masses and spaces is embodied in the ancient Chinese principles of yin and yang (negative and positive). I think of the garden masses (the planting or the structural features) as the "positives" and the spaces between them (the grass or paving) as the "negatives," and the balance between the two is an important factor in my garden designs.

Looking at shape and line
Garden designs are conceived as arrangements of abstract shapes; modern buildings and paintings, some natural objects, the rural and urban landscape, and the yin-yang symbol above can each give insight into the all-important relationship between shape and line.

PROPORTION

Proportionate shapes
Shapes evolving from, and proportionate to, the house create a sense of balance and harmony.

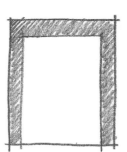

Disproportionate shapes
A dull plan. The narrow border relates to the boundary; the house is not linked to its garden space.

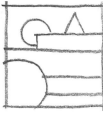

Abstract shapes
This garden concept illustrates how striking even a small space can be. It is the basic shapes (shown in outline, above) and the balance between the masses (plants, walls, and trees) and the spaces (the ground surface) that are of primary importance. Start by thinking in terms of abstract shape and only decide what form the shapes will take once you have a basic pattern.

ARRANGING SHAPES

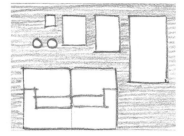

Making a composition
A satisfactory and balanced composition using shapes of different sizes is somehow instinctive in the home.

Altered impression
The impression is changed simply by reversing the relationship of the white spaces and dark masses.

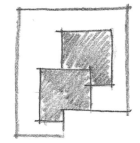

Central impact
As with interior design, so in garden design you need to construct a balanced composition from proportionate shapes.

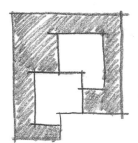

Boundary impact
Simply by changing the relationship between the masses and the spaces you can alter the composition

If you can start to get the relationship between positive masses and negative spaces correct, then your garden layout will start to look coherent. For example, think of your lawn as a negative space, but ensure that the positive masses that surround it, such as the planting beds or terrace, do not crowd it out or pinch it. It is often the relationship between the bulk and shape of the positive masses in a garden, contrasted with the open areas, that makes us feel enfolded, and to which we relate so favorably in a well-designed layout.

Starting Afresh

Later on you will need to consider practicalities, but for the time being think of your garden as an empty space and your only limiting factor its boundaries. A house *on* a blank space is simply *on* its site; your objective is to bring garden masses together to furnish the garden and make the house seem to be *in* its site. So think of the hard structures and the blocks of planting as furniture which you can position to balance harmoniously with the open spaces.

To get a feel for how radically you can change your garden, banishing all trace of what is there at the moment, try the simple exercise on the right. Imagine your garden as a stage and your house as a major prop, with the garden scenery coming in from the wings. As you compose different stage sets, you will start to see your garden's design potential emerging. On the stage you can use different elements, such as blocks of planting, to alter the foreground picture, the middle distance, and your perception of a distant view. As you build up a composition of shapes, it is important to think about the broad masses as well as the strong linear forms of the design.

Designing a garden, as opposed to just planting it, gives you the power to control the space you have before you. The way you perceive a garden space is determined by the juxtaposition of the different elements in it which divide the view into several layers (this effect is illustrated on the opposite page, top right). Quite often you can control the way you look at a view with something as simple as an arch.

GARDEN COMPOSITIONS

Making arrangements from a series of images on tracing paper shows how you can mold a landscape. In reality you might choose quite different features.

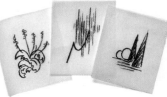

Landscape outline
Start by sketching the broad outlines of a view. Don't be too ambitious, just draw a simple silhouette.

Adding a building
On a piece of tracing paper draw the outline of a building. Sketch abstract forms of trees on other sheets.

Start a composition
Put the sketches together to try out different compositions. Notice my trees are not botanical drawings – my willow here conveys the essence of the shape only.

Foreground interest
On another sheet sketch in the outline of an architectural plant – mine is an acanthus with large leaves and spiky flowers – and move it around to create a foreground.

Layered landscape
Bring the house in its setting together with your trees and architectural plant in many different permutations, so that you begin to understand the layered effect of a landscape composition.

Another alternative
After doing several versions you will realize the potential you have to transform the design of your garden by altering the foreground, the middle distance, and the far view.

Parts of a view, above
A simple sketched and shaded outline identifies the foreground, middle distance, and far view of the garden shown on the left.

Altered impression, above
Changing the foreground features can transform a garden. The arch that frames this view increases the garden's apparent depth.

Manipulating space, left
The interlocking "layers" of interest – the planting and different types of trees – direct the eye to the point at which the path disappears from view.

SHAPES IN A SETTING

As the previous pages show, one of the first steps in designing a garden is to think in terms of shape. But which shapes? Where do you start? Look first at the surrounding landscape, for your composition of shapes should sit comfortably within this.

In the country the forms of the natural landscape can be echoed in the shapes used in the garden. A view of sharply angled field patterns, for example, might call for a sharply angled garden plan. But contrasts can work as well, as long as there is an underlying sense of proportion and the effect is strong enough to provide real visual excitement.

At the other end of the spectrum lies the man-made urban landscape. Here, you cannot rely on natural landscape forms, so you need to look for other strong design parameters. City gardens may be surrounded by high boundaries and the hard lines of other buildings. In this sort of setting, patterns with a geometry in them are visually more satisfying (and geometry does not mean just shapes with straight lines; it includes circles, or segments of circles, as well).

Scale is also important. In any setting, rural, urban, or suburban, the house will suggest the scale of the shapes you use in your design, for garden plans should always be proportionally linked to the proportions of the house. A design for a garden adjacent to a ranch house, for example, should probably contain smaller elements than one beneath an apartment building.

Linear interpretation
The strength of this composition of natural and man-made forms comes from its vertical and horizontal patterning. The vertical lines of the slender woodland trees which form the
backdrop to the clean horizontal lines of the house are restated in the verticals of the bold clumps of grasses in the foreground. The simplicity of the house throws the planting into sharp relief.

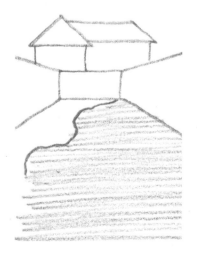

URBAN SETTINGS

In urban sites the geometry of boundaries and buildings should be reflected in the garden's design. Loose shapes are visually incompatible with such a cityscape and serve only to lead the eye to the boundary. But geometrical shapes (including small curves and circles) in proportion to the surroundings will blend visually and keep interest within the site.

RURAL SETTINGS

Echoing curves, left
In a country setting, let the forms of the natural landscape guide you in your choice of shapes. A gently rounded landscape calls for flowing shapes within the garden.

Reinterpreting angles, right
The strong, sharp shapes of distant conifers and mountains are captured in the zigzag of the path (which also reinterprets the angle of the roof).

Inspiration from nature
The shape of the cedar tree's branches which frame the view could have inspired the angular shapes used in this garden landscape, for the strong horizontals of the pool, the path, and the hedge are dominated by the horizontal line of the tree.

VISUAL DEVICES

Just as a dark color brings the end wall of a long room closer visually, there are a number of special visual devices that can be used to alter the apparent dimensions of a garden. There are some more general design principles, too.

Natural perspective makes parallel lines appear to converge, until they join at the vanishing point. But suppose you "redraw" these lines, making them physically converge or draw apart? These are devices that have been used by the designers of the great classic gardens to make a space look, respectively, longer or shorter. Similarly, you can make a narrow space appear wider by incorporating strong horizontals in the design.

Manipulating the Eye

Success in governing how the eye travels around the garden relies not only on a design's linear or ground patterning but on focal points which punctuate the garden layout rather like punctuation marks in a piece of writing. In a small garden there might be one visual sentence and the period might be a bench, whereas larger gardens might comprise a number of sentences complete with commas, and the period might be a view (in classic gardens it was often a vista).

Some gardens have an unavoidable eyesore such as an oil tank. With decorative screening it is all too easy to do the opposite of what you intended; a vine-covered trellis, for example, will only serve to *attract* the eye. Far better to place an intended focal point elsewhere and hide the ugly feature with a solid screen. High boundaries or a neighboring eyesore can be a problem too, for they draw the eye out of the garden. To anchor the eye in the site you will need a design that makes a strong three-dimensional composition, in which the elements are in scale with the boundary.

Increasing length
This short, high-walled entrance area is made to appear longer than it is by the small-scale fish sculpture which demands long-distance focus and the pale, receding pink.

L INEAR PATTERNING

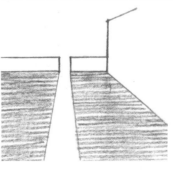

Long, straight lines
Parallel lines that run down the length of a site, for example in the form of a path, appear to draw together, thereby making the garden look longer; but they also divide it into three dull blocks.

Adding horizontal interest
A far better option is to stagger the shape of a path to integrate it with the areas on either side. This adds interest, while detracting little from the visual pull and without impeding physical access.

Point of focus
*Focal points serve to attract
attention to chosen areas, while
perhaps diverting attention
from others, and if they are as
striking as this clipped "window," they have an almost
magnetic effect. By allowing
the eye to take in some of the
view beyond, the window
prevents the garden from
seeming too enclosed, without
sacrificing privacy.*

Sense of space, above
*The emphatic horizontals of these steps
made from railroad ties create a sideways
movement, making the path's dimensions
look generous.*

Gentle horizontals, left
*The horizontal patterning of the flagstones
and the plants that flop over them ensure
the eye moves from side to side, rather than
down the path.*

KEEPING INTEREST IN A SITE

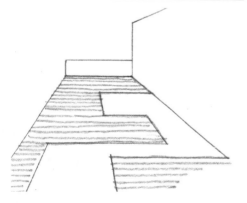

Bold shapes
*In urban gardens aim for a geometrical
design that is bold enough to keep interest
in the garden. Shapes with strong lateral
lines lead the eye in a gentle progression
down the site.*

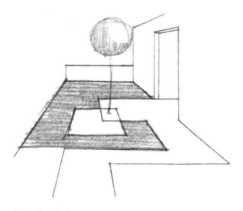

Vertical features
*Adding a tree and an arch in the wall starts
to give the two-dimensional ground pattern
vertical interest. Don't scale down the
elements, even in a small garden. Use fewer
of them, and use them boldly.*

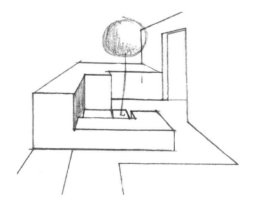

Bulking out the shapes
*Building up the design and bulking out the
shapes so that there is plenty of three-
dimensional interest prevent the small
garden from being overpowered by the
surrounding buildings.*

THE LANGUAGE OF DESIGN

Drawings enable you to formulate, express, and develop your sense of design until finally the garden is built and planted. Among the types of technical drawings you need to be able to prepare are plans, sections, and projections, which are all drawn to scale and are crucial for the accurate planning and construction of everything on the site. Between them they provide all the information that you, and any surveyor, contractor, or builder, may need. You will also be speaking the same language as an architect, with whom you may be in association. The schematic plan, which is the first drawing of the garden's design, shows only the main proposed features and planting areas. All subsequent drawings are based on this plan.

Many people are alarmed by the idea of making technical drawings – needlessly. They demand no particular artistic skill, for each type of technical drawing evolves in a logical sequence. Producing a freehand sketch is also, mistakenly, often seen as an obstacle. Yet it is an invaluable way to visualize new ideas. If sketching does not come naturally, or does not improve with practice, use the alternative procedure shown below.

Schematic plan
The first and most important drawing you will make of your garden's design. It must be accurate and to scale, as from this all your detailed drawings will derive.

The part of the plan shown in section starts here and runs towards the house.

Features shown in two dimensions on the plan are graphically illustrated in the projection.

The perspective drawing shows how the garden will look from this point.

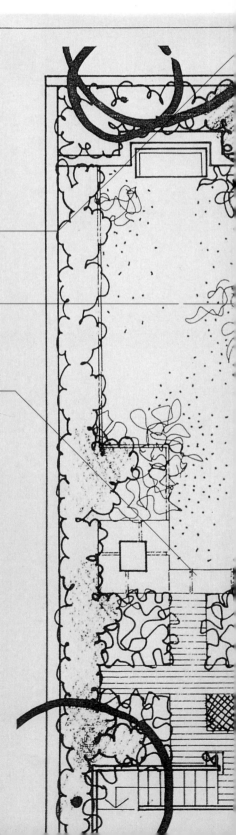

Quick visualization
This method enables you to experiment with plenty of design ideas. Lay a piece of tracing paper over a photograph of the site taken from the house, and draw in the view you envisage. The aim is to give an impression of the shapes of the composition, so use bold outlines (as in the drawings on page 42), and avoid fiddly, small, unnecessary details. Having a photograph of the house and the landscape outside the site's boundaries on hand will help you see whether your garden's design will integrate with the surroundings.

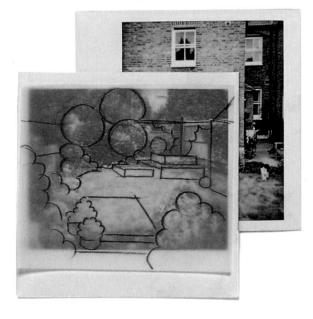

Projection
Unlike a plan, a projection shows the height of all the main features, as well as plan dimensions, but it has no perspective. Producing projections of details such as steps prompts you into resolving the dimensions of each part of your design. Instruction on how to draw a projection is given on page 325.

Section drawing
This is a "slice" through either the site, as here, or just part of it, and reveals all the changes of elevation. Sections are a useful way to check that the scale of your three-dimensional elements is correct. Instruction on how to draw a section is given on page 326.

Perspective drawing
A garden's design is really brought to life by this freehand sketch. Unlike the plan, the projection, and the section, it shows the features in perspective, and so gives an impression of what the onlooker will see. If freehand sketching does not come easily, use the snapshot-and-tracing-paper method on the opposite page; you will then begin to see how perspective works as well.

TYPES OF PLAN

After you have drawn a schematic plan of the design of your garden, you can go on to produce a structural plan and a planting plan on which to show all the working detail. On a structural plan you might see the positions of walls, steps, and the individual paving slabs, for example, and on a planting plan the locations of each shrub and group of perennials in a border. (Recommended scales for plans are given on page 152.)

Symbols are used to represent all the different types of hard and soft surfacing, garden elements, and plants. On pages 322-3 there is a glossary of the symbols I use; most of these are widely used in landscape drawing, so any contractor you might employ will be familiar with them. Whether you choose to use these symbols or devise your own, they must be drawn to scale so that stone paving, for instance, appears larger than bricks, and shrubs larger than perennials. If there is not room to show every necessary detail on a structural plan, supplement the symbols with labels. On a planting plan the name and quantity of each species is indicated.

Although plans are two-dimensional, they can give an impression of depth if the thickness and weight of the lines are varied according to how dominant the feature would look from above.

STRUCTURAL PLAN

The structural plan, drawn up from the basic schematic plan, shows in detail all the structural parts of the garden's design. As on the plan here, the position of the house, and the doors and windows that face the garden, are always included. Moving out from the house, structural plans show garden walls (with retaining walls differentiated from free-standing walls), fencing, edging, and steps, and garden structures such as pergolas and garden buildings. The surface materials of paths are clearly identified, along with areas of still or running water, and grass. The plan might also show how bricks or individual units of stone paving are to be arranged. Although this is primarily a plan of the hard surfaces, the spread of existing large trees over them is usually included.

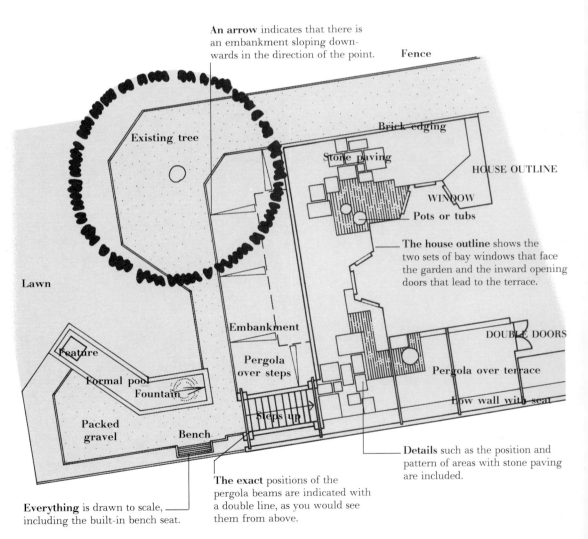

An arrow indicates that there is an embankment sloping downwards in the direction of the point.

Fence

Existing tree

Brick edging

Stone paving

HOUSE OUTLINE

WINDOW

Pots or tubs

The house outline shows the two sets of bay windows that face the garden and the inward opening doors that lead to the terrace.

Lawn

Embankment

DOUBLE DOORS

Pergola over steps

Pergola over terrace

Feature

Formal pool

Fountain

Low wall with seat

Packed gravel

Bench

Steps up

Details such as the position and pattern of areas with stone paving are included.

The exact positions of the pergola beams are indicated with a double line, as you would see them from above.

Everything is drawn to scale, including the built-in bench seat.

PLANTING PLAN

The schematic plan will also be the basis for the planting plan: on this symbols show the positions of individual trees, shrubs, perennials, and so on, although for a very detailed perennial border you might need to scale up the area. The outline of each symbol shows the plant's spread after a given time, and a dot, its planting position. The distribution of bulbs and small annuals, which are planted *en masse*, is only roughly shown, with a series of dots or cross hatching. For extra clarity, the symbols for groups of plants of the same species can be joined up at the centers. Each symbol or group of symbols is then labelled with the species name and number of plants (see the example on page 119). The completed planting plan serves not only as a shopping list but also as an accurate guide to where all the new plants are to be positioned.

TREE SYMBOLS

Here are some of the tree symbols that I use on plans. More symbols appear on page 323.

Schematic and planting plan

Conifers existing (heavy line) or planned

Deciduous trees existing (heavy line) or planned

Small tree

Schematic plan

Forest tree

Medium tree

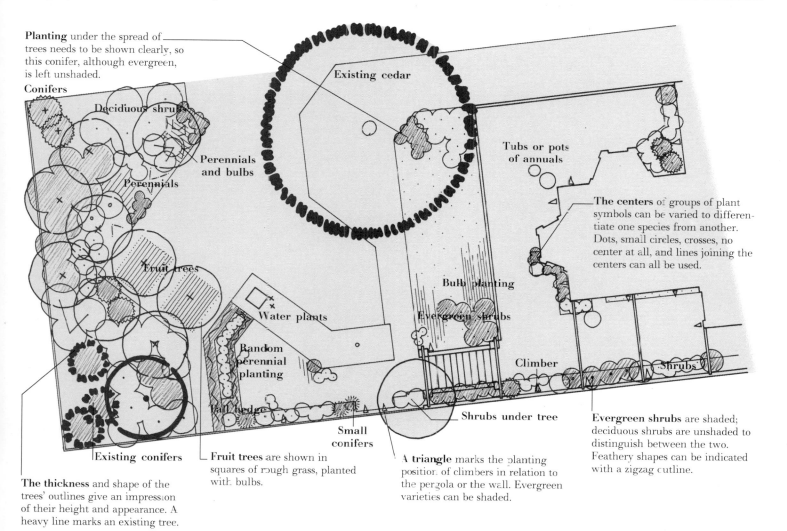

Planting under the spread of trees needs to be shown clearly, so this conifer, although evergreen, is left unshaded.

Conifers

Deciduous shrubs

Perennials

Perennials and bulbs

Existing cedar

Fruit trees

Water plants

Random perennial planting

Tall hedge

Small conifers

Tubs or pots of annuals

The centers of groups of plant symbols can be varied to differentiate one species from another. Dots, small circles, crosses, no center at all, and lines joining the centers can all be used.

Bulb planting

Evergreen shrubs

Climber

Shrubs

Shrubs under tree

Existing conifers

The thickness and shape of the trees' outlines give an impression of their height and appearance. A heavy line marks an existing tree.

Fruit trees are shown in squares of rough grass, planted with bulbs.

A triangle marks the planting position of climbers in relation to the pergola or the wall. Evergreen varieties can be shaded.

Evergreen shrubs are shaded; deciduous shrubs are unshaded to distinguish between the two. Feathery shapes can be indicated with a zigzag outline.

BASIC DRAWING SKILLS

Technical drawing is simply a matter of familiarity with the equipment used, and confidence. Once you have practiced the exercises here a few times you will feel completely at ease with the skills of basic draftsmanship.

It is easiest to draw accurately on an angled surface, so it is best to use a drawing board. Choose one not less than 3 feet (1m) across, with a T-square. Try the board at different angles until you feel comfortable; make sure it is well lit.

Tracing paper is commonly used as a basis for technical drawings, the thinnest being for the first drawings, the sturdiest for the final drawings. I often use thin sketch paper instead for the first drawings; it is just as suitable as tracing paper but less costly. You need a variety of pencils and a set of drafting pens with tips of different sizes. For accurate results, hold your pen or pencil upright, and if you have a dark drawing board, cover it with thick white card, so the lines you draw are visible.

SET OF EQUIPMENT

Several high-quality rulers (a 12-inch, 18-inch, and 24-inch) are essential. Only the final drawings are rendered in pen. Use an HB (softish) pencil for drafting; a softer 2B for sketching; and a 2H (medium hard) for detailed work.

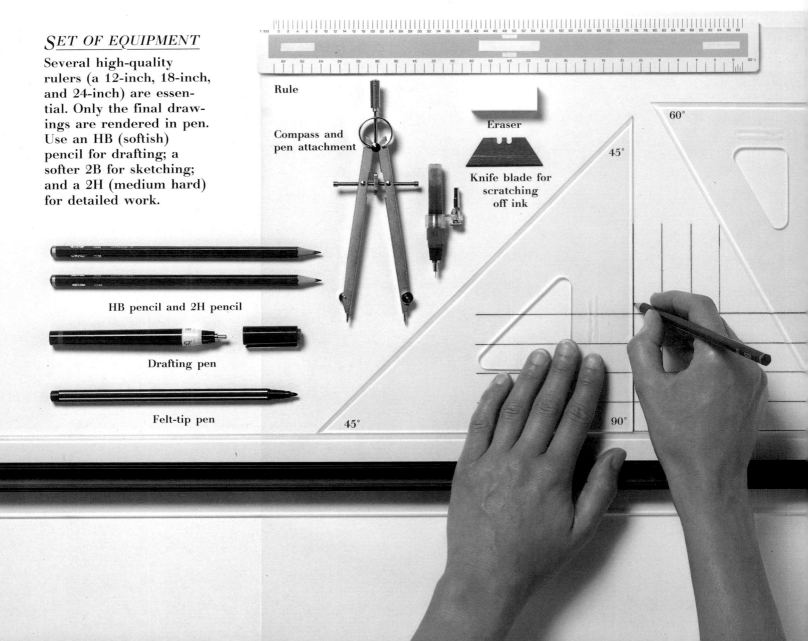

HB pencil and 2H pencil

Drafting pen

Felt-tip pen

Rule

Compass and pen attachment

Eraser

Knife blade for scratching off ink

60°

45°

45°

90°

1 Horizontal lines
Steady the T-square and draw equally spaced lines. Keep the pencil sharp by rotating it as you draw, and work from top to bottom.

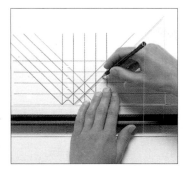

2 Verticals and diagonals
Using a triangle, draw vertical lines with the straight 90° edge. To make a 45° angle, rest the triangle on the T-square.

3 75° angle
Combine the different edges of the two triangles to produce a greater number of angles. Use simple addition: here 45 and 30 make 75.

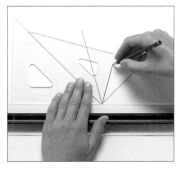

4 105° angle
For 105°, place the 45° edge of the right-angled triangle on the T-square; butt the 60° edge of the other triangle against it.

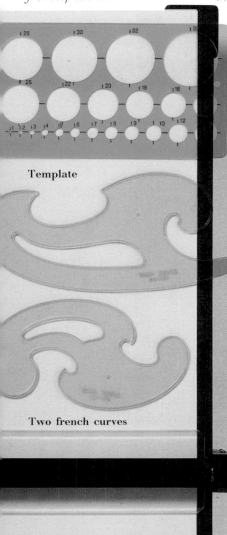

Template

Two french curves

Geometry, above and right
Place the point of the compass at the center of a square. Rotate the apex of the compass as shown to draw a circle.

Choose a drawing board that has a T-square.

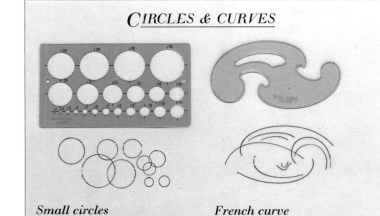

CIRCLES & CURVES

Small circles
A template is a timesaving alternative to a compass.

French curve
This is a useful aid to drawing many types of curve.

EVOLVING SHAPE & PATTERN

Here is a loosening up exercise that will give you confidence in the transition from drawing lines to making abstract patterns. It will also introduce you to the satisfying logic of creating free shapes within the discipline of a grid. Working with letter forms will get you used to using open angles and clear shapes; small angles and mean shapes are not practical in a garden. Aim to make a design that you would be as happy to see reproduced in any other medium as realized in a garden design.

From line to abstract pattern
Letters on a grid used to make a pattern.

MAKING A LOGO INTO A PATTERN

1 *Draw four lines 1in (2.5mm) apart. Between these draw the alphabet freehand; every letter is made up of circles and lines.*

2 *Now, draw four lines 2in (50mm) apart. Draw the alphabet using a tri-angle and compass. Give the letters a standard thickness.*

3 *On a piece of tracing paper, draw a grid of six 2in (50mm) squares; use a triangle for verticals and the T-square for horizontals.*

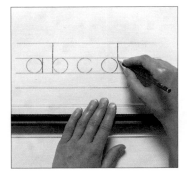

4 *On this grid trace four letters from step 2. They can face any way but the circles must fit in the grid squares. Don't use m or w.*

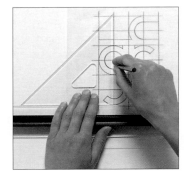

5 *Next, divide the grid squares in half, horizon-tally and vertically; the lines should cross at the centers of the circles.*

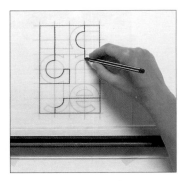

6 *Trace over parts of the letters and the grid to produce an abstract design. Ensure no lines meet the grid edge at under 45°.*

WORKING WITH ABSTRACT SHAPES

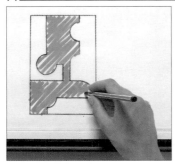   

1 Roughly shade in the pattern you have made with a colored felt-tip pen to give the shape definition.

2 Add complexity: trace over the step 6 outline again, and try tracing over that upside down.

3 Shade in the new shapes. As all the shapes came from the grid, they will relate geometrically.

4 Color in the shapes, bringing the abstract pattern to life. Try out negative versions (below left).

CHOOSING & USING A GRID

The secret ingredient in your garden's design is a dimension that is unique to a particular site, expressed in the form of a grid. The size of the grid squares should relate to a dominant feature of the house, this being the most important structure on the site. By using shapes within that grid or a multiple thereof, you will evolve a design that has a proportionate visual unity with the house. The grid will also encourage you to unfold your design from your living space instead of relating it to the boundaries, the downfall of many garden designs. The grid is drawn on tracing paper and used in conjunction with the scaled layout of the site.

But how do you decide which feature to take as your grid dimension? Look at the house in conjunction with the scale plan and try to find a recurring dimension. This may be in something as simple as the window-wall spacing. Then look at the house from a distance, where it is easier to see structural spacing such as the verticals of a verandah construction. The plan of the rear of some houses might be L-shaped, and you might well use one of these dimensions for your grid. The house has probably been designed and built on a module – try to discover that from the plan. Alternatively, use the dimension of the most striking feature or one that you wish to become a focus of attention.

If the dimension of the grid that you choose is too small, it will produce a fussy design with little angles which are both visually irritating and in practice awkward to construct and maintain. Where the site relates to a view of some scale you may double the grid size towards the view so as to increase the size of the shapes within it, although they will all still have a proportional relationship.

Whatever the size or shape of your garden, evolve the grid at 90° to the house; it may be turned at an angle of 45° should you wish to direct the pattern in a particular way – to a view or a special tree, for instance. Your grid is a tool to be used to help you to develop a sense of proportion. It is not necessarily a straitjacket. Later, you will see how you evolve the design of a garden beyond the dictates of the grid, rationalizing a basic concept into practical shapes and spaces.

CHOOSING THE SIZE OF THE SQUARE

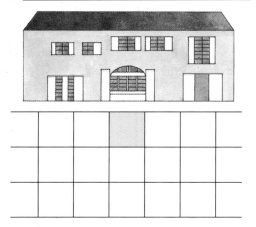

Window width
The central windows were chosen for the grid dimension as they are the most important feature on this elevation of the house.

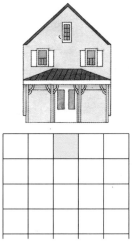

Verandah measurement
The distance between the posts of the verandah gives the elevation of the house a visual rhythm, so this measurement was taken for the grid square dimension.

Structural bay
If the house elevation has no obvious proportional relationship between its features, use the measurement of the most dominant feature – like the width of the bay here.

*T*HE GRID & THE PLAN

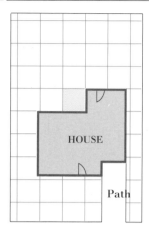

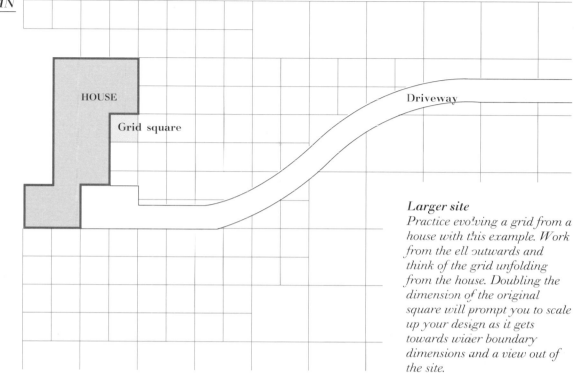

Small site
The grid dimension was taken from, and lined up with, the ell at the back of the house; it does not matter that there is only part of a square along the boundaries. On such a small site, the same size grid square is used throughout.

Larger site
Practice evolving a grid from a house with this example. Work from the ell outwards and think of the grid unfolding from the house. Doubling the dimension of the original square will prompt you to scale up your design as it gets towards wider boundary dimensions and a view out of the site.

A visual unity,
above and right
The grid system helps evolve a design that works well because it relates the garden strongly to the house. The garden here unfolds naturally from the house because the width of the window, which was used as the grid dimension, is echoed in the width of the gravelled area, the paving, and the spacing of the pergola beams.

PATTERNS ON A GRID

The pattern of your garden's design will start to determine the garden's mood and style long before you consider the materials from which it will be made or the style of the planting. Using shapes that are multiples of your grid squares will ensure that your garden design of whatever size is closely related to the proportions of the house. But the next step is to arrange the shapes to mold a character.

Broadly speaking, patterns can be divided into those with a sense of movement and those that are static. Patterns that contain flowing curves tend to create that movement because their lines draw the eye through the space. Straight-edged shapes arranged in a directional pattern have a similar effect; straight lines give the fastest movement, both physically and visually, while diagonal lines create a slower, crablike movement.

Patterns with movement require a purpose, perhaps drawing attention to a special feature, or leading to a view. Those with expansive, serpentine curves are not suited to small gardens, for there is just not enough space for the pattern to reach a satisfying conclusion.

Static patterns can be more restful. They are usually balanced compositions and keep interest firmly rooted in the site, which should be your aim if your garden is small or surrounded by tall boundaries or unattractive views.

Garden Masses and Spaces

In any pattern the relationship between positive masses and the negative spaces that flow between them is important (see pages 40-1). Eventually, on a garden plan, the light, gridded areas of these patterns would become the positive masses and the dark shapes, the negative spaces. In the simplest terms the masses might be beds of planting divided by retaining walls, and the spaces, paving or grass. Visualize the patterns here like this; then try reversing the relationship so that the gridded areas become the spaces and the dark shapes, the masses. You will find that many of the patterns are functional as embryonic garden designs shaded this way around and assume quite a different character.

PRINCIPLES OF PATTERN

These patterns are made from shapes proportionate to the grid. Try them out using a gridded sheet and paper shapes. Halve the grid square at times for smaller shapes. The exercise will give you a feel for pattern and you will soon evolve new versions of your own.

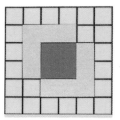

4. Interlocking squares
Two overlapping squares make a central one; all are proportionate to the boundary square.

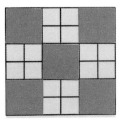

1. Symmetrical and static
A formal pattern using the grid square quadrupled holds attention in the site – perfect for a small garden.

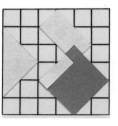

5. Shapes at 45°
Turn the squares to a 45° angle to the boundary square. They are no less proportionate to it and create an abstract pattern.

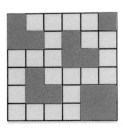

2. Diagonal counterbalance
By leaving space between L-shapes that occupy three grid squares you will create a pattern with gentle movement.

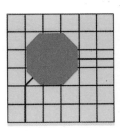

6. Simple geometry
Octagons have a satisfying geometry – four sides halve the grid square diagonally, four touch its sides.

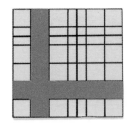

3. Controlled movement
Straight lines give the fastest visual movement; cross the lines for slightly slower movement.

7. Loosening up
Two half circles are shown connecting along a grid line.

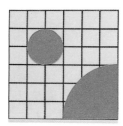

8. Double curve
A small circle fits within the grid, with a segment of a larger one opposite it.

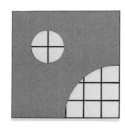

9. Circles reversed
Reverse the circular design shown above and appreciate the positive/negative relationship of the shapes.

Serpentine curves
Curves on this scale are suitable only for large gardens This design could be used in its negative form as well (visualize the colored shape as the positive mass), creating a different effect. Practice drawing the curves accurately with a compass set to the width of the grid squares. Although the shapes are "free," there is a strong geometry in this pattern.

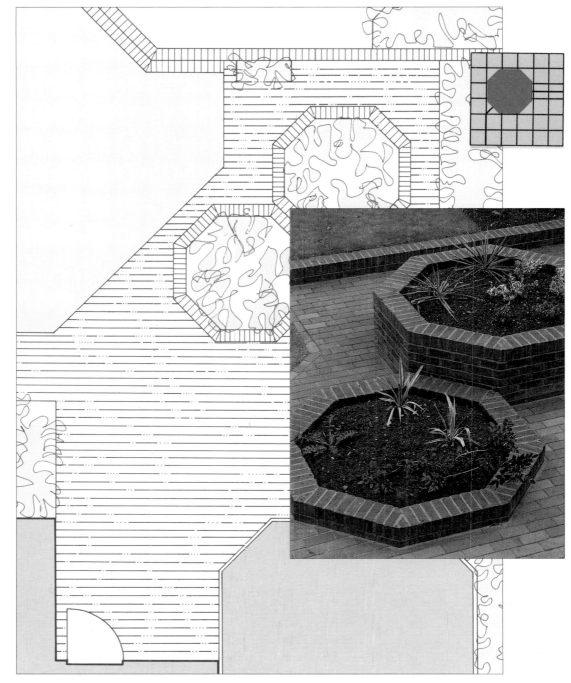

Static geometrical pattern
From this section of the plan of a garden you can see how the angles of the house are echoed in a pair of octagons and the angled edge of the brick paving. An octagon is shown as the negative space on the hypothetical mini-grid but in the finished garden, octagonal

brick beds constitute the positive masses, and hold interest firmly within the site. When the aim is to provide a focal point, it is important to be bold and ensure that most of your shapes occupy at least one grid square and, like the brick octagons, are fairly large in relation to the overall design.

PATTERNS IN A SITE

Having seen how to draw abstract shapes and devise a grid, and how patterns work in theory, the next step is to formulate a pattern that works in a site. By enabling you to experiment and discover different design options, this technique helps you forget what is there already and encourages a completely fresh approach.

At this early stage you are seeking to come up with a visually satisfying pattern which you can rationalize and refine later as you work towards a garden plan. While the shapes should be a multiple of your grid square, you do not have to follow the grid system slavishly – it is simply an aid to starting a design and working with proportion.

When you run out of ideas for just sketching with a pencil, shapes cut from paper really come into their own – by trying them on different parts of the grid, perhaps overlapping them with existing shapes, you quickly generate new alternatives. Tracing over parts of the pattern to make a clean version and developing this with new shapes enables you to experiment without starting again from scratch. The shape of the site here is typical of the sort of irregular corner plot that poses a real design challenge. Try the technique on an imaginary site, and perhaps on an outline of your own garden.

First Steps

The house and boundary outline and the grid are drawn accurately on a raised drawing board using a T-square and a triangle; the final version of the pattern (see step 8) is done with a dark felt-tip pen and straightedge. All the experimental patterns are drawn freehand, although you may find it easier to make circles with a compass set to the width of the grid squares. From step 4 onwards, lower the drawing board so the paper shapes do not slide.

Because the garden spaces on either side of the house are linked and can be seen together, one tracing paper grid was used and the two spaces were designed as one. But if you have two completely separate garden spaces, design one at a time; you may use the same grid for both, simply realigning the house (see step 2), or use two different grids.

DESIGNING WITH SHAPES

This technique is the key to exploring the design possibilities of a site.

Your aim at this stage is to make a visually satisfying abstract pattern.

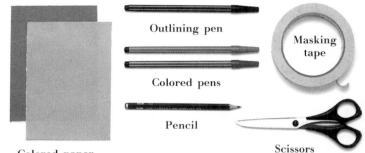

Outlining pen

Masking tape

Colored pens

Pencil

Colored paper

Scissors

CREATING A PATTERN

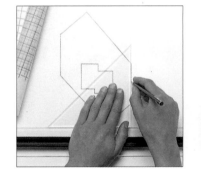

1 *Decide on your grid square dimension and draw a grid on tracing paper. On a clean sheet draw a scale outline of your house and the boundary of the site.*

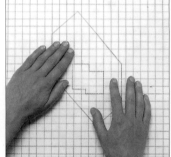

2 *Place the house and boundary outline under your grid; line up the squares at 90° to an important feature, like the ell. Secure with masking tape.*

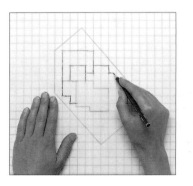

3 *Place a clean piece of tracing paper over the top and, using the grid lines as a guide, draw abstract shapes to create a pattern. Start near the house and work outwards.*

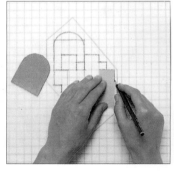

4 *Also try cutting out some shapes (based on the grid) from paper and experiment with them in different positions. Draw around them on your tracing paper.*

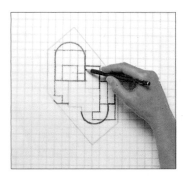 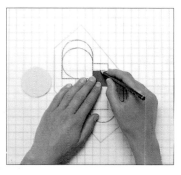 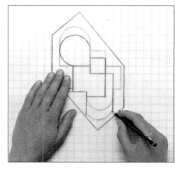 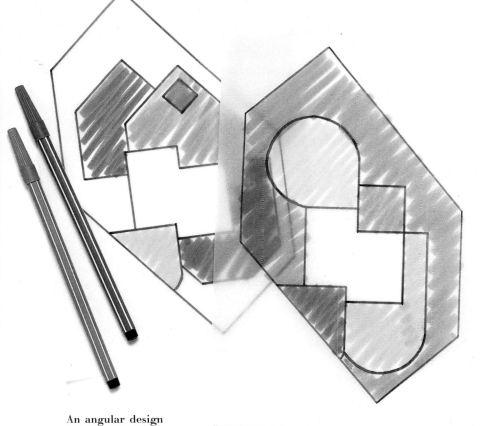

5 Continue trying out different combinations of paper shapes, looking as much at the spaces you create between the shapes as at the shapes themselves. Then clarify a pattern you like by drawing thickly over the parts you want to keep. The design can still be modified further.

6 Take a clean sheet of tracing paper and trace over the thick lines you made in step 5; to improve the design you can alter the shapes as you go along. Remove the trace of the rough version and work up the pattern on your clean tracing paper by drawing around more paper shapes.

7 Once you are satisfied — and not before — make a neat copy. On fresh tracing paper trace off the outline of the house and boundary, and your new garden shapes. Again, you can refine and adjust the shapes as you go. You might try several variations before you are ready for a final version.

8 Trace the pattern neatly using a dark felt-tip pen and a straightedge; remove the other sheets of paper. With a few colors, define the shapes by shading them in. Take care not to mix more than two styles of pattern or you will lose the clarity of the design.

A mixed design
of circles and squares.

Contrasting patterns

With circles that fit in the grid squares, as in the design near left, you can introduce the limited movement suitable for a fairly small site. The angular design on the far left has been created with the grid set at 45° to the house.

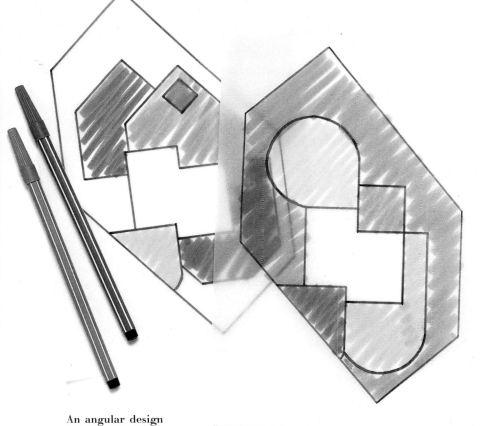

An angular design
at 45° to the house.

THE GRID AT 45°

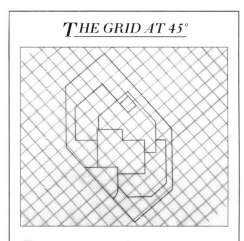

To see your garden's design in a new light, experiment with shapes on a grid that is evolved at 90° to the house but then positioned at 45° to it. With the grid in this new relationship to the house, you can make angular patterns.

INTERPRETING SHAPES

The carefully positioned proportional shapes of these examples of garden design generate a strength and a clarity that is rarely achieved using a piecemeal approach. All have a strong geometry that comes from an underlying grid. Any one pattern on paper can be interpreted in numerous ways outside according to whether the shapes are raised, sunken, or flat. And the character of the pattern is influenced by whether the materials used are hard, soft, reflective, smooth, or rough. Patterns do not have to be complex to be effective – often the simplest ones make the greatest impact when realized as three-dimensional shapes in the garden.

Linear directions, left
The pattern of this garden – a single, long, straight line balanced by a series of short horizontal lines – takes the form of stone paths that contrast with and contain the soft shapes of different types of planting.

Dynamic pattern, above
The impact of any pattern on paper is intensified in the garden. The powerful effect of these squares of wooden decking across water belies the simplicity of the pattern.

Geometrical balance, right
There is a wonderful counterbalance of proportionate shapes in this composition, since its geometry of hedging and planting expresses the underlying grid powerfully.

Echoed semicircles, left
A pattern of semicircles used in two flights of steps, one stone, one brick, has graphic simplicity, enlivened by the visual witticism of the brick steps continuing below the water.

DESIGN ALTERNATIVES

On these and the following pages are some garden plans that reveal how all the theoretical principles explained in this chapter come together to make a true garden design. Each plan was evolved using a grid, as shown on pages 56-7. The grids are shown with the plans.

To check that the terraces, lawns, and other spaces are a practical size, you may make paper cut-outs to scale of what they need to accommodate. For the terrace, a chaise longue for instance, and to set on the poolside paving, chairs and a table.

SMALL TOWN GARDEN

In a small garden use geometrical shapes to evolve a design that holds the eye in the site, for there is no point in introducing linear movement if there is nowhere for the eye to go. Accordingly, all three designs here are inward-looking, although two of them incorporate a sense of movement. Small gardens can usually be seen in their entirety from the house so it is important that every component be hard-working, that pots are grouped as focal points, and permanent furniture is treated as an integral part of the layout. And it is important not to have lines that meet the boundary at less than 90° to avoid mean, impractical corners.

Small-garden grid
The façade of this house is divided visually into three parts, each the width of a window. This dimension is halved for the grid as it would have produced shapes too large for a small garden. The designs are more closely related to the grid squares than the larger and freer designs on pages 66-9.

Geometrical transitions
As the working drawing shows, having several distinct yet linked areas in a small garden creates a deceptive air of spaciousness. The sense of movement created by the steppingstones across the water and the interlocking rectangle and squares is counterpoised by the large trees positioned diagonally at each end of the garden.

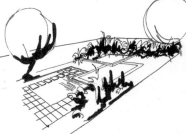

Geometric shapes in a walled town garden

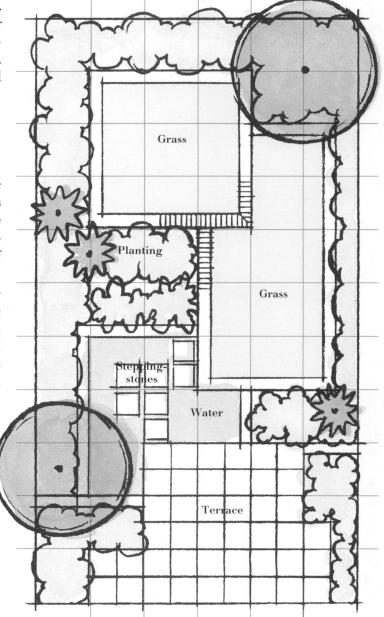

Grass

Planting

Grass

Stepping-stones

Water

Terrace

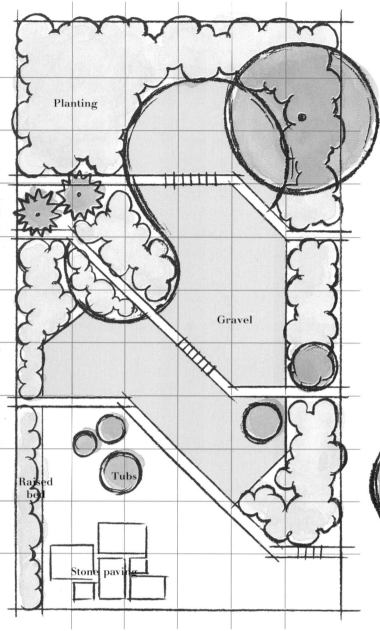

Planting

Gravel

Raised bed

Tubs

Stone paving

Traditional approach, below
This design has the satisfying symmetry of a traditional formal garden. The layout is divided into two "rooms," the first with tubs containing clipped trees, the second conceived as a formal herb garden. Each element in the garden, including the benches and the pedestal, contributes to the emphatic stillness of the pattern.

Formal motifs enhance a symmetrical layout

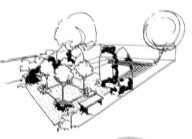

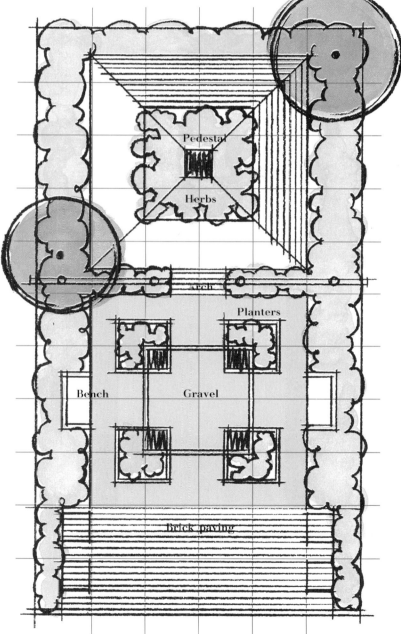

Pedestal

Herbs

Arch

Planters

Bench   Gravel

Brick paving

Asymmetrical diagonals contrast with curves

Mixed pattern, above
Generally, two types of pattern can be mixed; any more will look fussy. The tight, emphatic curve at the far end of the garden makes the design inward-looking by drawing the eye to the middle of the site. Symmetry is not an aim here: the trees are deliberately sited in an irregular pattern to enhance the drama of the curves and diagonals.

MEDIUM-SIZED GARDEN

When designing a garden of this size you may start to introduce some movement and to increase the scale of the shapes as they move away from the house. Movement can be created with curves and circles, or with straight lines and angular shapes. The flowing curves in the layout below would suit a medium-sized garden, perhaps without a boundary fence or wall and in a location with a soft natural landscape, say woodland. The angular design, top right, is also dynamic, but this time it is more urban in character.

The Design Process

As usual, I started off using the grid as a guide to choosing shapes proportionate to the house, but soon found I needed to move off the grid when positioning them – remember, the grid is only a way to achieve a plan proportionate to the house, it is not a design straitjacket. Once I had a rough pattern that suited the site and its location, and met the basic requirements (a terrace, a pool, and hard surfacing connecting front and back), I began to ask myself some specific questions. Is the poolside terrace large enough for a table and chairs? Is the pathway connecting the two sides of the house a practical width? Are the lawns of sufficient size? Then I adjusted and adapted the designs accordingly, and began to loosen up the pattern and to introduce new elements, such as a pergola, trees, and other areas of planting, into the basic arrangement of shapes.

The grid
The dominant feature at the front of this house is the division of the verandah into five sections by a series of columns. The square of the grid is equivalent to two of these sections, so it also happens to equal the width of the house extension (see the plan) as seen from the front.

Curved movement
This design of gentle curves is for a garden outside town. I derived the pattern from circles that fit in the grid squares, but shifted the main one nearest the house off the grid lines to center it on the house extension – the view from the back windows is the most important. The other circles at the back shifted accordingly.

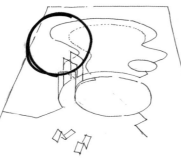

Circles off-center open out into fluid curves

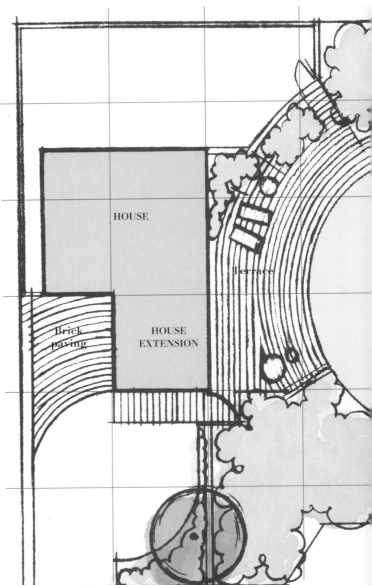

HOUSE

Brick paving

HOUSE EXTENSION

Terrace

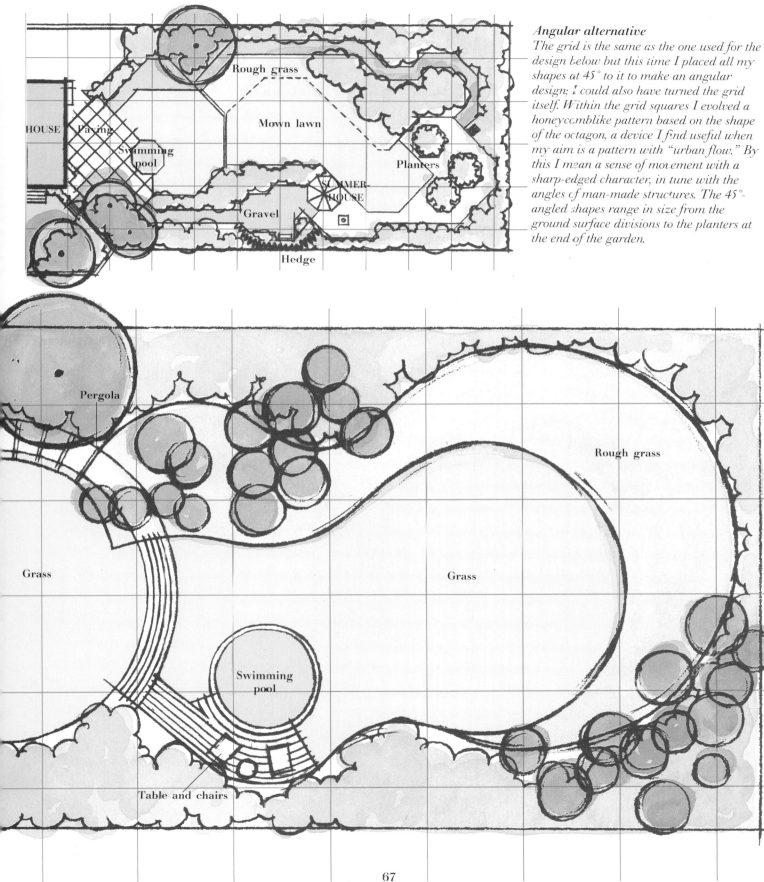

Rough grass

Mown lawn

HOUSE Paving

Swimming
pool

Planters

Gravel

SUMMER-
HOUSE

Hedge

Angular alternative

The grid is the same as the one used for the design below but this time I placed all my shapes at 45° to it to make an angular design; I could also have turned the grid itself. Within the grid squares I evolved a honeycomblike pattern based on the shape of the octagon, a device I find useful when my aim is a pattern with "urban flow." By this I mean a sense of movement with a sharp-edged character, in tune with the angles of man-made structures. The 45°-angled shapes range in size from the ground surface divisions to the planters at the end of the garden.

Pergola

Rough grass

Grass

Grass

Swimming
pool

Table and chairs

COUNTRY GARDEN

The larger the site, the more elements you have space to include. By working loosely within the grid, adapting shapes as and when you need to, you can ensure that each part of the garden has a proportionate relationship to the house.

This is the sort of large country house that commands a wide view of the countryside beyond. My design parameters were to integrate into the design the large existing driveway that fragments the site and to open up much of the garden to the views, while providing some shelter against the strong prevailing winds which would otherwise make the garden an uncomfortable place to sit. It is better to integrate necessary evils like a driveway into a design rather than conceal them behind the standard devices of hedges or rows of trees.

This brief seemed to rule out a formal, symmetrical composition. Instead, I sought to establish a pattern that is visually stronger than the driveway. Within the large, loose scheme, which incorporates the sweeping drive and massed planting (for shelter) as part of the layout, there is a relatively formal arrangement of geometrical shapes in the walled garden.

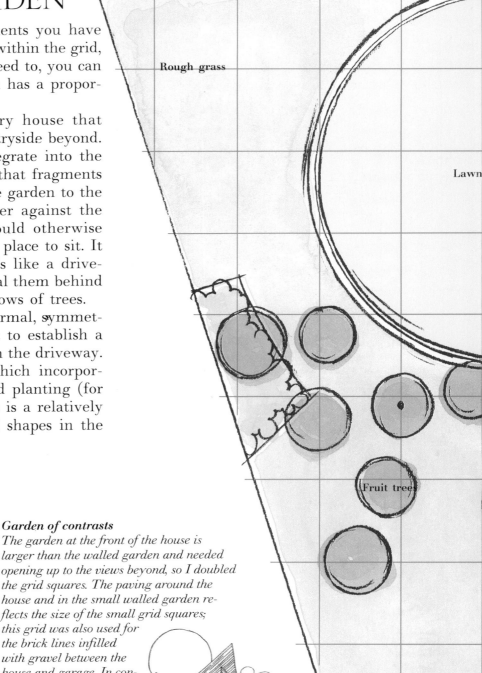

Rough grass

Lawn

Fruit trees

The grid
The dimension of the smaller projecting bay on the house was halved for the basic grid square, and doubled for the larger, open garden space. I chose this feature in preference to others because a smaller square for the walled area would have resulted in too fussy a plan, and a larger square for the open area, a design that lacked subtlety.

Garden of contrasts
The garden at the front of the house is larger than the walled garden and needed opening up to the views beyond, so I doubled the grid squares. The paving around the house and in the small walled garden reflects the size of the small grid squares; this grid was also used for the brick lines infilled with gravel between the house and garage. In contrast, on the other side there is a composition of generous, sweeping shapes (developed on the large grid), which includes the driveway that leads visitors, via the turnaround, to the house, and the grass circle that leads the eye to the country beyond.

Garden rooms
open out of each other

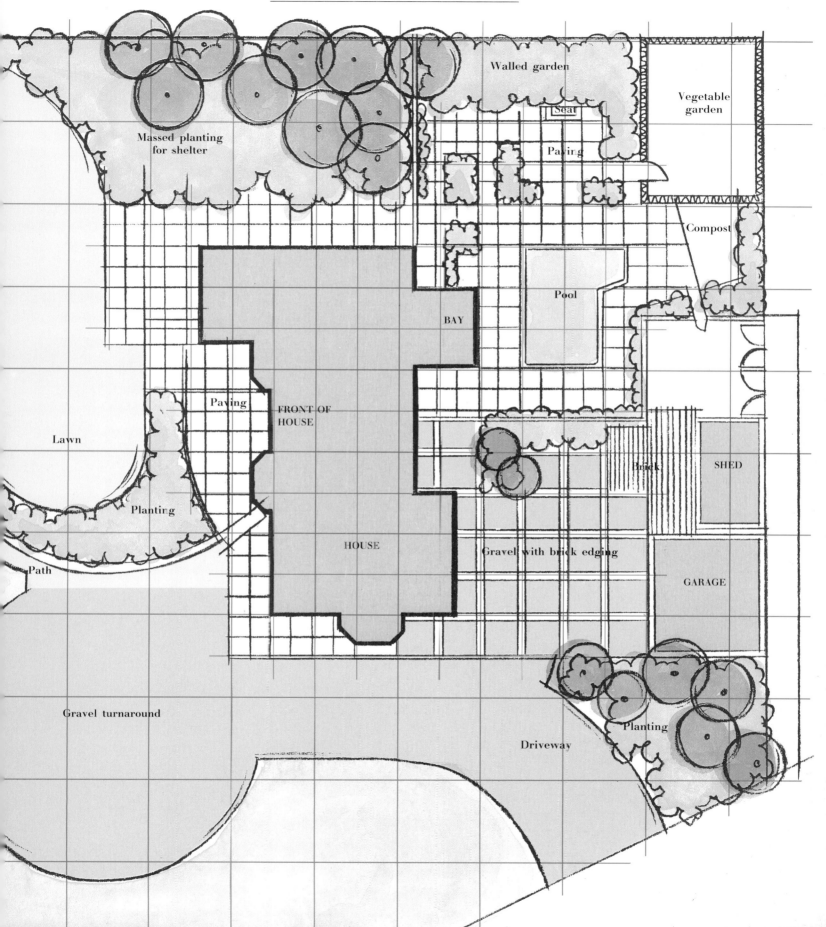

Massed planting for shelter

Walled garden

Vegetable garden

Seat

Paving

Compost

Pool

BAY

Paving

FRONT OF HOUSE

Lawn

Planting

Brick

SHED

Path

HOUSE

Gravel with brick edging

GARAGE

Gravel turnaround

Planting

Driveway

3

STYLING
THE GARDEN

*The basic rules of designing a garden may be
interpreted in many different ways – modern or historical,
national or regional; and within each of those
there are other moods as well.*

PRINCIPLES OF STYLE

In the last chapter I set out to explain the technique and theory of evolving a garden plan successfully. But governing your decisions on layout is a style concept, an idea in your mind's eye that you need to think about long before you set pen to paper – for style affects the form of the layout as well as its subsequent furnishings.

In Part One I showed how gardens that echo their settings have an integrity and a logic to them that are visually satisfying. My approach is a far cry from that which sees no paradox in slapping a preconceived notion upon an unwilling site – the English cottage garden in Arizona, for example – and manipulating the site to accommodate the design. But while slavish copies might be inappropriate, there is much that can be learned from national and historic styles around the world. It is a question of reinterpretation: the Japanese garden holds important lessons in achieving an effect of controlled calm and taut symbolism, even if many Western versions of it have become pastiche.

In order to show the potential and creativity of the styling process, on the following pages are collections of artifacts, structural materials, surfaces, and plants which should evoke a garden mood to suit a particular garden in a particular location.

Rural Styles

Country styles will to a large extent be dictated by the geology of the region and the use to which the surrounding land has been put over the generations. These man-made manipulations of the natural landscape add up to its visual value, and by echoing them in your garden's design you can make a satisfying link between setting and garden (see pages 10–15).

National, traditional (probably designated as "country"), and regional styles of garden were always born out of their site. Layouts and materials originally had to be local,

since it was almost inconceivable to transport materials from one region to another. Ideas certainly moved about, but they were reinterpreted with the available materials and in the light of different lifestyles. The style concept can be strengthened immeasurably by using materials from the surrounding area only. Apart from guaranteeing a strong union with the setting, they always look better together, too, since local stone color will generally blend with tiles made from local clays, and gravel colors will match those of the soil.

Styles for Urban Settings

Indigenous country styles are comparatively easy to analyze; it is a question of looking out beyond your boundary. With enclosed town gardens and those that surround houses in suburban areas, the most appropriate style might be harder to visualize. But actually it is easy – you can do whatever suits you! Evolve your plan according to your practical needs, then style it to reflect the structure of your house. Where the space is completely enclosed, the garden can be as exotic as you care to make it, since it functions on its own with little relationship to neighboring gardens.

In some city gardens the style is often dictated by the scale of the space. Rather than being a scaled-down version of a country garden, the town garden relates to the interior of the house; it is the room outside, in fact. Materials and furnishings may echo the interior, but should also, if possible, pick up on the period of the structure. We find it relatively easy to make decisions about the styles that are right for the interiors of our houses, only to lose confidence in our judgment when we go outside. Yet the same prompts are there. The location, the site, and the house, plus our own likes and dislikes, all hold the essential clues to the style that will best suit a garden.

COUNTRY STYLE

Rough stone walls and wooden fences embody the essence of the country garden, which is open to wood- or farmland, or may be near the ocean. The overall mood is unsophisticated, perhaps rather unkempt, with a marvelous mosaic of color. Yet beneath the apparent randomness there should be a strong framework controlling and unifying the whole, the color and texture of key ingredients such as walls and fencing echoing those of the house and the landscape from which the garden has evolved. To accentuate the country feel, choose old-fashioned plants – daisy-like flowers, sweet peas, hollyhocks, pot marigolds – and let them grow in flowering profusion. The colors can be clashing and bright, but site strong foliage forms with the perennials. For outdoor furniture, stained wood gives a more elegant feel, but bleached pine chairs and a table are equally fitting.

Furniture
Natural materials are the obvious choice for the country-style garden; anything worn and weathered can also look good.

Containers
Use anything and everything as containers. Plain clay pots provide the right note of simplicity, while herbs and flowers can burst out of old cans.

Surfacing
Stone paving looks very "country," and gravel allows plants to seed randomly in it. Lay paving bricks in a herringbone pattern with plants creeping through the cracks.

Boundaries
*Open wood fencing, such as
post-and-rail, will play down
the division between garden
and countryside.*

Accessories
*Tools and functional objects
can all have a visual as well
as a practical role if sympathetic materials and styles
are chosen.*

Country grouping, left
"Country" style changes according to location, but in this very English garden lies its very essence: exuberant plantings and random seating for a summer day's enjoyment. It is cheerfully planted with abundant flowers, shrubs, and herbs, some of which have seeded casually between the pavings and in the border behind the stone wall.

Garden meets country, right
Country style is taken to its ultimate conclusion in this dramatic merge of garden with the rolling hills beyond. Two structural elements make it possible: a ha-ha wall, just visible across the middle of this picture, and a terrace that projects right into the view.

A romantic mood, left
For many, country style means "secret" gardens, creaking gates, mellow brick, and frothing roses. It is a romantic and nostalgic image, but one that relies heavily on existing structures and appropriate styling.

MODERN STYLE

Characteristic of the modern-style garden are simplicity of line and an almost sculptural quality of space. On plan or three-dimensionally, shapes are simple and geometric, or flowing and organic – but just as the house is a "machine for living," in Le Corbusier's words, so form follows function in the garden, for this is a room outside, a place for active enjoyment. The swimming pool and the jacuzzi most definitely fit into the look, along with a tennis court, perhaps. Colors are crisp and clean, featuring strong contrasts. Vegetation is massive, architectural, and strong in line, large-leaved hostas and spiky grasses being fashionable examples. Accessories are allowed, but restraint is the order of the day; one carefully chosen item will reinforce the modernist concept that "less is more."

Containers

Large concrete tubs help create the modern setting, while terracotta can work visually if the shapes are appropriately clean and bold.

Boundaries

Aim for simplicity, with boundaries that will accentuate the strong, uncluttered lines of your design. A black trellis against a white wall is crisp, almost Oriental in feel.

Surfacing
Square tiles divide up space geometrically; concrete paving makes a simple, crisply austere background.

Furniture
Look for comfort, clean lines, and absence of decoration, for function is all-important. Classic modern designs — here a director's chair — make a strong statement.

79

Line and shape, left
The strong lines of modernist architecture call for an architect's approach to planting as well. Here grasses make the perfect foil for uncompromising lines: bristly in outline, they form dense, bulky mounds that contrast well with the tracery of the fence. Cordylines provide further spikiness and a visual link between the areas on either side of the wall.

Minimalist harmony, right
All nonessentials are stripped away in this American garden. The uncluttered outline of the rectangular pool is echoed in the sculptural shapes of the planting masses. The seating is simple and functional.

Enclosed space, left
Organic and inorganic forms come together to create this superb courtyard composition. The harmony between the tree, stairs, and oversized pot makes an object lesson for any designer in the art of sculpting space.

FORMAL STYLE

Certain houses seem to call for a formal, classic garden to surround them — certain people seem to as well. This is a universal style, always owing as much to the layout of the garden as to the choice of accessories. While personally I object to always having to move in straight lines, I can appreciate the classic elegance of the look: Man dominating his landscape with a perfect symmetry. Geometry, balance, and proportion are all part of this style, plus a certain staginess. The formal garden might have a terrace with balustrading, gracious steps, statuary, even a pavilion. A formal pool could reflect the symmetry, and ideally vistas will be hedged with yew — and punctuated with a suitable accessory. A touch of Fragonard softens the whole — tumbling roses and wisteria, perhaps — but sober clipped trees in tubs will keep such waywardness in check.

Surfacing
Coarse gray gravel or a mixture of sand and pebbles is suitable for parterres and yew-edged axial paths.

Boundaries
White finialled trellis or decorative wrought iron evokes a formal urban mood. Stone balustrading suggests classicism and makes a grand statement.

Sculpture and furniture
Punctuate vistas and views with
statuary or formal features.
Outdoor furniture can
carry classical motifs.

Containers
Echo a symmetrical layout
with square-molded terra-cotta
tubs planted with clipped box.
A venerable planter sounds a
classic Italianate note.

Sculptural formal, above
Traditional themes can be given a successful updated architectural treatment. In this quiet and moving formal garden, clipped hedges and large topiary shapes impart a modern sculptural quality when reinterpreted in twentieth-century terms.

Theatrical style, left
Playful reinterpretations of motifs from the classical world update the formal look for a California context. Devoid of unnecessary prettiness, this swimming pool has a wonderful theatricality.

Urban formal, above
Here the look is neat and tidy New England formal. To reinforce the look, the planting is strictly contained within its designated areas, the horticultural interest conforming to human design.

COLONIAL STYLE

Homey, neat, clean, and tidy are all adjectives that come to mind when I think of the colonial style. With its suggestions of American cottage garden, Northeast colonial offers a comfortable and comforting look, in gentle harmony with its location. Because colonial homes were so plain and unadorned, their owners took great pains to create an aura of elegance with exterior details. Latticework and picket fences are familiar motifs, and an historic method of defining property and garden boundaries. These are particularly typical in small New England hamlets. Southern colonial style is a much more formal one, however, so the garden echoes the formality and gracious living in arches, arbors, and box edgings – but the overall feel is generally looser and more random than in the formal style.

Boundaries and surfacing
Simplicity and natural materials are the key. White picket fencing has a clean, crisp, colonial look. Wood decking gives a relaxed, countrified feel and provides a visual link with a woodland setting; wood chips for paths have the same effect. Slate makes handsome paving.

Containers
White-painted terra-cotta pots or a half barrel both suggest simplicity. Colonial style is a variant on a country theme, so tiered planters, with culinary herbs, perhaps, would be appropriate too.

Furniture and accessories
When the living is easy: a tradi-
tional hammock carries connotations of
the Deep South, and for relaxing in style dur-
ing long summer evenings on the verandah, wicker
lounge chairs would be perfect. Wood seems the natu-
ral choice for other furniture.

A garden for relaxation
This quiet, sunny verandah has all the qualities of the Southern colonial style: generous proportions inviting rest and relaxation, plants allowed to sprawl and climb aimlessly, and touches of more formal living in the tubs and verdigrised bench.

Grand style, above
New England colonial style started as the classic seventeenth-century English look; to be precise, the town-house style of the well-to-do merchant. Here, huge trees and wide lawns sound the appropriately self-confident note.

The common touch, above
*A pleasing jumble of pots and
objects brings character to this
garden. Notice the formal
touches which gently counterpoise the comfortable clutter
and homey air.*

MEDITERRANEAN STYLE

Whether in California, Australia, or France, a Mediterranean-style garden is most definitely a garden for lounging on a terrace or by the swimming pool, the air heady with the fragrance of citrus and cypress. For eating out, there should be a welcoming spot, be it under a tree or a large sun umbrella. Against a backdrop of white or sun-baked walls and spiky vegetation, the garden will ooze with vibrant colors cascading from terra-cotta pots. Blues, yellows, oranges, deep pinks, and reds are the classic Mediterranean colors, since delicate hues tend to be devoured by the strong sunlight, while purples and dark blues become somber.

Surfacing
Terra cotta and ceramic suggest an authentic setting, while colored tiles and pebbles complement the natural vibrancy of sea and sky.

Furniture

Shade is a key design element of this style, so parasols — or even huge linen umbrellas if you have the space — work well. Chairs and tables can be strongly colored, perhaps café style.

Containers

Pots can give regional impressions: the olive oil jar evokes Provence, the flower pots suggest Moorish influences, and the verdigris head (a wall pot) is a reminder of the classical Mediterranean world.

91

Mediterranean flavor, left
What could be more Mediterranean than this row of lemon trees planted in swagged terracotta tubs? The random stone paving, the tiled roof, and cypress in the background complete the setting perfectly.

Pool-side shade, above
The swimming pool is the dominant feature of the walled area of this garden. The chaise longue and linen umbrella offer protection against the powerful African sun, while the succulents planted in pots are displayed almost like pieces of extravagant statuary.

Spring colors, left
In another interpretation of the style, this pretty garden displays the floral abundance of a Mediterranean-type garden in spring. Colors are bright and crisp. White walls reflect the heat away from the house, seating is sited for shade, and a passageway with terra-cotta tiles provides a cool retreat from the sun.

ORIENTAL STYLE

S cale is the common theme that links the gardens of the East, for the typical Oriental garden is not large. This is not to say that it should be styled with little bridges, lanterns, and umbrellas, like a scene from *Madame Butterfly*; the style is far more vigorous. Think of banana leaves sprouting from Tokyo gardens, of huge fan palms and lush undergrowth, of fish-filled pools and vibrant orchids. The man-made aspects are deliberate, restrained, and immaculate, with a conscious use of pavings, gravel (in Japan it is raked), and large, smooth boulders, all these features the result of ancient and complex Oriental philosophies. Overall, the effect is one of controlled calm, meticulous maintenance, repose, and, to me, centuries-old tension. Textures are all-important: bamboo fences lashed with knots, cool moss under pine trees. Splashes of rich, vibrant color are used occasionally and with unswerving exactness: a swath of iris, say, or something painted a brilliant orange to create a conscious highlight.

Containers
Look for textural detailing when choosing pots. Stone troughs or wooden planters are both good: the materials and somber colors fit in well.

Boundaries
Brushwood fencing and bamboo canes make strong textural statements; lightweight screens can be useful as dividers within the garden.

Furniture
Exploit the natural textures and rough shapes of rocks and driftwood to make seats and features; keep seating low.

Surfacing
Rocks are important styling details for their mass and sculptural shapes. Stained decking and gravel are appropriate.

Line and texture, right
*The crisp lines and emphasis
on form, both so characteristic
of the Oriental style, were one
inspiration for the modernists.
In this garden corner, linear
forms – decking, fencing, and
raised plank pathways – are
complemented by vegetation
which has been manipulated
to create an overall balance.*

A palace garden, left
The traditional Japanese look
of rock and raked gravel
reveals the Oriental emphasis
on space and austere simplicity. Naturally sculpted forms
suggest a symbiosis of landscape and man-made garden.

Foliage textures, above
Here an Oriental mood has
been achieved with temperate
plants selected for their shape
and architectural potential.
Central to the effect is the play
on leaf forms: the foreground
feathery Japanese maple, the
glaucous hosta, and the spiky
fern. Bamboo fencing makes
the reference clear.

4

DESIGNING WITH PLANTS

*The way in which we use plants is as much a styling
exercise as creating the plan and choosing its
furnishings, for they are all part of one composition.
There are, however, priorities in their selection and use.
Here we discuss what those might be.*

A DESIGNER'S APPROACH

It is the introduction of plant material into a pattern that excites many garden designers, for in their mind's eye the static pattern takes life and the imaginative juices start to flow. Of course, it is not just a question of filling in the spaces: the arrangement and style of the living materials have to be part of the design concept from the start.

Depending on the site, your two-dimensional plan may have a third dimension of height in the form of retaining walls and changes of level, but it is the planting that will introduce bulk; your initial plant selection should seek to extend the plan's intention upwards. It is this bulk that starts to define both the positive forms on a site and the negative spaces, or voids, between them; suddenly, your outside room not only has walls but furniture as well, through which you will thread your way. Appreciated in this light, a garden's design becomes a sculptural concept.

The mood or style of your garden might be historical, or it might be national; it might be related to a particular site condition, or to a style of planting – examples of these follow on the next few pages. Whichever may be the case, you need to have a clear idea of the look you seek.

Historical styles will be dictated by your house principally, but for the purist the selection of the correct plants for the period is a consideration. It was only in the late eighteenth century that decorative plant gardening became fashionable, and increasing numbers of plants were introduced from abroad, and later hybridized. For myself, I am happy with the essence of a period, and after that I work with the available palette. For example, rhododendrons, azaleas, conifers, and bedding roses all evoke the 1920s to me, and would look wrong in certain period layouts, while near an eighteenth-century house in England I would use some woody material favored by the fashionable of the era – a cedar of Lebanon perhaps or, in a city, a *Magnolia grandiflora*, originally imported from America.

National styles evolve from local roots, so location and climatic zone are factors affecting their eventual look – for inevitably what grows has to do with what will survive in the given conditions. As I have noted earlier, the Italian garden has many historical forms, but its range of plants has stayed broadly the same, and a typical Australian garden would undoubtedly have eucalyptus in it, although other vegetation would vary with the area.

Leading the eye
A tree sited in the center of this lawn acts as a foreground to the rounded, shrubby shapes of the mixed border planting beyond, the tree's shape echoed in turn by the vertical spires of the yellow verbascum.

A period
A concrete sphere provides an abstract punctuation point in a planting scheme, accentuating the loose, gentle outlines of the plants around it and providing a counterpoise between nature and man.

Enhancing sculpture
Plant forms can be selected to enhance a man-made feature, drawing the eye towards it while playing a subservient role to it. Here the generous leaves of ligularia surround a mysterious standing figure.

Plants for punctuation
An Irish yew provides another type of punctuation – almost an exclamation mark – among a mass of low-growing flowering plants. Its vertical shape echoes its urban setting, and it will give valuable winter form.

Color and shape,
left and above
*Strong architectural forms call
for a robust approach to planting. Here plants of startling
color contrasts are arranged in
generous swaths, the hummocks
of grass echoing the rounded
window arches on the office
building behind, and the
foreground spires of lythrum
the structure between them.*

Clipped shapes, above
*Box clipped into gentle domes
provides an abstract backdrop
for the sculptural leaves of a
globe artichoke, illustrating the
potential of free plant forms
counterpoised with structural
foliage effects.*

ARCHITECTURAL STYLE

While other styles of planting soften and contrast with the ground plan, in the architectural style the plants are there to further the two-dimensional plan concept, to extend it into three dimensions.

Broadly speaking, one can identify three types of architectural style. Firstly, there are the plants that are architectural in themselves, their characteristically strong shapes providing a structure for looser schemes or making a statement on their own. Many of these plants originate in hot and dry or humid, tropical regions, and their strong leaf forms or dominating outlines are often the result of the plants' adaptations to the climate. Next come the parterres and *allées*, pleaching and topiary of the architectural style of renaissance and formal layouts. Here the style has more to do with the control and shaping of the plants than their intrinsic architectural qualities. Finally, there is the controlled look of the Japanese planting style, an asymmetrical concept that clips and restrains what would otherwise be too loose.

English formal
Box and yew have been clipped into strongly geometrical shapes and combined with fruit trees to compose this cottage style version of an architectural look.

102

Block planting
The line of a swimming pool
in this garden is reinforced by
the strong blocks of planting—
bamboos and, in front of them,
Rudbeckia fulgida *var.*
sullivanti '*Goldsturm*'.

Subtropical look, left
The strong forms of agaves,
yuccas, and aloe combine to
make the characteristically
lush, architectural look of hot,
subtropical regions.

WATERY STYLE

Watery plant groupings often derive much of their visual strength from the horizontal line of the water itself; since many of the water-loving plants have large leaves and strong outlines, good contrasts are created with little help from the designer.

Many of the plants in this range will also grow in constantly damp earth. It is worth noting, however, that few of them retain their leaves through winter in a temperate climate. Bamboo will of course remain, but it is invasive; and there is a compensation in the twigs of shrubby willows and dogwoods, both of which like damp conditions.

Aside from the classic water plants – such as reeds, rushes, and waterlilies – you can create a watery look using grasses in damp areas, but they need to be planted with gravel and rock to be convincing. *Iris germanica* could also be used, planted for a stream effect. Growing water plants in waterproof pots is another option – no one has said that pots need to have annuals in them alone.

Simple planting
The plants at the side of this simple waterfall act as a contrast to both its strong lines and that of the watercourse itself. The larger plant is the water iris, Iris ensata, *which forms a background to* Astilbe x arendsii *'Brautschleier'.*

Rocky water feature
In these warm subtropical waters, long-stemmed lotus (Nelumbo) *grow with cyperus behind the rocks. Spiky vertical reeds and rushes contrast with the horizontal line of the water, while the flat waterlilies are more restful in appearance.*

A profusion of plants
The horizontal water plane is echoed by the deck bridge in this Dutch garden – both combine to contrast with the exuberance of plantings in the water and around it. The spikes of blue flowers in the foreground come from Pontederia cordata; *beyond is a bamboo,* Sinarundinaria nitida, *and to its right the rounded leaves of* Ligularia dentata *'Desdemona'. The grass with spotted leaves beyond the deck bridge is* Miscanthus sinensis *'Zebrinus'.*

COTTAGE STYLE

Traditionally, the cottage garden was a colorful jumble of vegetables, herbs, fruits, and companion flowering plants, such as pot marigolds, which acted as deterrents to pests. No doubt there would have been seasonal flowers too, snowdrops or bluebells in spring, but flowers for their own sake were a rich man's pursuit; the cottager would have used his garden to produce food for the family. Cottage garden style today takes the best of the traditional approach, but extends the range of material, for winter interest is important too. Old-fashioned plants — in other words, those that existed before the hybridizer got to them — still form the essence of the look, for example, pinks, shrub roses, love-in-a-mist, monkshood, and *Lilium candidum.* Herbs such as rosemary, lavender, sage, parsley, and chives are also quintessential. Contemporary additions include the hellebores, certain shrubs, and a far greater range of climbers and bulbs throughout the year. The effect is a vibrant muddle, overflowing, alive with insects, and heady with fragrance.

Decorative herbs
Herbs add flower color, form, and texture to a cottage garden, and are right for the style too. In the foreground are chives, with Welsh onions beyond.

Contemporary cottage garden style, left
A modern cottage garden arrangement, including lupines and delphiniums, with creeping masses of pinks at the edge of the path. Colors are mixed and vibrant, although softened with gray herbal foliages and foaming green alchemilla flowers.

Lines of color, above
*In front of a pink rose is the summer foliage of the California tree poppy (*Romneya coulteri*) and the variegated form of* Iris pallida *with clumps of lavender.*

PLANTING IN GRAVEL

Gravel is nature's seedbed. It offers ideal conditions for plants to establish themselves naturally, self-seeding outwards in a controlled anarchy of quirky plant groupings, the same plant repeating itself around the garden. The look changes naturally too, since the planting masses grow and move each season; from time to time they can be thinned out to create yet another look.

Self-seeders can be accompanied with shrubs for a more structured effect: instead of planting up prepared beds, use woody shrubs or climbers with gravel under them for a clean look, and one that will save on maintenance.

Plants that flourish in gravel are those that prefer shallow, well-drained soil; in winter gravel protects the seeds from rotting, and it acts as a protective mulch for seedlings in summer. In sun, many gray-foliaged plants will thrive – in short, most plants of the Mediterranean.

Traditionally, gravel was also used to infill decorative parterres of box.

Golden daffodils
As these clumps of daffodils planted in gravel die down, *emerging perennials, particularly the clumps of* Alchemilla mollis, *will hide their leaves.*

Gravelled corner
The controlled anarchy of gravel plantings is shown by Sisyrinchium striatum, *a great self-seeder which keeps its irislike leaves throughout winter and is an admirable plant for the gravel technique. The gray spires with yellow flowers are* Verbascum olympicum. *The gold-leaved tree on the right is* Catalpa bignonioides *'Aurea'.*

NATURAL PLANT GROUPINGS

There is a natural, informal way of arranging plants that recreates the feel of the wildflower meadow and country hedgerow, where native plants – wild-flowers, brambles, and so on – often interspersed with roughly cut grass are left to their own devices. The success of a wild planting scheme depends upon its location, for it should appear to be of it, not imposed upon it. In most temperate parts of the world that do not have extreme soil conditions, the natural plant horizon extends from low herbs and wildflowers through shrubs to small and then forest trees. To create a natural plant grouping, include plants from this spectrum, and group them according to the way they would naturally grow: some increase by runners, like brambles; ferns procreate by spores; bulbs produce bulbils; certain flowers self-seed, each producing a particular seedling pattern; and so on. You can plant a new wild area to create such a growing pattern artificially, and nature will soon infuse your selection with other native plants. It is sobering to realize that the gardener calls these natives "weeds" if they turn up among his petunias, and pulls them out, replacing them with alien species. Maintenance then becomes an attempt to hold off the locals. It surely makes sense then to go with the indigenous plants, or their hybridized forms.

Meadow look
Daisies and bluebells growing in roughly cut grass. Sustain a wildflower garden by mowing so that woody plants do not impinge. Wildflower mixes are available; make sure the one you choose is suitable for your soil and location.

Native planting with rock
"Wild" changes according to location: in this California garden, sedums, mosses, and grasses burgeon forth from a rocky buttress, spreading themselves into every crack and crevice in a planting of great character. Each location will have its own selection of native plant material that is most suited to that spot.

A natural tapestry
A bank of native plants, including English bluebells, brambles, red campion, dandelion seed heads, and bracken. Such a natural grouping, though a planted one, can provide a good transition between a more structured garden planting and the freer look of the surrounding countryside.

WOODLAND STYLE

There is no better example of woodland planting than the way in which nature does it; you might reinterpret the look with the plants you use, but study the way the plant masses have grouped themselves in the wild, and adapt the style to your own garden. A woodland style varies according to the wood itself, however, and the age, height, and density of the trees. In a temperate zone, the ideal is a light woodland – one that is not too densely planted – of preferably deciduous trees with clearings, for light is important to anything growing on the woodland floor. When establishing such a woodland, the types of trees you plant to create it will of course depend upon the situation. Where there is space, plant forest trees for future generations, interplanting perhaps with quicker-growing softwoods which can later be thinned. In smaller areas, medium-sized trees with smaller, possibly flowering, trees at the edge of the wood are appropriate. Where space is very limited, create a small thicket, with multistemmed hazels, perhaps. The natural fertility of the soil also influences the planting; an established woodland will probably have a moist and well-mulched soil thanks to an accumulation of plant litter, but a new woodland floor can be extremely dry at times, unless you doctor it.

Woodland grouping
Tiarella, with foxgloves
(Digitalis) *and Solomon's seal* (Polygonatum) *in the background, in a moist, lightly shaded location.*

Spring scene
Euphorbias, green-flowered
Helleborus argutifolius, *and,*
in the foreground, Paeonia
mlokosewitschii *together*
make an artful woodland
planting beneath high-
canopied trees.

A host of hostas, left
Massed hostas growing
beneath the light leaf canopy of
a rhododendron planting
create a magical effect in
spring. Woodland plantings
tend to be at their best in this
season, before the trees come
into leaf and cast their shade.

BUILDING A FRAMEWORK

Plants are so diverse that it is all too easy to become absorbed in the highly pleasurable details of a decorative planting scheme at an early stage. There lies the route to a restless garden with little unity of thought between concept, plan, and planting. Instead, begin by thinking of the planted areas of your garden as bulky, three-dimensional shapes, to be manipulated as an extension of your design concept – I will explain this on page 116. To give a structure and an order to your planting, and to help you compose with broad brushstrokes, use a selection of plants according to their functions within the overall design.

Whether I am planning a planting scheme from scratch or looking at established gardens, in my mind there are five key plant categories, and I ask myself how the planting scheme functions in their terms. The first category at planning stage is the "specials" – the star performers that form focal points for the garden's design and are crucial to the direction of the eye within and around the site. The second category is that of the "skeleton" planting, or what one might think of as the green background that will ensure year-round enclosure, provide a windscreen, and generally mold the garden space. The "decoratives" are those to be displayed in front of the skeleton, and after them come the "pretties," the perennials for flower and foliage interest in spring and summer. Lastly, I think of the infill plantings, the transitory splashes of color as the seasons change, and the invaluable gap-fillers for new schemes.

The categories are discussed in greater detail on pages 120-33. Do not worry unduly about which category a plant fits into, for there are no rules: a special plant in a small garden might function simply as a pretty in another. The categories form a structure for your thinking, a way to break down the planning process into stages that reflect your concerns when designing a garden.

THE FIVE CATEGORIES OF PLANTING

  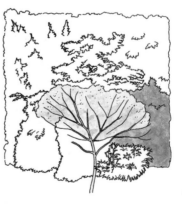 

The specials
In the planting opposite, the dominant element is the standard gold form of Robinia pseudoacacia 'Frisia' – so this must be the special.

The skeletons
The background framework that holds this concept together comprises a cypress, holly, purple pittosporum, cotoneaster, and olearia.

The decoratives
Escallonia would be planned in at the decorative stage. When in flower, as here, the perennial Crambe cordifolia also plays a decorative role.

The pretties
The perennials here include Hosta sieboldiana, Argyranthemum frutescens, and golden marjoram. Sweet Williams add more pretty interest.

An established plant grouping in spring

Analyzing existing plant groupings will help you to understand successful plant combinations as structural frameworks, with plants from every category working in balance together. In this example, as always in my plantings, evergreen elements with good foliage color and texture play an important though background role; by spring they are eclipsed by the more transient qualities of various flowering perennials and annuals.

The infill

Foxgloves have self-seeded around and through the grouping. Alchemilla mollis and Asphodeline lutea also fill any gaps.

SCALE, SHAPE, & MASS

The planting masses enclose, frame, and shelter your garden, and balance the central spaces in a new design. As I explained earlier, it is the right proportion of mass in relation to the void that makes a garden a satisfactory space to be in, and with the planting it is mass we are considering.

The sketches below will help you to see the planted areas as blocks of green matter – there is no need to draw these stages for your own design. Once you have grasped this concept, you can compose a picture of plant shapes on an elevation drawn from your plan (opposite). You will not only see the heights of the lumps of vegetation that are

necessary to screen a view, to relate to existing large plantings, or to link a building to the site and so on, but you will also see the areas of new planting that are necessary and the shape they should be to fit the style of your layout.

The specials will be the first key plants to position, so look for the correct places for focal points. These can dominate the layout or counterpoise an existing feature. Go on to fill in the elevation sketch to make a pleasing composition of forms. Experiment with different shapes – lollipop, circular, triangular, columnar, and spiky shapes will all be useful – and try a variety of sizes too. Pair small shapes with large ones, or use them separately as counterbalances; smaller shapes can be interpreted

*P*LANTING AS BULK & SHAPE

The sketches below explain my concept of the planting as bulky masses that extend the plan upwards. There is no need to draw these stages for your own design.

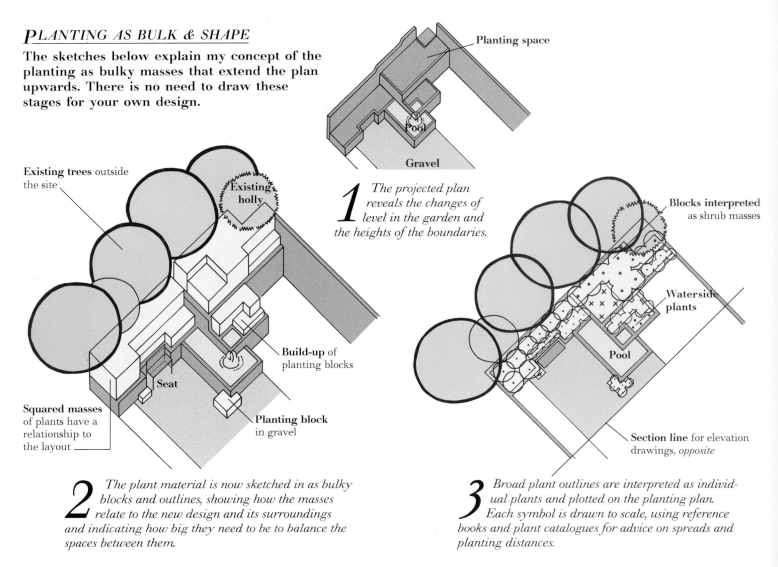

Planting space

Pool

Gravel

Existing trees outside the site

Existing holly

Build-up of planting blocks

Seat

Squared masses of plants have a relationship to the layout

Planting block in gravel

1 The projected plan reveals the changes of level in the garden and the heights of the boundaries.

2 The plant material is now sketched in as bulky blocks and outlines, showing how the masses relate to the new design and its surroundings and indicating how big they need to be to balance the spaces between them.

Blocks interpreted as shrub masses

Waterside plants

Pool

Section line for elevation drawings, *opposite*

3 Broad plant outlines are interpreted as individual plants and plotted on the planting plan. Each symbol is drawn to scale, using reference books and plant catalogues for advice on spreads and planting distances.

PLANT SHAPES ON AN ELEVATION

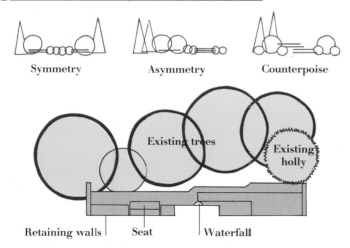

Symmetry   Asymmetry   Counterpoise

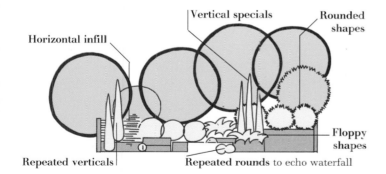

Existing trees

Existing holly

Retaining walls   Seat   Waterfall

1 *The elevation Draw an elevation from your plan (see page 326) of each main view in the new design. Sketch in, to scale, existing plants in or outside the site, as these will dictate the proportions for the new plantings.*

Vertical specials   Rounded shapes

Horizontal infill

Floppy shapes

Repeated verticals   Repeated rounds to echo waterfall

2 *Arranging shapes On tracing paper, sketch a composition of different plant shapes, keeping each one simple and abstract. Compose a pleasing picture, perhaps shading evergreens to balance deciduous shapes.*

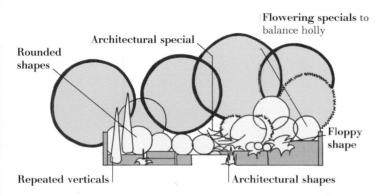

Flowering specials to balance holly

Architectural special

Rounded shapes

Floppy shape

Repeated verticals   Architectural shapes

A mixed example Less architectural than the previous version, this example has more rounded plant shapes and fewer dominating verticals. Either would work well as a planting design.

as lower-growing plants in the final planting plan. There can be no correct permutation of shapes for your plant compositions – the right one is that which looks best to you.

From your final sketch you can go on to identify the skeleton and decorative elements among your abstract plant outlines; your garden will still need fleshing out with pretties and infill planting, but they can wait until you work up the planting plan in detail.

The Planting Plan

Once you have an idea of how you want the planting to look overall, you can start to consider which plants will achieve those particular effects for you. Your outlines are all drawn roughly to scale by virtue of working from an accurate plan, so you can calculate the approximate height and spread that a plant will need to fulfil its allotted role, and go on to choose the individual plants.

An early consideration has to be the time frame for the scheme. For smaller gardens, I use a five-year plan when determining planting distances and choosing plants. I position the plants at close enough distances to enable them to become a group by that time; thereafter, they will probably have to be cut back, thinned out, or moved. In the intervening years, I fill any gaps with ground cover, annuals, or self-seeding biennials. A longer time frame may well be needed for a very large garden, or when planting up a woodland area as you would certainly not want to move the trees around.

The example on pages 158-60 shows a plan built up over the five years of the planting framework.

You do not need to be familiar with a vast range of plants to evolve a workable planting scheme. Just by visiting gardens you can learn a great deal – take a catalogue with you to check which plants are commercially available. As a general guide, the fewer the varieties the better. Once your initial plan is complete, go over it again, halving the number of species used, and doubling the quantities of those that remain. This will encourage you to repeat the same plant around the garden – always a strong unifying device – and to plant in broad blocks of color rather than little patches.

THE MATURING GARDEN

It takes several years for a planting scheme mapped out on paper to mature to the image you have of it in your mind's eye. To show the stages of development, I have taken as an example an urban garden with a harsh industrial backdrop. I set the garden strongly in its location by using the abstract patterns of the warehouse roof lines beyond the boundary as a basis for the layout.

The planting needed to be both simple and fast-growing, to give a sense of privacy to the garden as quickly as possible, screening the parking space but allowing enough room for a child to play.

Smoky brown brickwork and general urban drabness called for bright colors to cheer up the space, so I used two golden-leaved robinias as my specials: they arrived as large nursery-stock trees, not semimature size, but a spindly 15ft (5m) high. These were backed up by quick-growing conifers (which I do not normally advocate, but they were needed here to make up for the slow growth of most of the rest of the evergreen skeleton material). The decorative planting concentrated on gold and green foliage, with white flowers.

The first months
The garden a few weeks after planting shows the zigzag layout stark and hard-edged. As the planting matures and fills in over the next few years, the layout will soften, though still echo the outlines of the industrial roof lines beyond.

Before I finally plant them, I position the plants in their pots at their appropriate planting distances, both to check for sufficient spacing and to make any last-minute adjustments.

In the microclimate of a city, plants grow fast, but some infill was still necessary to create a jungle straightaway. As always, I relied on annuals between the young shrubs, plenty of bulbs in spring, and pots of geraniums for the terrace.

To give an idea of how the planting will develop over a three-year span, I have sketched the changing plant shapes on tracing paper over a photograph of the garden shortly after planting (see below).

*T*HE PLANTING OVER THREE YEARS

A nursery-stock *Robinia pseudoacacia* 'Frisia'

Three *Griselinia littoralis* 'Variegata' are well spaced out

Malus – relocated for greater emphasis

The x *Cupressocyparis leylandii* is still very small

Nicotiana and white snapdragons provide low flowering interest

Sunflowers for temporary drama, and height

Year one: Initial planting
The far left-hand corner of the garden shows the immature plants, nursery-stock robinia and transplanted malus, all well spaced out leaving room for growth.

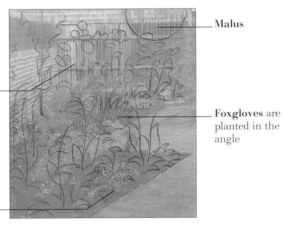

Malus

Foxgloves are planted in the angle

Year one: Infill planting
Fast-growing plants can be used to fill in the gaps and provide short-term interest in the first few seasons. Sunflowers and foxgloves are useful because of their height.

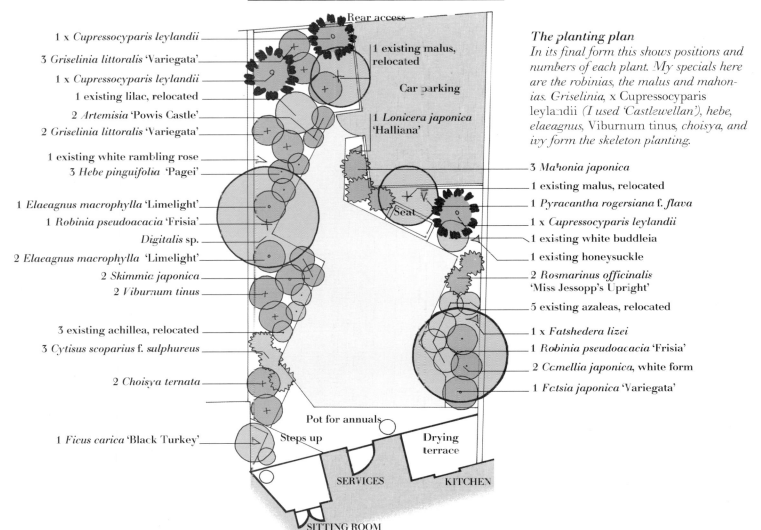

1 x *Cupressocyparis leylandii*

3 *Griselinia littoralis* 'Variegata'

1 x *Cupressocyparis leylandii*

1 existing lilac, relocated

2 *Artemisia* 'Powis Castle'

2 *Griselinia littoralis* 'Variegata'

1 existing white rambling rose

3 *Hebe pinguifolia* 'Pagei'

1 *Elaeagnus macrophylla* 'Limelight'

1 *Robinia pseudoacacia* 'Frisia'

Digitalis sp.

2 *Elaeagnus macrophylla* 'Limelight'

2 *Skimmia japonica*

2 *Viburnum tinus*

3 existing achillea, relocated

3 *Cytisus scoparius* f. *sulphureus*

2 *Choisya ternata*

1 *Ficus carica* 'Black Turkey'

Rear access

1 existing malus, relocated

Car parking

1 *Lonicera japonica* 'Halliana'

Seat

Pot for annuals

Steps up

Drying terrace

SERVICES

KITCHEN

SITTING ROOM

The planting plan

In its final form this shows positions and numbers of each plant. My specials here are the robinias, the malus and mahonias. Griselinia, x Cupressocyparis leylandii (I used 'Castlewellan'), hebe, elaeagnus, Viburnum tinus, choisya, and ivy form the skeleton planting.

3 *Mahonia japonica*

1 existing malus, relocated

1 *Pyracantha rogersiana* f. *flava*

1 x *Cupressocyparis leylandii*

1 existing white buddleia

1 existing honeysuckle

2 *Rosmarinus officinalis* 'Miss Jessopp's Upright'

5 existing azaleas, relocated

1 x *Fatshedera lizei*

1 *Robinia pseudoacacia* 'Frisia'

2 *Camellia japonica*, white form

1 *Fatsia japonica* 'Variegata'

The trees are screening the parking area

Griselinia littoralis 'Variegata' are bulking up

Year two: Greater bulk

The shrubs will be bulking up by now, though slowly since they are evergreen. So annuals for infill are still invaluable, particularly to flop over border edges.

The x *Cupressocyparis leylandii* mark the garden boundary

Annual infill is still necessary to highlight the seat

The robinias frame the garden picture, keeping the eye within the site

The shrubs are spreading slowly

The seat is enfolded by burgeoning plant masses

Camellias make glossy green mounds at the foot of one robinia

Plant shapes balance the lawn space

Year three: Design realized

The garden should be alive with sunny yellow foliage. The planting bulk will create areas of shadow, allowing the whole to read as a sculptural mass.

SPECIALS

O n the following pages I have tried to analyze and present guidelines for my five key planting categories. Of course, every design calls for its own individual mix of plants, but I hope some of my suggestions will help you.

The plants I term the specials form the linchpins of the planting scheme. They lead the eye around the garden and function as focal points in the design; they also give sequence to a garden's planting by punctuating what might otherwise just be a green fuzz.

Depending on the layout, the garden could have one major special, it could have several specials positioned as a culmination of the design, or a series of them sited around the garden. But always remember that in any production there need only be one or two prima donnas, supported by a large chorus. Too many prima donnas, all clamoring for attention at once, become far too demanding for the viewer. Where they are the same – a mass of Mediterranean cypresses, for instance – they form a unity in themselves and create their own style.

If you are planning your garden from scratch, you will want your specials to link the proportions of the house to those of the garden. A tree that is too large, like a willow in a small garden, will quickly engulf and unbalance the scheme, whereas too small a plant will not be strong enough visually to fulfil the intention. Existing established trees might well be the specials; they could even be outside the site, although this has its own risks, as your pivotal tree might be cut down one day. Perhaps more safely make your special a repeat of an off-site tree, a sort of counterpoise.

Coming down in scale, the planting areas will each have a special within them, it in its turn relating back to the larger specials. Even large plants in pots can perform as focal points on a terrace.

Any plant chosen as a special needs to have architectural value and a good outline to give it year-round dominance, although it need not necessarily be evergreen. The actual tree or plant you choose

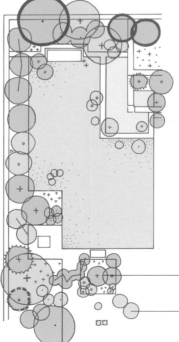

An immature framework
There is always a time lag between what one conceives and the achievement of that goal, but even at this early stage this framework is working well. The two Cordyline australis *and the tubs of chrysanthemums provide the visual "period," creating a foreground for the garden. Eventually the eye will be caught by a clump of* Euphorbia characias *subsp.* wulfenii, *sited to accentuate the seat and to pair with the foreground incident.*

— Two *Cordyline australis*

— Two tubs of chrysanthemums

Two *Betula pendula*

A larger view

*A composition without props, such as a seat or structure, but dominated instead by two graceful, focal-point silver birches (*Betula pendula*), and a strong but simply shaped lawn. Ground-cover planting enhances the special role of the trees, and, to lead the eye towards them, paving has been laid through the shrub masses that frame the foreground.*

Special trees and garden features
In this garden the focal points already existed in the form of a large garden pavilion and an armillary sphere. In the planting I sought to link these two features and enhance their visual roles by using trees with bold outlines and strong forms. The fastigiate beech and cedar are thus the specials, filling in the space between the pavilion and the sphere. The juniper, with its spreading branches, plays a quieter skeleton role, though one just as important.

Garden pavilion

Fagus sylvatica 'Dawyckii'

Cedrus deodara

Armillary sphere, on paving

Juniperus x *media*

Repeating forms

Specials off-site
*Here the strong vertical forms
of two* Calocedrus decurrens,
*the California incense cedar,
dominate. A skeleton hedge
and some clipped box balls
in the border serve to pull
these specials visually into the
scheme, in so doing drawing
the eye across the site.*

A tropical feel
*The strong leaf shapes of many
tropical plants make them
exciting material for a focal
point in a garden or border.
Here the dramatic spiky foliage of the background yuccas
has been consciously emphasized by that of the agave in
the foreground.*

will be a matter of personal preference, but an indication of what *not* to do might be helpful. I would
advise against some of the more obvious prima
donnas: I find trees with purple or variegated foliage difficult to place, since they tend to be unspec-
tacular in shape, though their leaves are real show
stoppers. Imagine *Acer negundo* 'Variegatum' with
a purple plum: anything else must be a comedown.
Too many conifers can be a great mistake, too, as
their strong colors and shapes make a planting stac-
cato and restless.

Shrubs with good form and interesting foliage
are contenders. *Euphorbia characias* and its sub-
species *wulfenii*, melianthus, and the upright forms
of rosemary and yew are all good; and anything
spiky, such as yuccas, makes a great eye-catcher,
although in temperate climates these need to be
sited near the house as their exotic quality may
provide too strong a contrast against a backdrop of
broad-leaved natives. (See also pages 280-3.)

SKELETONS

Once you have located and selected your focal points of emphasis within the design, you can establish the structure that will last the year round with what I call the skeleton planting. This not only puts flesh on the bones of the design, but provides a permanent framework for the garden as a whole and the individual beds and borders within it. What the garden will look like in winter is the key guideline for your skeleton planting; good evergreen foliage and winter interest will therefore be the characteristics you seek, and the skeleton plants will usually be sited for maximum effect for viewing from the house.

The skeletons have a background role to play, steadying the design and performing quietly, if unremarkably, throughout the year. In summer, they will be eclipsed by more attention-seeking shrubs, but in winter they come into their own, either for their form, foliage, stems, flowers, or berries. Hedging is therefore an important skeletal element, vital for its green bulk and as a provider of privacy and shelter – and sometimes to further the design concept (see pages 158-9).

Plants to be considered at the skeleton stage will be evergreen shrubs and trees, such as holly, yew, hemlock, and juniper, and perhaps some of the colored foliage subjects like *Lonicera nitida* 'Baggesen's Gold' or gray elaeagnus. As a general rule, I recommend natives for this category: they have a stocky vigor that withstands climatic excess, and since much of this skeleton material will be at the perimeter of the garden, they help to integrate it

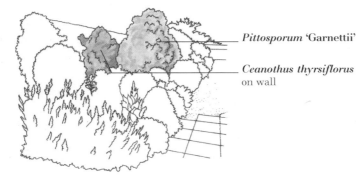

Pittosporum 'Garnettii'

Ceanothus thyrsiflorus
on wall

Pittosporum 'Garnettii'

Ceanothus thyrsiflorus
on wall

A mixed border
The backbone plant in this border is Pittosporum *'Garnettii', making a year-round contribution to the structure of the planting. The ceanothus is another evergreen skeleton element.*

Skeletons for form
The sculptural mass of golden box (the skeleton) sets off the star performer in this grouping – a crab apple putting on a spectacular show of spring blossom.

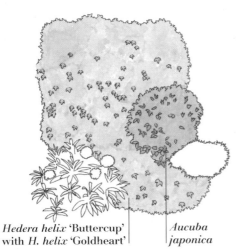

Hedera helix 'Buttercup'   *Aucuba*
with *H. helix* 'Goldheart'   *japonica*

Skeletons for the smaller garden

*An evergreen framework has been pro-
vided by several forms of ivy (*Hedera
helix *'Goldheart' and* H. h. *'Buttercup')
and* Aucuba japonica, *with* Euphorbia
mellifera *in front. Contrasts of leaf shape
and color as well planned as these do
not need the distraction of brightly
colored flowers.*

Sculptural effects, right

*The tall verticals of bamboo stems contrast
dramatically with the horizontal, but equally angular, spreading form of* Juniperus x
media. *The result is an abstract composition of linear forms.*

with its surroundings too. For small gardens the key skeleton plants may have to be smaller in scale as well: variegated euonymus, cotoneasters, even ivy all work well, as do bay and box grown as clipped container subjects. Among the evergreen flowering shrubs there are plants with excellent skeleton potential. Mahonias, with their architectural shape, glossy foliage, and scented winter flowers are among the best – dramatic enough to act as a special in a small garden – and the Mexican orange blossom (*Choisya ternata*) is another good all-rounder. *Viburnum tinus, V. x burkwoodii*, and the Portuguese laurel (*Prunus lusitanica*) are also among my favorites. Within borders, the smaller evergreens and shrubby evergreen herbs such as hebes and rosemary can be used as a backbone, but avoid anything that looks dog-eared out of season.

Winter performers provide the next layer of skeletal planting. *Viburnum x bodnantense, Garrya elliptica, Jasminum nudiflorum*, and wintersweet (*Chimonanthus praecox*), are cherished favorites for their flowers, and I consider all the hellebores wonderful garden plants with – or indeed on its own – *Iris foetidissima*: insignificant in flower, but with good straplike, year-round foliage and ostentatious seeds. Then a clutch of plants, dogwoods and rubus among them, will provide dramatic stems in winter. (See also pages 288-93.)

The background element
The dark green of a yew hedge (Taxus baccata) – the skeleton – provides the backdrop to the bare winter branches of Cornus mas.

DECORATIVES

O nce the specials and the skeleton structure are established on the plan, the next stage is the introduction of decorative flowering shrubs – the colorful material that will lighten up the skeleton framework against which it is seen. While the bulkier decoratives still have a structural function, they also add the first layer of flowering bulk to the garden, for many will be eye-catching in their season of interest.

The decorative qualities of a plant are very diverse – what are they? Flower color and quality of course come high up the list, but flowers are a transitory feature, and a plant should have attractive foliage and a pleasing overall shape too. I would include tall ornamental grasses in this category, as their character is so distinctive.

Perhaps it is enough to say that the decoratives should be plants that you like, the final choices coming down to personal preference.

One of my favorite decoratives is broom (*Cytisus*), particularly when it is cut back after flowering – I love that Mohican haircut look. The softer, floppier forms of lilac (*Syringa*) and mock orange (the creamy-flowered *Philadelphus coronarius* is one of the best) both have the added virtue of fragrance in season, and buddleias, too, give a good summer show. As with all decorative shrubs, they should be kept cut back and not allowed to get too woody. All the species shrub roses are high on my list: they are tough, have a good shape if controlled, and some produce excellent hips in autumn.

Some climbers and wall-trained shrubs come into this decorative category. Climbing roses – one I particularly love is 'Madame Alfred Carrière' – give wonderful scent and cascades of flowers, the honeysuckles likewise. Azara is good for a wall or fence as it is evergreen and has vanilla-scented flowers; ceanothus might also be a decorative in some gardens. *Clematis montana* needs siting as a decorative, for its vigor gives it a structural role, but I find that the other clematis species are thinner, and so should be planned in at the next stage.

Gray foliage continuing zigzagging line

Santolina

Sculptural masses

Santolina and artemisia form low, spreading mounds of decorative gray planting, a zigzagging line leading around and towards the phormiums and cypresses (both specials) in this California garden.

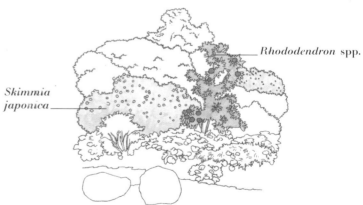

Rhododendron spp.

Skimmia japonica

Complementary color, left and above

Decorative masses of azaleas and a mound of Skimmia japonica *in flower bring both bulk and color to this composition, complementing the central rhododendron.*

129

PRETTIES

With the pretties come the star performers of the late spring and summer months, the herbaceous perennials. Again, I think of this as a planning stage, not an immutable group of certain plants: the objectives here are color harmonies and a continuity of flowering interest around the garden.

For me, the pretties are primarily a whole range of plants that rely on their flowers as their main feature. Also in this category, though, are several invaluable foliage plants, included here because their lack of winter form makes them inappropriate at an earlier stage of the planning. I am thinking of hostas, fennel, and angelica, for instance.

Leaving the inclusion of so many glorious perennials, such as delphiniums, lupines, asters, and so on, until this fourth stage might seem to be a put-down, for many pretties are established favorites. But of course it isn't. The point I want to make is that these plants, which have the disadvantage of leaving gaps once they have finished flowering, will look so much better in front of the right decoratives, which in turn are sheltered by the skeleton planting; it is a continuity of thought.

When it comes to actual plants, the choice is, again, vast. My own favorites include alchemilla – a plant I would not be without for its foaming, generous nature – kniphofia (particularly *K. caulescens*), Japanese anemones for shade, and stachys. Acanthus might be planned in at this stage, depending on the garden; its form and flower spikes qualify it as a special in some settings.

Ground-cover planting is planned in with the pretties. It is more lasting than the infill planting, for one is not seeking the drama of an individual plant, rather the quality of the total mass.

At the pretties stage, you can afford to experiment and even take the odd chance, without altering the overall structure of the planting. Indeed, if the previous categories of planning have been a success, the design will be strong enough to hold a variety of approaches with the pretties.

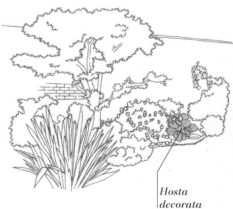

Hosta decorata

The pretties in context
The pretties might lack year-round structure, but that does not mean any loss of impact. This garden shows all five categories at work, from the eye-catching phormium (the special) to the hosta as the pretty, and the alchemilla as infill.

Pretties for summer display
*A wonderful grouping of
perennials, all qualifying as
pretties since none is woody or
evident in the winter months.
The scale of the concept and
the subtlety of the color
harmonies are the work of a
master. Seen in late spring, it is
an essay in contrasting vertical
forms with horizontal bands of
color, the foliage tones providing a strengthening element.
The plants include (from the
top):* Veronicastrum virgini-
cum '*Album*', Campanula
lactiflora, Astrantia *spp.,* Salvia
nemorosa, *and* Sedum
spectabile.

INFILL

No matter how good your selection of plants, there will always be periods when extra drama with a splash of color is appropriate, and while your planting is young, instant plants will give color and interest. Infill planting satisfies both needs. It has a more random quality than the other categories, accentuating by contrast the rigidity of a formal layout, or continuing the intention of a freer planting.

Bulbs, annuals, self-seeding plants, and biennials all come into this category, infilling between shrubs, perennials, or ground cover, coming up between paving slabs, or massed in rough grass. Sometimes the display will be short-lived but seasonal, as with crocus, narcissus, and tulips. Or the infill may provide ground cover — forget-me-nots, nicotiana, or saxifrage. Lastly, there is infill of the "cheeky incident" variety. In my own garden verbascums, onopordum, and silybum all seed themselves around in a wonderfully anarchic way; alchemilla is sometimes just a little *too* cheeky.

Early in the year, bulbs are the preeminent infillers, starting with the dainty winter-flowering crocus, not the vulgar large-flowering cultivars. (I confess a peculiar dislike for autumn crocus; their color seems curiously out of character with the season.) For mixed plantings I love lily-flowered tulips and the exotic parrot forms; where space is limited I use the smaller species. Then there are all the handsome alliums, and the crown imperials (*Fritillaria imperialis*), their great heads of drooping bells so right for the cottage garden.

Bulbs for summer include *Gladiolus communis* subsp. *byzantinus*, small but superbly wine-colored, and excellent for naturalizing. Of the lilies, my favorites are the trumpet varieties, with the old *Lilium regale* still the best; the scent is magical.

Among annuals, the taller plants are very useful, particularly for instant height in new borders. Foxgloves and sunflowers are both invaluable.

Finally, pots have great infill potential, providing temporary color as the garden matures.

Spring infill
The lily-flowered forms of tulip are excellent for spring color and elegant form in mixed borders, looking best when planted in loose, random drifts. In this border they contrast well with the rounded outlines of the permanent planting, giving it a much-needed lift in spring.

Contrast of forms
The succulent, silvery foliage of Echeveria elegans and the woolly leaves of stachys creep and sprawl around a spiky agave. Despite the strong contrasts of form and texture, the infill in this hot, dry site is appropriate stylistically for the special it surrounds.

SEASONAL INTEREST

An important element of any planting scheme is not simply the contributions that the plants make to the garden in summer, but how they perform, both independently and together, through the other seasons as well. A carefully orchestrated planting scheme can use the seasonal attributes of different plants to great advantage, and can also compensate for any out-of-season dullness: for example, the ubiquitous spring-flowering cherry can be planted in a group that offers summer flowers beneath it and autumn foliage interest as well.

Once you are aware of the seasonal attributes of plants, you can organize groupings that make use of the shift in color and form from, for example, flower color to seed heads, or from spring foliage to autumn color.

Bark color, evergreen leaves, and berries may not seem very important in summer, but in winter they assume far greater significance. It is in winter, too, that you will first see whether the skeleton planting of the garden is providing an adequate framework to hold the design together.

In a large garden it will be possible to plan the planting for different areas of emphasis throughout the year. A small garden offers rather more of a challenge, as everything is seen at once.

Once you start to think through your palette of plants, the number that have interest during more than one season is not so great – and the smaller the area you have to plant, the greater the value of a dual or even triple usage. By selecting your plants to provide at least two seasons of interest you will get maximum value from each – though still within orchestrated groupings. And here spring and summer bulbs come into their own, for their flowers come up through other plantings, which in turn hide their dying foliage.

Here and on the overleaf I show how the changing seasons make their mark on the garden.

DOUBLE BORDER

Summer

Autumn

A view in my own garden shows, in spring, tulips providing the focal point against a backdrop of shrubs; Daphne laureola is flowering to the left. By summer (top) the many yellow foliage tones are highlighted by the verbascums and alchemilla, providing a zigzag of yellow incident leading the eye towards the Robinia pseudoacacia 'Frisia' beyond. In autumn (above), gray foliage and rust colors come to the fore.

Spring

AN INDIVIDUAL PLANTING

A structural framework both ensures that a grouping looks good from all sides, and orchestrates the planting seasonally. As you plan your own schemes, bear in mind the overall structure, as well as each plant's appearance before, during, and after flowering. In this group I sought strong plant forms softened by perennials, a composition of shapes that can be abstracted into a simple dome with verticals and horizontals *(right)*.

Spring, left
The main view of this gravel planting shows the clipped box (Buxus sempervirens *'Gold Tip') acting as a backdrop to the greeny gray foliage of* Euphorbia characias *subsp.* wulfenii *and its crowning glory of lime-green flower heads.*

Summer, right and far right
The acid tones of spring fade to softer golds and mauves, the euphorbias changing color dramatically, while the pretties come into their own. Seen from the rear, the planting is more restrained, alchemilla *and* Allium christophii *enlivening a swath of low* Cotoneaster dammeri *in front.*

Autumn, right and far right
With the euphorbias now deadheaded, the scheme becomes one of striking blocks of color, almost monochromatic in its overall impression. The gray Atriplex halimus *counterpoises new euphorbia foliage, with Michaelmas daisies providing a clean white. To the rear, the just-dying flower heads of* Sedum spectabile *supply bronze and rust tones.*

Summer, front view

Summer, rear view

Autumn, front view

Autumn, rear view

THE SEASON'S PERFORMERS

Different textures and colors take center stage in any planting as the year progresses. Plan for a sprinkling of star performers for every season, backed by sympathetic foliage forms and tones. The key performers in the individual planting here are indicated right.

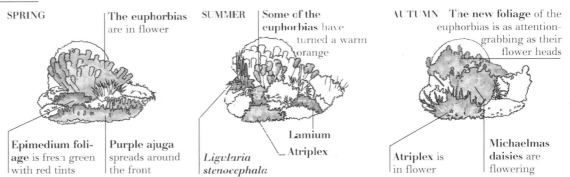

SPRING

The euphorbias are in flower

Epimedium foliage is fresh green with red tints

Purple ajuga spreads around the front

SUMMER

Some of the euphorbias have turned a warm orange

Lamium

Atriplex

Ligularia stenocephala

AUTUMN   The new foliage of the euphorbias is as attention-grabbing as their flower heads

Atriplex is in flower

Michaelmas daisies are flowering

WORKING WITH COLOR

Volumes have been written on the theory of color, on color harmonies, and color contrasts, but ultimately color appreciation is highly personal, not to say subjective. Some people love strong, bright colors; others prefer softer pinks and grays. It has often to do with age.

I have found that as I get older my appreciation of color subtleties changes. Shocking the viewer with color clashes and too much strength, I hope I have outgrown, but equally I am not yet into menopausal mauves or parlor pinks. The colors I like early in the morning and evening are very different from those that are appealing at noon. Similarly, the plant colors I would use beside high-action swimming pool areas have little in common with those I consider right for a view of a meadow beyond. Are my preferences governed by rules or do I mix and match in the way I pick the day's shirt and tie? What I choose you might loathe! And yet I do have some rules for myself.

The first is to accept that the green of foliage is a color just as much as that of flowers, and is the color we all use most. Fresh spring green turns into heavy summer green before firing up to gold in autumn – and within that range are palest yellow greens through to purple ones.

I tend to use color as a complement to my design, not as an end in itself. The color selection I make will be based on the color of the fence or wall behind the border, the color of the material of the house, and, most important of all, the color range that my client likes. The interior of the house tells me a lot about the colors for plants on the terrace outside – as it does about the color and type of paving and the style of pots into which all this planted color goes.

Then there is the intensity of light, which varies in different parts of the world: the stronger the light, the clearer the colors, for light affects our perception of color enormously.

The size of the garden affects my color choice. In small, enclosed areas my color range will relate back to the house and its interior; in larger spaces the house relationship will finish at the terrace, and the color range will probably get paler as it reaches the boundary. Too much strong color at a distance foreshortens the space. And if there is a view, color has to be seen in association with that too. The damp, misty atmosphere of Britain, for example, gives a bluish tinge to distant views; at boundary areas this effect has to be worked *with* in the planting, not against.

Foliage color, right
This cool foliage combination makes an interesting play on green and white, the variegation of the hosta picked up in the flowers of the trillium (see also page 265). It demonstrates how with careful selection of tones of green, light can be reflected into a shady corner.

One-color scheme, right
A single-color planting mass can have great impact. This planting was selected for quick effect, to screen a service building. The yellow flowers of senecio, Hypericum 'Hidcote', santolina, and violas are blended with gray foliage and golden sage.

Dot color effects, right
A pretty cottage garden muddle of herbaceous perennials shows the dot or patch approach to planting for color effect: each plant is planted in drifts that run into the next, creating a visual feast of color.

Slabs of color, right
I particularly like to see color used in generous swaths, the masses making shapes of their own and creating strong contrasts. Here lavender makes a sculptural shape in relation to the yew hedge behind it.

Seasonal color changes have a role to play, for there seems to be a definite natural cycle, at least in temperate parts of the world. Creams and pale lemons characterize the beginning of the year, blues the midsummer, running through to the warmer oranges and coppery autumn colors. But there is no truth in the much-quoted phrase that all nature's colors go together. They do not, particularly after the hybridizer has had a go at them! I am sure that there is a place for candy pink cherries with egg-yolk yellow daffodils – a standard horror – but I have not found it.

To most color combinations I add white (my infillers perhaps), gray (decoratives or pretties), and a tiny touch of purple (a decorative). The color I use will be in foliage as well as flower, and it will always be in association with green, preferably the dark green of a yew hedge backdrop, but more usually the fresh green of grass.

Creating Different Effects

I am particularly fond of limiting myself to single color arrangements, although I would not dream of planting up a whole garden this way, just areas of it. Yellow and lemon are my favorites, but with them comes gold and gray foliage, and of course green. You can make a similar collection of plants with blue flowers, or even pink ones, but as soon as you add gray foliage with green and even a touch of purple, you are beginning to complicate the issue. White flowers alone are very popular, but the range of whites is enormous, from blue-white through to creamy white. Monochromatic color schemes are not, therefore, an easy option, for the subtle shades need careful orchestration.

As opposed to single flower color arrangements, you can compose with foliage color too: gray, gold, and purple, as well as green. These associations of leaf colors can be spectacular, provided that varying flower colors do not disrupt the purity of the effect. Remember, too, that different tones of green do not always look good together.

You can use your plant color in large block masses to create a directional effect; you can work in blobs or patches; or you can infuse one color through another rather more naturally. The success of any color scheme will depend upon the scale with which you are working. As a broad guide, most color concepts start off with far too many different plants. In a single bed try to use fewer color varieties but in bigger masses. Even be bold enough to use one huge mass of, say, nepeta, with perhaps just a few lilies through it – it is a technique that can be spectacular but calls for bravery, and is really at the other end of the spectrum from the cottage garden muddle.

Individual garden designers have their own techniques, and they are constantly striving to perfect old ideas while exploring new combinations and unusual associations of plants. But their secret is to start off with a simple framework, and experiment with variations later.

5
DESIGNING STEP BY STEP

In this chapter we discuss the nuts and bolts of creating a garden's design from start to finish. What are the processes of getting ideas down on paper, and how do you develop and interpret them?

SITE ASSESSMENT

I have now outlined a broad philosophy that places the garden in its setting, and shown how that setting reciprocally can influence the look of both the house and the garden that surrounds it; I have also looked in detail at the principles of good design, of style, and of planting theory. In this chapter I will put all the elements together on a test case garden to show the process of producing a design for it.

The first stage is a full assessment of the site and your objectives for it – what one might call the design program, which will include a site analysis sketch – and an accurate site survey.

The Design Program

One is often more sure about what one does not want in a garden than what one does, so start by listing those aspects of the site of which you are in doubt. Follow this with another list (see the chart on page 147) of things you definitely do want – a terrace, perhaps, and if so, in sun or shade? What about a vegetable patch? Are you keen to incorporate water, or do children make this impractical? Most fundamental of all, do you even like gardens, or gardening? Your garden might be a place to sit, or the hard work of gardening might be your first pleasure, but even if it is, how much time can you realistically give to it?

Next come the styling decisions, because the initial, and to some extent subjective, ideas of how you want your new garden to look will be the guiding forces behind your design process.

The first place to start is with yourself. Are you a formal person, or more casual? Do you like plants spilling out at random, or do you prefer a neater, more structured look? Next, ask yourself what the house and garden surroundings are telling you. I find that a look at the interior of a client's home – the age and period of the furniture, the color scheme, the pictures on the wall, even the curtains – tells me a lot about them and their lifestyle. Look at the style of the house, its period and materials,

its roof, eaves, and so on, and record your initial reactions. Look, too, for dominant features to echo in the garden's design.

Site Analysis

An analysis of your site, that is, getting a feeling for its setting within a broader framework when looking out of it, and conversely the detail of the site and the place of the house within it, is crucial. The best way is to make a rough sketch plan of the garden and mark all the relevant information on it (see page 146).

The view out. Country gardens will need to reflect their landscape setting; urban gardens must also be consonant with their surroundings and may have strong period or architectural overtones. The area between these two, the universal suburb, can look remarkably similar all around the world, although the suburban garden will still be subject to its own climate and topography; it may be inland or near the ocean, for example.

Orientation. Use a compass to indicate the direction of the sun at noon in relation to the garden. The further north you are in the northern hemisphere and the further south in the southern, the lower the sun's arc as it traverses the sky in winter. This can be significant in overshadowed urban gardens, or in those with existing trees.

Topographical conditions. Look at the site on a local map (see opposite) and note any features outside the site that might affect your design decisions. A hill marked as "Windy Ridge" on the map, or a dip called "Foggy Bottom," is saying something about the local conditions.

Prevailing winds. Wind can render a garden unusable, so check your site to find where winds come from. If the site is exposed, the shape of the trees is a good indication. Near the ocean, winds will be salt-laden; these present a restriction as only certain plants will thrive under such circumstances.

Boundaries. Are they too open or too closed? In a country setting the open or closed boundary is

SITE ANALYSIS

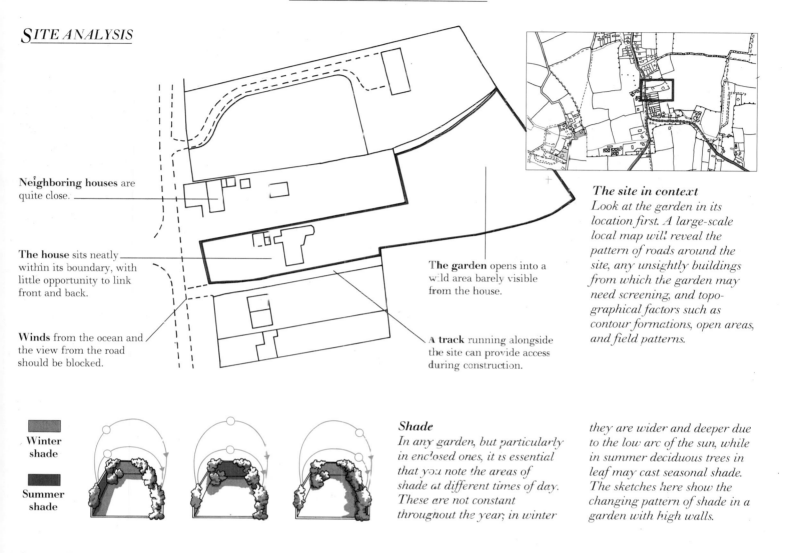

Neighboring houses are quite close.

The house sits neatly within its boundary, with little opportunity to link front and back.

Winds from the ocean and the view from the road should be blocked.

The garden opens into a wild area barely visible from the house.

A track running alongside the site can provide access during construction.

The site in context
Look at the garden in its location first. A large-scale local map will reveal the pattern of roads around the site, any unsightly buildings from which the garden may need screening, and topographical factors such as contour formations, open areas, and field patterns.

Winter shade

Summer shade

Shade
In any garden, but particularly in enclosed ones, it is essential that you note the areas of shade at different times of day. These are not constant throughout the year; in winter they are wider and deeper due to the low arc of the sun, while in summer deciduous trees in leaf may cast seasonal shade. The sketches here show the changing pattern of shade in a garden with high walls.

dictated by views in and out of the site, the need to provide shelter from prevailing winds, and to keep livestock out. In an urban situation, privacy is often the key requirement, so open boundaries are not an option. This puts a premium on the materials from which the boundaries are constructed. If they are walls, are they sound, too high, or too low? If fencing, is it in character with the building? (Many fences are perfectly functional but in my view hideous to look at.)

Drainage and irrigation. Other factors that will influence your design, depending on your part of the world, are whether irrigation is necessary (see pages 332-3) and whether a major drainage operation should be undertaken. If the latter is needed – and I have seldom found it to be so on domestic sites – perhaps you should consider a bog-type

garden, going with the site rather than fighting against it. A permutation of this is the low-lying site near ocean or river, where the garden or parts of it are subject to flood or a high water table. This is even more restricting, as many plants will not appreciate the changes in water level; deeper-rooting types will need to be elevated above the water table by landscaping.

Elevation. Note down any steps or obvious slopes in the existing garden, since the potential for a change of level in a new design will have a strong impact on the way you approach it. Even a flat site, like our test case garden, can sometimes have a grade change introduced without major landscaping needing to be undertaken.

Utilities. A normal household functions with various underground utilities, and before committing

SITE ANALYSIS

The house
The proportions, style, and layout of the house are the starting points for a new design. Here a strong but informal design is suitable; nothing historical, fussy, or too symmetrical. Polaroid photographs provide useful reference.

This border planting would be fine if cut back and reshuffled. Established shrubs are a good counterpoise to the walnut opposite. The main colors here are white and pink.

According to the owner, the short hedge and paving are a good sheltered sitting area at certain times of year, so I will keep them. As the hedge is a strong yellow, I will work with it.

This area catches the sun most of the day.

The line of the new extension is at an angle; I might use this in the design.

The wild area
The garden extends through a gap in the hedges into a wild area of large-scale informal shrub plantings and meadow, with a natural-looking pond at the center.

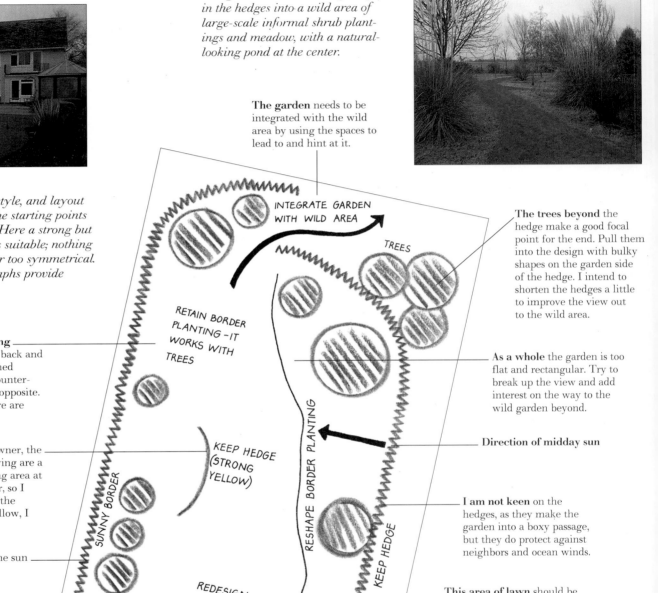

The garden needs to be integrated with the wild area by using the spaces to lead to and hint at it.

INTEGRATE GARDEN WITH WILD AREA

TREES

RETAIN BORDER PLANTING – IT WORKS WITH TREES

KEEP HEDGE (STRONG YELLOW)

RESHAPE BORDER PLANTING

SUNNY BORDER

KEEP HEDGE

REDESIGN LAWN

SEPTIC TANK COVER ✗

CONSERVATORY

BREAK UP PLAIN FRONTAGE

HOUSE

The trees beyond the hedge make a good focal point for the end. Pull them into the design with bulky shapes on the garden side of the hedge. I intend to shorten the hedges a little to improve the view out to the wild area.

As a whole the garden is too flat and rectangular. Try to break up the view and add interest on the way to the wild garden beyond.

Direction of midday sun

I am not keen on the hedges, as they make the garden into a boxy passage, but they do protect against neighbors and ocean winds.

This area of lawn should be redesigned completely as it is so flat.

The owners like plants, so the main interest should be near the house. Yellow used here will reflect sunshine and work with the gold hedge opposite.

The terrace has unsympathetic lines; I will try orienting it to the new conservatory.

I will use climbers and pots across the back of the house.

yourself to a design that involves major earth moving, consider what is practical in order to avoid expensive rerouting of pipes or cables. At this stage a rough idea of where water, gas, electrical, and telephone lines run is all that is needed; later, if major earthworks are contemplated, it may be necessary to contact the relevant utility to pinpoint the location of a line.

Running from the house will be surface water drainage, probably from the roof. Indicate any drainage system on you plan, in addition to the location of your septic tank cover, if you've got your own septic tank – somehow it is always just where you want your terrace!

Soil

While the composition and condition of a soil do not necessarily affect how people use a site, they do affect the designer's thinking about the ultimate styling of the garden, and an analysis of the soil in your garden is an important part of your assessment of the site. The plants and the style of planting are an essential part of your overall design, and it is pointless to invest a lot of time in a garden plan that you cannot realize.

The constituents of a soil vary enormously around the world, for soil is, after all, the surface layers of geological substrata. For example, older igneous rocks such as granite and sandstone tend to form an acid soil above them, while limestone and chalk produce an alkaline one. Between these extremes are other soil types, conditioned in other ways.

To a degree, the existing vegetation will tell you a lot about the soil in which it is growing. Natives and weeds are clues, as are introduced plants in neighboring gardens. Plants can suggest the soil's condition, its acidity or alkalinity, and whether the ground is dry or waterlogged – all factors which help you to read your site. Heathers and rhododendrons are classic indicators of an acid soil, nettles of a rich soil, buttercups of a wet soil, and viburnum of an alkaline soil, for instance. But to be accurate in your analysis you should test the soil.

Testing the Soil

The soil test will tell you the degree of acidity or alkalinity on a sliding scale known as a pH value. A reading is given on either side of neutral value pH 7, becoming more alkaline as the reading goes up, until absolute alkalinity is reached at pH 14, and getting more acid as the reading drops lower. A pH reading below 4.5 means the soil is too acid for plant growth. An ideal soil has a pH value between 6 and 6.5.

In any garden larger than an urban back yard, test the soil in three or four different places and mark each place and your test result on your analysis plan. Always take your results from soil 3-6in (70-150mm) below the surface. One testing method is to use a pH meter, pushed into the ground to give a reading. Also available are simple kits, in which dry samples of soil are agitated in a solution, and the resulting color compared to a chart – rather like a litmus test.

Soil Texture

The condition and potential of your soil are not only a matter of pH value; its textural quality is of primary importance as well.

Texture has to do with the size of the granules of which the soil is composed. A sandy soil, for instance, is made up of coarse grains of the parent rock, while clay is composed of minute particles. This textural quality directly affects the roots of a plant growing in it, since food is taken up in soluble form by feeder roots from moisture which surrounds each grain, along with air. And, very crudely, that food is converted by a photosynthetic process through the leaf of the plant into carbohydrates. The layers of moisture surrounding coarse grains of sandy soil can very easily leach away, and such a soil is said to be poor, although it is also a warm soil since spring air can circulate through it earlier than through a water-retentive clay one. Where the particles are very small, moisture collects in excessive amounts; the soil becomes sticky and difficult to work until it has dried out.

Both these extremes of condition may be improved by the addition of organic matter, and once you come to construct and plant your garden's design you should dig in a proportion of humus as a soil conditioner. Fibrous organic matter binds together loose grains of an open soil, while it lets air into a clay soil by pushing the grains apart. Some types of humus add food, others small organisms, but all types will help convert an unsatisfactory soil into a healthy and fertile one.

So the ideal soil has a pH value of 6.5, is rich in organic matter, crumbly to the touch, dark in color, and, believe it or not, smells good as well – so don't forget the nose test.

If your garden is a neglected urban space, the soil will probably appear sandy and sour, since without regular additions of organic matter soil becomes impoverished and dusty – making an ideal litter box. Do not go to the expense of having the soil replaced, just feed it and dig in plenty of humus.

THE SITE SURVEY

The next step is to make an accurate site survey, with all the information you will need to draw up an accurate scale plan. I advise taking measurements of all the features in the existing garden, even if there are some that you don't intend to keep in the new design – you may change your mind.

Check whether plans have ever been drawn up for the site or part of it, perhaps for a house extension or as part of a sale. These can be a helpful starting point, particularly for pinpointing boundaries on an irregular or overgrown site, although they should be checked with your own measurements. All too often a client points to a jungle of poison ivy in dense woodland, telling me that a stake somewhere in there marks the boundary.

Clarity is essential when measuring a garden, since any mistakes will result in an inaccurate scale plan. Make a working sketch of the garden as you see it, and record the measurements on this. On a large or complicated site, you will need to make separate sketches of individual areas, or of the triangulated points, to keep your main sketch from becoming a forest of incomprehensible figures.

Be careful to take running measurements (that is, measurements that build up across the façade or down the garden), rather than individual ones, and mark them clearly on your plan – otherwise you will get back to the drawing board to find the survey does not add up. Record your measurements in a clear, concise way with a fine pencil point, so you can understand them later. This sounds obvious, but I have found that in the freezing cold, when it is windy, the paper damp, and the site the last place I want to be, it is all too easy to make a symbol that could be 5 or 3, 1 or 7.

When you think you have finished, check your sketch for all the details you may have forgotten, such as access doors, the widths of the trees, and whether French windows open in or out.

How you measure is the same for any site. The procedure is purely logical, and as long as you take it slowly, at your own pace, and with every scrap of your concentration to ensure that you do not miss a measurement, you cannot go wrong.

HOW TO MEASURE A GARDEN

These steps show some broad techniques for measuring which can be applied to any site, but you will need to decide which method – taking offsets or triangulating – is appropriate in any area of the site. In addition to the items below, you will find a small metal tape measure for window heights useful; and if you will be taking rough levels (see page 151), a plank of wood, some wooden pegs, and a mallet are needed.

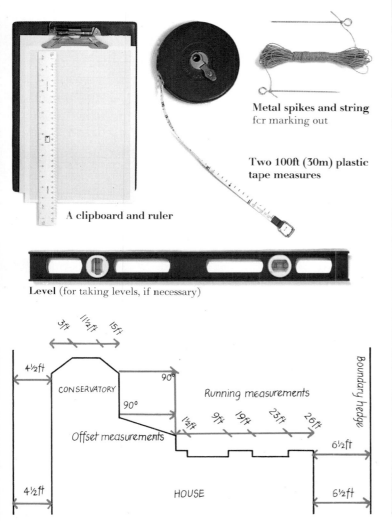

Metal spikes and string for marking out

Two 100ft (30m) plastic tape measures

A clipboard and ruler

Level (for taking levels, if necessary)

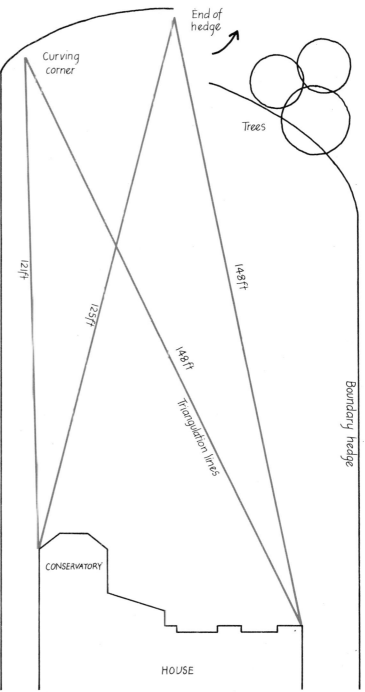

1 **Measuring the house**
Peg one end of the tape measure down securely, and run it across the façade. Take spot measurements at each feature – windows, doors, etc. – and mark them down. Do this on all the important faces. Where a house has an angle other than 90°, take offsets to the corners from established points (see step 4). The angle can be checked by assuming a triangle between it and a house corner on either side, and measuring all three sides. Measure from the sides of the house to the boundary.

2 **Triangulating boundary points**
Even if the site looks regular, use the triangulation technique to position the far boundary corners as a check. Measure from one corner of the house to the point you want to fix, then measure to it from another corner. Clearly note the measurements. Make a wide triangle: if too narrow, it will not be accurate when you transfer the measurement to the scale plan. Then measure around the boundary, noting where fence becomes wall, wall becomes hedge, and so on.

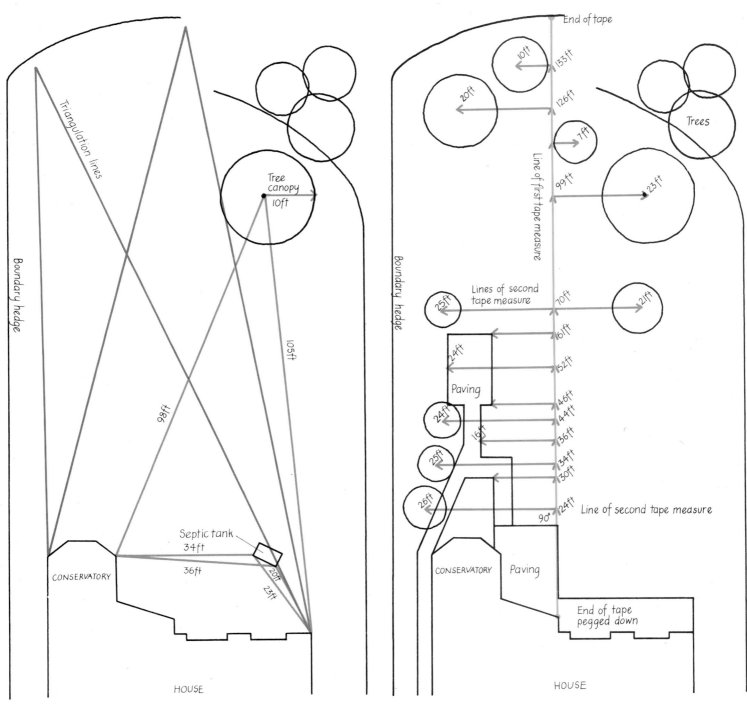

3 Triangulating trees
The triangulation technique also enables you to position trees and other elements accurately. Measure from the trunk of each tree to two corners of the house, for clarity noting the measurements on a separate sheet if necessary. It is important to measure the spread of each tree, too, remembering that it may not have grown evenly. All tree canopies must be drawn to scale on your plan to avoid mistakes with planting schemes.

4 Taking offsets
Some rectangular sites, and some areas of gardens of any shape, can be measured simply by taking offsets at 90° to the house. Peg the end of the tape down securely at a known point (mark it on your sketch plan), then run the tape up the garden at right angles to the house or other known feature. Wherever a feature hits the tape, mark down the measurement. With a second tape, take offsets at 90° to the first tape, measuring across to trees or other features in the garden.

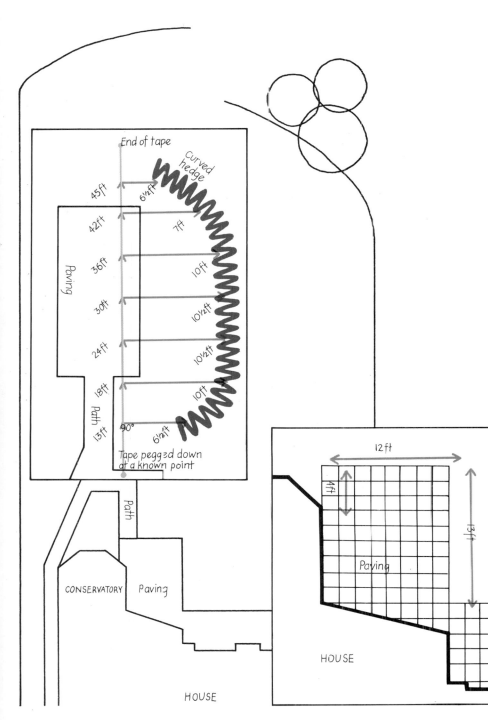

Measuring curves
5 Establish a line for the tape that is parallel or at right angles to a known feature. Taking offsets, measure to the curve at regular intervals — say every 2 feet or 500mm Use this technique in reverse for pegging out a new feature.

Other features
6 Sketch individual areas on separate sheets so you have room for the figures. Measure paving stones, threshold details, and so on. Take vertical measurements too — the height of the hedge and windows, for instance.

MEASURING ELEVATIONS

Any site with obvious changes of elevation will need professional surveying before a landscaping plan is done, but at this stage a rough idea of the potential for elevation changes is all that is required. The following simple methods will suffice.

1 Use two wooden stakes and a plank of wood with the longest round measure — say 3 feet (1m) — marked off on it At the top of the slope lay the plank down, and use the mark on it to position a peg 3 feet (1m) below. Hammer in the peg until the plank is level when its end is on the peg (check this with a level).

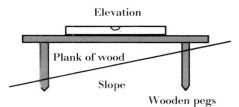

2 Measure the amount of peg above the ground — this gives you the total fall over 3 feet (1m). Continue down the slope using both pegs to rest the plank on and checking for elevation each time: the fall is the height of the lower peg minus that of the higher one.

3 Add together the falls to get the total fall in the ground over however many feet (meters) measured.

Alternative method for gentle slopes
This method is very rough and ready, but it can be useful if all you need is a general indication of a change of elevation. Ask someone to stand at the top of the change of elevation and hold the end of the tape measure. Stand at the bottom of the slope and hold the tape out until it is horizontal, using a level held along the tape to check. With a second tape measure, measure from your end of the tape to the ground to find the total change of elevation.

THE SCALE PLAN

With all your measurements taken, you are now in a position to make a scale plan.

Deciding on a Scale

Working to scale simply means using one unit of measurement on your plan for every so many units on the site; so that, for example, ¼ in on the scale rule equals 1ft on the site.

In the course of the design process you may find it necessary to work to different scales for different plans; sometimes it is simply a question of fitting the plan on the page, sometimes a change of scale is needed to reveal details in areas such as paving or planting. The following is a guide to the scales most commonly used:

⅛"–1'0". Use for the scale and schematic plans of a medium-sized garden between 30 and 90 feet long. I also recommend using this scale for your rough sketch stage, whatever scale you use for your scale plan, for it will keep you from getting bogged down in unnecessary details that distract from the overall design; on a smaller garden, though, you can work to scale ¼"–1'0" throughout, for I would not suggest drawing it twice. For larger gardens, those over 90 feet, break the garden down into smaller areas and draw each area up at ⅛"–1'0". The equivalent metric scale is expressed as 1:100.

¼"–1'0". Use for the schematic plan of a small garden up to about 30 feet long. Also use this scale for planting details of beds, borders, and so forth, and for scaled construction drawings. The metric equivalent is 1:50.

½"–1'0". Use for drawing any individual features to highlight their details, for example, a pergola.

1"–1'0". Use for detailed construction drawings or section drawings of such elements as walling: it is a large enough scale to show the width and depth of a mortar infill, for example.

Drawing the Scale Plan

Start with your drawing board correctly positioned and well lit, and all your equipment at hand (see pages 52-3).

Draw the scale plan on thin tracing paper in roughly the order you measured it, always cross-checking positions against other measurements. If you find a major discrepancy, never guess; check the measurements again on site.

Every garden will be different, but by showing the basic techniques for turning your site measurements into a scale plan I hope it will be possible for you to interpret the process on your own site.

*T*ECHNIQUES

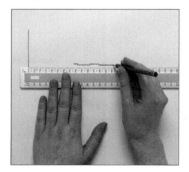

1 **Drawing the house** *Always start with this. Using a pencil and a ruler, establish a horizontal, then draw the outline of the back of the house following your running measurements. Mark all windows and doors and their recesses.*

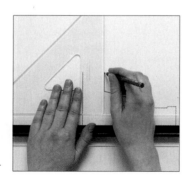

2 **House outline** *Draw right angles using a triangle set against the T-square of the drawing board. With the ruler, mark off the correct measurement on the verticals. For other angles, transfer offset measurements accurately.*

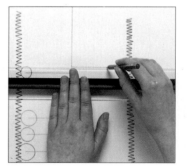

3 **Transferring offsets** *Draw a line on your plan corresponding to the position of your tape measure on the ground. Work up it: use the T-square or a triangle at 90° to the line and a ruler to draw in each feature at the correct point.*

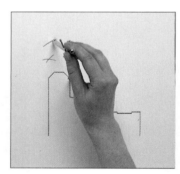

4 **Triangulated points** *Set a compass to the correct scale measurement. Put the compass point on the house corner and make an arc. Make a second arc for the other measurement: where the two arcs cross is the position of the tree or other feature.*

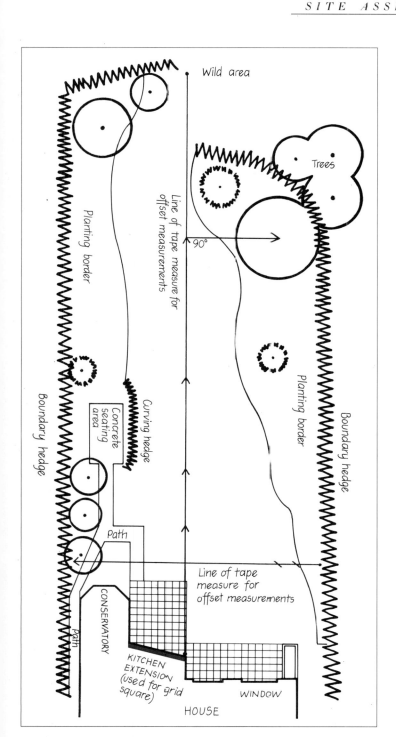

Wild area

Line of tape measure for offset measurements

Trees

90°

Planting border

Boundary hedge

Planting border

Boundary hedge

Curving hedge

Concrete seating area

Path

Line of tape measure for offset measurements

Path

CONSERVATORY

KITCHEN EXTENSION (used for grid square)

WINDOW

HOUSE

THE BUBBLE DIAGRAM

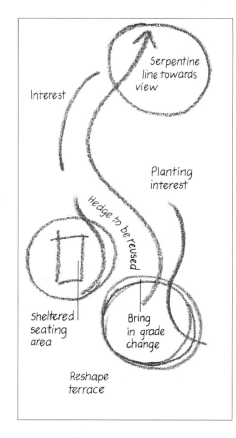

Interest

Serpentine line towards view

Planting interest

Hedge to be reused

sheltered seating area

Bring in grade change

Reshape terrace

On tracing paper over the scale plan, make a bubble diagram. This shows the ideal positions for all the elements required in the new design. It therefore brings together the objectives of the design program with the scale plan of the garden.

PREPARING TO DESIGN

You will now have before you a scale plan of the existing garden, a bubble diagram showing the aims of the new design, and a grid drawn up on another sheet of tracing paper.

5 **The finished scale plan**
Continue transferring all your garden's measurements onto the scale plan, double-checking each one for accuracy. At this stage, draw in every existing feature on the site, as decisions about what you may or may not keep in the new design will come later. Once the plan is done, choose the feature that will produce the grid square (see pages 56-7); in the garden shown here, the sloping kitchen extension was a strong element, and its dimension would also produce a grid of a suitable size.

DEVELOPING THE DESIGN

The drawings below show how to set about producing an initial design for the test case garden. I used the method explained on pages 60-1: on tracing paper I worked up embryonic layouts using freehand shapes to realize new ideas, then worked the designs up a little further into positive and negative spaces. Any one of the three designs shown here would have worked admirably as a garden.

I hope these examples show that it is not enough to produce one workable solution and stop there. Being a designer is a constant process of thinking again, producing different solutions, and trying new permutations to evolve a layout that is pleasing in plan form, and has open, workable spaces in it.

Throughout this initial sketching stage, the eventual interpretation of the shapes and spaces you are creating is always at the back of your mind, but for now your initial priority is a beautiful plan; practicality comes later.

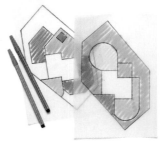

Methods of working
Follow the instructions on pages 60-1 for your working method at the initial design stage. On top of your scaled survey, lay your bubble diagram, and then your grid. Cover this with fresh tracing paper on which to draw.

THE EMBRYONIC DESIGNS

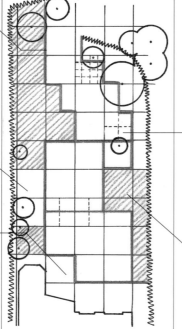

The straight edge of the end planting bed helps lead the eye into the wild area, but is a little hard and uncompromising. It doesn't help to break up the boxy feel of the hedges, one of my initial objectives.

I liked the potential of bringing a sitting or grassed area right up to the boundary; it gives a sense of breadth.

This area could be a terrace extending out from the house: with the grid laid at 90° to the house, I would be able to keep the existing paving.

A broad curve across the garden helped with the strong directional flow, as well as suggesting breadth.

With such a narrow, rectangular site I found myself working very strongly with the grid squares, divided into quarters or eighths where appropriate.

The planting areas break across the view from the house, providing a frame and a foreground to the view beyond.

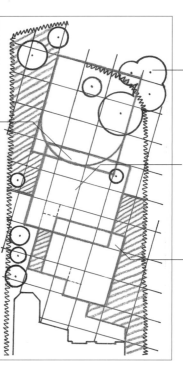

The grid set at an angle allowed the trees beyond the hedge to be incorporated into the design visually.

More open space in the middle of the design would, I hoped, help increase the feeling of space and width.

Using fractions of the grid square was even more necessary here to accommodate interesting shapes.

Design One. I began with the grid coming off the house at 90°, subdividing it where it seemed appropriate. This design achieves my objective of creating movement from house to wild area, and the planting beds break into the view to slow down the eye.

Design Two. With the kitchen extension set at an angle, I had a strong – even quirky – angle at which to set the grid. This immediately made the design flow from the house better. I could now break up the rectangular feel of Design One with curving shapes.

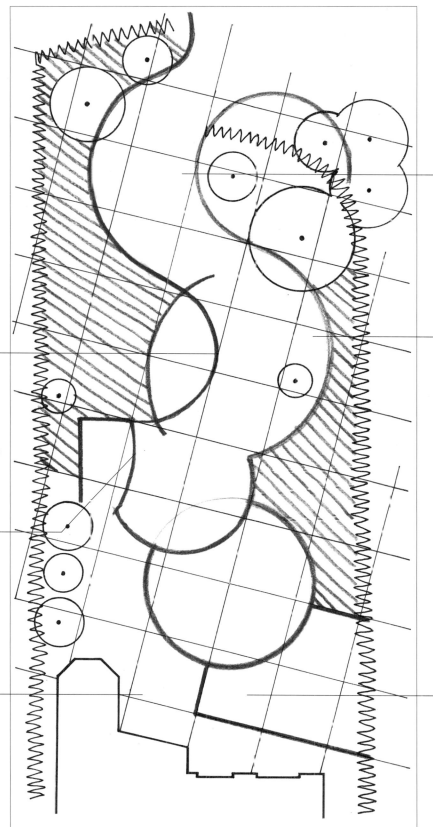

Design Three

Using curves in the design opened up a host of possibilities ripe for exploitation. I definitely preferred the grid set at an angle, and so, with my compass set to multiples of the grid squares – and often fractions of the squares – I tried a design of intersecting arcs. The arrangement of positive and negative spaces worked best in Design One, so I used this as a starting point.

I arranged the arcs and circles as planting beds that repeated the zigzag progression I liked in Design One. This was even stronger with the grid coming at an angle from the house: the eye was led from the terrace to the right-hand bed, then on to the planting at the end of the garden and beyond.

I liked the idea of keeping and echoing the existing curved hedge to give the design integrity.

Keeping the areas near the house open and uncluttered would, I hoped, give a sense of breadth and break up the long, narrow feel of the existing garden.

From Design Two, I kept the strong directional pull towards the trees at the right-hand end of the garden.

An exaggerated meander sweeping off into the wild area gave the sense of movement I wanted to create. I liked the increasing complexity of the curves moving away from the house: it seemed to highlight the transition from tame to wild.

A right-angled area was appropriate near the house, to ease the transition from straight lines to curving ones.

PRODUCING THE SCHEMATIC PLAN

With the design concept decided upon, the next step is to go on to refine the sketch into a workable garden design. Your rough shapes now have to become accurately planned garden areas, so a degree of adaptation and alteration is inevitable.

The objective is the finished schematic plan, drawn to scale and incorporating universally understood symbols and drawing conventions (see pages 322-3). This schematic plan will be the basis for all later drawings and the planting plan.

Shallow step
A key part of the design was a shallow curving step. Although it is a flat site, by grading the gravel area down I could build soil up behind a brick riser.

The hedge
The repeated curves make the existing curving hedge a strong focal point.

Brick curves
The first curve on the rough design was interpreted as concentric lines of bricks, achieving a satisfying contrast as paving butts in.

Existing paving
The curving design involved taking up some of the existing terrace so that it no longer ran straight across the house. It was reshaped to echo the curved step around the conservatory.

Gravelled area
The foreground circle linking to the terrace was interpreted as a gravelled area furnished with plants, sinks, and small-scale features.

Curving border
This bed now bends around to culminate in the planting area on the right of the step when looking from the house.

Border shaping
The top area of the garden had a considerable amount of existing plant material which the owners wanted to retain. The curves on my rough design became interpreted here partly as reshaping for the planting area, and partly as curving swaths of rough grass (the dotted lines).

Sketch of planned garden
This is how I expect the sitting area behind the small hedge to look: the lines of brick sweep up from the conservatory towards this sheltered space, helping to make it a point of interest from the house. Brick or other small unit paving offers the most flexibility for curves. Concrete slabs may be cut to shape or laid with the mortar taking up the curve, but unless the arc is extremely gentle, you have a problem with the wide joints at the outer edge.

Existing trees
With the existing trees at the top right-hand corner of the garden I had a ready-made planting mass, the green punctuated by the existing gold conifer. I shortened the boundary hedges here to allow a better view through them.

The garden from the same point as the sketch.

THE PLANTING PLAN

As so often happens, the theory of developing a planting plan differs from the actual practice, for there are always established elements that need accommodating. This garden had a considerable amount of existing plant material, which the client was understandably reluctant to ignore; so rather than start from scratch, many of the smaller shrubs and the perennials were lifted and reused. Among the older shrubs some were still worth keeping but could not be moved, so these were cut back and new material grouped around them; shrubs such as old roses, mock orange, and buddleia all need fairly brutal treatment from time to time in any event. Of course, it is often easier to remove old shrubs, for it would be a pity to sacrifice your new design concept for lovely, but perhaps inappropriate plants.

The structural elements
A sketch of the proposed planting shows the bulky masses zigzagging down the garden, the plant forms and shapes put together to make balanced three-dimensional pictures (see pages 116-17).

KEY   ● **Plants featured in each category**   ● **Evergreen**   ● **Other**

Specials
After the cutting back and heeling in of plants we wanted to keep but move, the garden had as its main features the surrounding hedge, a malus, and a gold conifer at the end.

I decided that the curving lonicera hedge and conifer were the main eye-catchers, and complemented them with the bush form of the gold catalpa in the corner, and two clumps of variegated gold Phormium tenax.

The arrangement of golds zigzags down the garden – I always think that if something is worth having once, it is worth repeating. By so doing, the concept is steadied and the garden unified.

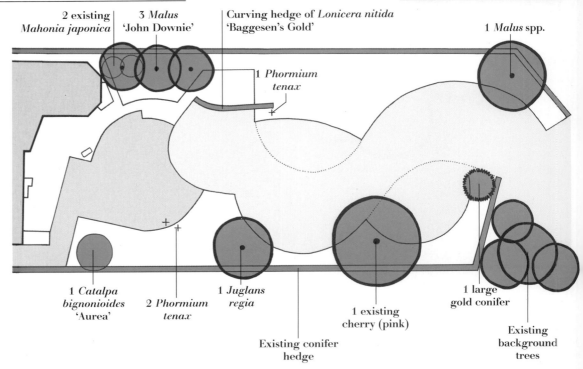

2 existing *Mahonia japonica*

3 *Malus* 'John Downie'

Curving hedge of *Lonicera nitida* 'Baggesen's Gold'

1 *Malus* spp.

1 *Phormium tenax*

1 *Catalpa bignonioides* 'Aurea'

2 *Phormium tenax*

1 *Juglans regia*

Existing conifer hedge

1 existing cherry (pink)

1 large gold conifer

Existing background trees

158

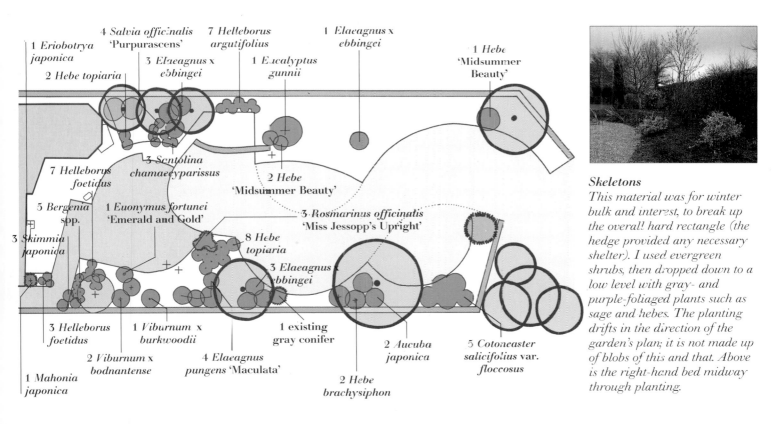

1 *Eriobotrya japonica*

4 *Salvia officinalis* 'Purpurascens'

2 *Hebe topiaria*

3 *Elaeagnus* x *ebbingei*

7 *Helleborus argutifolius*

1 *Eucalyptus gunnii*

1 *Elaeagnus* x *ebbingei*

1 *Hebe* 'Midsummer Beauty'

3 *Santolina chamaecyparissus*

7 *Helleborus foetidus*

5 *Bergenia* spp.

1 *Euonymus fortunei* 'Emerald and Gold'

2 *Hebe* 'Midsummer Beauty'

3 *Rosmarinus officinalis* 'Miss Jessopp's Upright'

8 *Hebe topiaria*

3 *Elaeagnus* x *ebbingei*

3 *Skimmia japonica*

3 *Helleborus foetidus*

1 *Viburnum* x *burkwoodii*

1 existing gray conifer

2 *Viburnum* x *bodnantense*

4 *Elaeagnus pungens* 'Maculata'

1 *Mahonia japonica*

2 *Aucuba japonica*

2 *Hebe brachysiphon*

5 *Cotoneaster salicifolius* var. *floccosus*

Skeletons
This material was for winter bulk and interest, to break up the overall hard rectangle (the hedge provided any necessary shelter). I used evergreen shrubs, then dropped down to a low level with gray- and purple-foliaged plants such as sage and hebes. The planting drifts in the direction of the garden's plan; it is not made up of blobs of this and that. Above is the right-hand bed midway through planting.

Decoratives
Many of the decoratives in this garden are the original shrubs, particularly in the left-hand border. I thickened the structure provided by a huge berberis and old roses (above is Rosa *'Pink Grootendorst' with sambucus and aquilegias for temporary infill) with lavender, potentilla, and my favorite geranium, 'Johnson's Blue'. The right-hand bed needed to be brighter to work with the catalpa and to lighten the shade from the hedge, so I used a creamy hydrangea to reflect light in.*

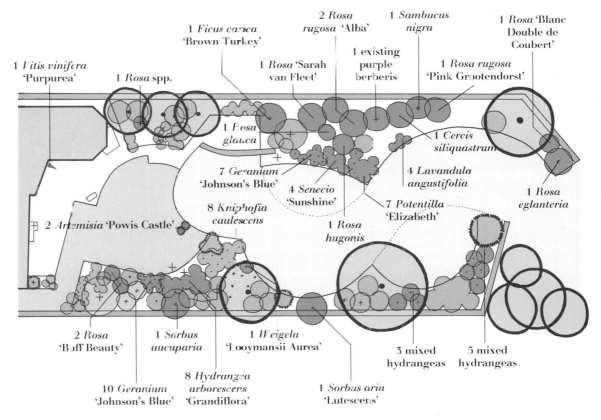

1 *Vitis vinifera* 'Purpurea'

1 *Ficus carica* 'Brown Turkey'

2 *Rosa rugosa* 'Alba'

1 *Sambucus nigra*

1 *Rosa* 'Blanc Double de Coubert'

1 *Rosa* spp.

1 *Rosa* 'Sarah van Fleet'

1 existing purple berberis

1 *Rosa rugosa* 'Pink Grootendorst'

1 *Rosa glauca*

1 *Cercis siliquastrum*

7 *Geranium* 'Johnson's Blue'

4 *Senecio* 'Sunshine'

4 *Lavandula angustifolia*

8 *Kniphofia caulescens*

7 *Potentilla* 'Elizabeth'

1 *Rosa eglanteria*

2 *Artemisia* 'Powis Castle'

1 *Rosa hugonis*

2 *Rosa* 'Buff Beauty'

1 *Sorbus aucuparia*

1 *Weigela* 'Looymansii Aurea'

3 mixed hydrangeas

5 mixed hydrangeas

1 *Sorbus aria* 'Lutescens'

10 *Geranium* 'Johnson's Blue'

8 *Hydrangea arborescens* 'Grandiflora'

Pretties

With this category the gravel became a focus: I planted gray stachys to echo the artemisia, and libertia for its dense, spiky foliage. A handsome acanthus interrupts the line of the step across the garden. For spring interest in the right-hand bed I planned in the gold variegated leaves of brunnera, whose blue flowers match those of the geranium. Perennial foliage of green, gray, and purple was used throughout to punctuate the entire garden.

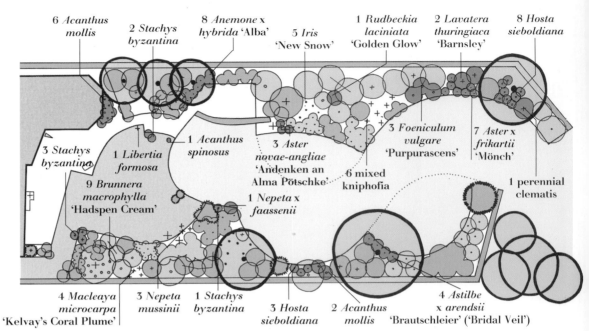

6 *Acanthus mollis*
2 *Stachys byzantina*
8 *Anemone* x *hybrida* 'Alba'
5 *Iris* 'New Snow'
1 *Rudbeckia laciniata* 'Golden Glow'
2 *Lavatera thuringiaca* 'Barnsley'
8 *Hosta sieboldiana*
3 *Stachys byzantina*
1 *Libertia formosa*
1 *Acanthus spinosus*
3 *Aster novae-angliae* 'Andenken an Alma Pötschke'
3 *Foeniculum vulgare* 'Purpurascens'
7 *Aster* x *frikartii* 'Mönch'
9 *Brunnera macrophylla* 'Hadspen Cream'
6 mixed kniphofia
1 perennial clematis
1 *Nepeta* x *faassenii*
4 *Macleaya microcarpa* 'Kelvay's Coral Plume'
3 *Nepeta mussinii*
1 *Stachys byzantina*
3 *Hosta sieboldiana*
2 *Acanthus mollis*
4 *Astilbe* x *arendsii* 'Brautschleier' ('Bridal Veil')

Looking over the libertia

Aquilegias for infill

Beyond the curving hedge

The gravel planting

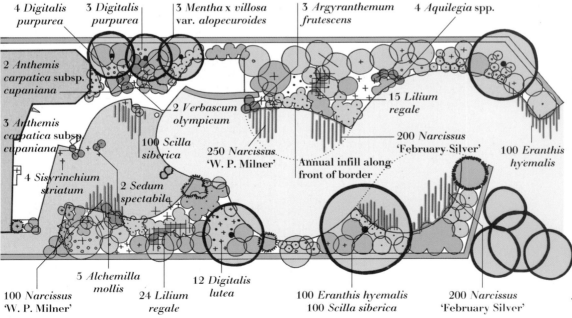

4 *Digitalis purpurea*
3 *Digitalis purpurea*
3 *Mentha* x *villosa* var. *alopecuroides*
3 *Argyranthemum frutescens*
4 *Aquilegia* spp.
2 *Anthemis carpatica* subsp. *cupaniana*
3 *Anthemis carpatica* subsp. *cupaniana*
2 *Verbascum olympicum*
15 *Lilium regale*
100 *Scilla siberica*
250 *Narcissus* 'W. P. Milner'
200 *Narcissus* 'February Silver'
100 *Eranthis hyemalis*
4 *Sisyrinchium striatum*
2 *Sedum spectabile*
Annual infill along front of border
100 *Narcissus* 'W. P. Milner'
5 *Alchemilla mollis*
24 *Lilium regale*
12 *Digitalis lutea*
100 *Eranthis hyemalis*
100 *Scilla siberica*
200 *Narcissus* 'February Silver'

Infill

For early spring interest I planted the pattern of rough grass and gravel with masses of winter aconite (Eranthis hyemalis), pale blue scilla, and early narcissus. I specifically use early-flowering species of narcissus for naturalizing since they stand the wind better and are not blown over, and they die down early so the grass does not become too long and untidy before it can be cut.

For infill in the gravel I added anthemis and the sworded foliage and cream flowers of sisyrinchium, and in the borders Lilium regale.

Planting beneath the walnut tree, right
A splash of color was called for here to lighten the shade cast by the hedge and established walnut tree. Some heeled-in kniphofia make a suitably bright statement; a yellow foxglove, Digitalis lutea, *will appear later.*

The young planting shows the hebe plants widely spaced, with the rosemary creating a vertical counterbalance to their neat, buttonlike mounds. Nepeta mussinii *adds a froth of purple color.*

THE FINISHED GARDEN

By the end of the first summer after its completion, the garden is already looking established – thanks, in part, to the proportion of existing plant material that I was able to incorporate. The gravel planting needs more time to spread and sprawl – it still looks rather thin in relation to the space – but the curves of brick outline the area well. At this time of the year the rough grass has been mown as lawn, but in the spring its swaths, interplanted with bulbs, will heighten the effect of the graceful curves that lead the eye at a leisurely pace towards the wild area beyond.

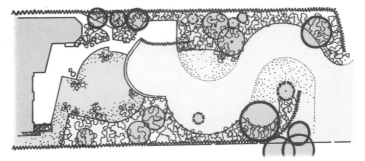

The plan and garden, above and opposite
The view down the garden reveals the stages of gradual transition: the terrace to gravel, the low step leading to lawn. Gold plants form a zigzag that enhances the directional flow.

Paving detail
The curving lines of brick are punctuated by a change in the width of the path – announced by the tuftlike foliage of Libertia formosa – and softened by anthemis. An immature acanthus will in time form a stately summer focal point.

Looking back to the house
Neither the house nor its location had a strong stylistic message to continue, so the new design needed a character of its own. This view shows how the planting masses successfully frame the house, the gravel making an informal transitional space.

Planting group
The right-hand bed is an important visual break across the garden. Kniphofia and hydrangeas catch the attention when in flower, but for year-round impact a gold phormium is planted in front, supported visually by the low mass of quietly skeletal hebes.

6
DESIGN & STYLING SOLUTIONS

*Here we examine some garden design case histories.
You will see that a hard basic layout matures
into a perfect combination of plant material
overlaying design structure. It is a reciprocal and
mutually enhancing process.*

A GARDEN WITH A VIEW

The view of softly rolling farmland, a rural tapestry of hedged fields, was the main feature that persuaded my clients to buy this farmhouse. To make the garden a part of this backdrop was therefore my principal consideration.

The house was derelict when the owners acquired it, and the grounds neglected. An extensive area had once been cultivated, running down to a small stream in the valley, but the owners felt that this was too large an area to maintain – and, in any case, too much garden within such a stupendous view would have been almost an imposition. So first I cut the garden right down in size by constructing a ha-ha just beyond an old weeping ash tree, leaving everything outside it as rough pasture. This has allowed an unimpeded view from the house, the grazing sheep now serving almost as a living garden feature.

Across the rear of the house a raised, stone-paved terrace (left) was then built in a wide semicircle, its low, bounding stone wall at sitting height. With this dramatic promontory as the main feature of the garden, and with no interrupting boundary fences, there is the feeling of stepping from the house right into the country. To the side of the house are the working areas of the garden, but nothing obstructs the view over the gently falling lawn to the fields beyond.

PLAN ANALYSIS

The semicircular terrace dominates the plan. To strengthen the link between house, garden, and view, I took the proportions for the plan from the dining room that occupies the rear corner position of the house and is one of the most important viewing points from within. The curve of the terrace is repeated in the shape of the border next to it, which in turn bounds a level sunbathing lawn. With this border planted decoratively, the vegetable gardens and greenhouse are screened.

The front part of the garden, with its collection of old farm buildings, is mostly separated from the rear by a tall brick wall. A new orchard of fruit trees becomes the one linking element, planted across the path and through the gap in the wall. Beyond them is a view to the spire of the church.

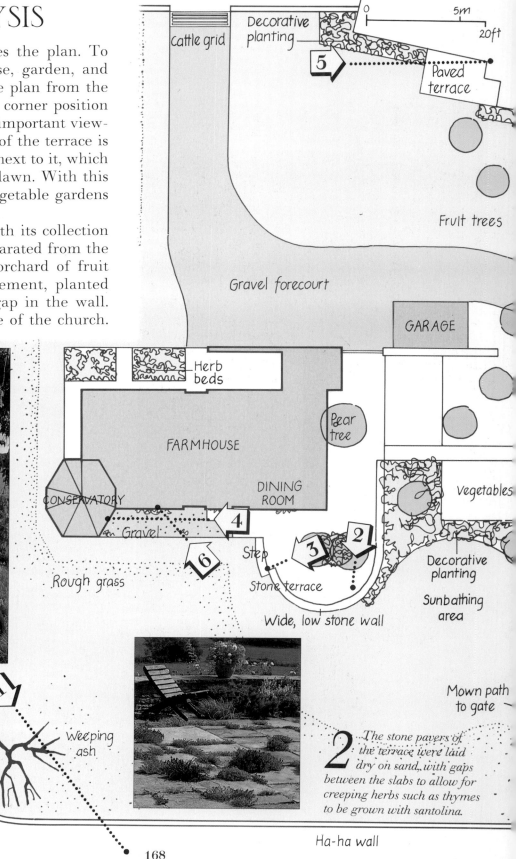

Cattle grid

Decorative planting

5m

20ft

5

Paved terrace

Fruit trees

Gravel forecourt

GARAGE

Herb beds

Pear tree

FARMHOUSE

DINING ROOM

Vegetables

CONSERVATORY

Gravel

4

3

2

6

Step

Decorative planting

Rough grass

Stone terrace

Sunbathing area

Wide, low stone wall

Mown path to gate

1 To integrate the garden with its setting, a ha-ha substitutes for a fence. The ground falls away here, so a ditch wasn't necessary; instead, a wall of concrete blocks (the top just visible here) was built into the slope to a height of 4ft (1.25m). The Fraxinus excelsior 'Pendula' marks its end.

1

Weeping ash

2 The stone pavers of the terrace were laid dry on sand, with gaps between the slabs to allow for creeping herbs such as thymes to be grown with santolina.

Ha-ha wall

3 The stone coping of the terrace wall makes a platform for pots of geraniums and a variegated agave, brought outside for the summer.

GARAGE

Greenhouse

Vegetables

N

5 The house faces a collection of old farm buildings. Their stone walls and tile roofs make a mellow backdrop for a decorative shrub planting: hebe, senecio, and roses all feature here.

4 A paved and gravelled path links the terrace and conservatory across the back of the house.

6 A garden bench nestles against the house amid the climbing rose 'Zéphirine Drouhin' and valerian, Centranthus ruber. On the left is a shrimp plant.

A WALLED GARDEN

An air of tranquility and spaciousness characterizes this town garden, which lies behind an Edwardian house. Once dominated by a dull rectangular lawn, with regimented herbaceous borders flanking the boundary walls, the garden was transformed by replacing these with an informal arrangement of stone, brick, and gravel (all ideal surfaces for furniture and pots).

As well as to cater to the owners' lifestyle, my aim was to complement the house and evoke the mood of an Edwardian garden rather than to copy the original. The greenhouse windows, which match those of the house, and the metal bench are in period style, while the modern slatted furniture is a loose visual reference to the balcony woodwork. The emphasis on foliage plants (many of which are shade tolerant) reflects the Edwardians' penchant for exotic leaf shapes, but in a modern way, for the plants have strong architectural qualities; they are not botanical oddities.

Strength of design was called for to prevent the enormous trees that surround and shade the site from dominating it, and to focus attention within the area – for this garden is always viewed from above, from a kitchen and sitting room on the second floor. The open gravelled areas, the robust patterning of the surface materials, and the chain of focal points all contribute to the layout's impact.

PLAN ANALYSIS

My aim was to break up the rectangular shape of the site and to create a sense of spaciousness. The key to this is the strong ground pattern, which comprises a terrace of stone running across the garden to emphasize its breadth, and, running down the garden to emphasize its length, brick and gravelled areas of overlapping rectangles. To enhance the feeling of space, these open areas are punctuated by a shallow step, an arrangement of pots and furniture, and incidental plantings.

The layout for the garden was devised on a grid of squares that are half the width of the house extension, and multiples and divisions of the square were used to make the proportional shapes. Given that the garden is surrounded by walls at right angles, I used straight-edged shapes, but the overall impression is gentle rather than hard, because I chose mellow-colored construction materials, made gradual changes of level, and introduced planting as an integral part of the central area, in beds, growing through gaps left in the stone paving, in groups of containers, and through the gravel.

1 The strong lines of Cordyline australis provide a dramatic focal point to the informal arrangement of plants behind an old water-filled sink, and echo the angular patterning of the wooden stairway and balcony above.

2 Choice of garden accessories is crucial to the mood evoked in a design. The simple, classic style of this hardwood furniture enhances the air of uncluttered tranquility that pervades the garden.

Boundary wall

Planting

Feature

Shallow step

1

3

5

Planting beds

Steps up

4

BALCONY

Stone terrace with brick

HOUSE

2

Pear tree

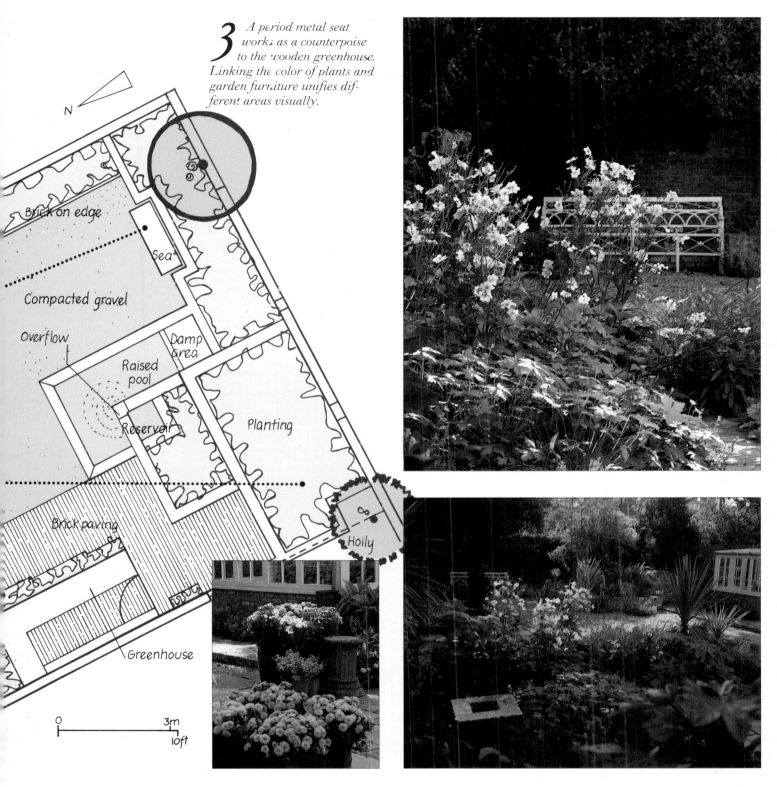

3 *A period metal seat works as a counterpoise to the wooden greenhouse. Linking the color of plants and garden furniture unifies different areas visually.*

N

Brick on edge

Seat

Compacted gravel

Overflow

Damp area

Raised pool

Reservoir

Planting

Brick paving

Holly

Greenhouse

0   3m

10ft

4 *Informal groupings of pots and stone features provide a contrast to the expanses of open space.*

5 *This view shows the potential of using focal points on either side of an open space. The foreground* Cordyline australis *interrupts the view to the water feature and brick beds, increasing the site's apparent length.*

A COUNTRY GARDEN

T his garden surrounds a modern house built within the grounds of a nineteenth-century farm. Once a series of walled enclosures with a large pond screened by old hedgerow trees, the garden needed cohesion to allow a logical progression around it and views to the countryside.

Wide steppingstones now strike off from the terrace towards a pastel-colored mixed border, the paving visually linking house to garden. The border ends at an old wall (left) that I finished with a finial ball to make a "period," because through an arch in the wall, surmounted by an open wooden pavilion, a change of mood occurs. This next space is dominated by a huge copper beech, and the planting needed much stronger coloring to work with it. I made it a gravelled area, planted with predominantly yellow flowers, all centered on an old well. Behind the copper beech is a window in the wall, giving a glimpse of the cows as they graze in the field beyond.

From the well area a path leads under an existing pergola to a new feature, a second wooden pavilion, sited to partner the first in the winter view. Beyond this and the excavated pond, the distinction between field and garden is barely discernible.

The garden, already large, seems larger still now that views to the countryside allow it to flow out towards the farmland beyond.

PLAN ANALYSIS

The plan for the garden evolved broadly in two halves, bisected by the pergola walk. This was an existing feature, but its alignment on the central bay window of the house makes it a useful axis. Wooden pavilions link the two halves visually.

The area to the right of the pergola walk developed from a collage of squares and rectangles, with some elements proportional to the square around the well. The left-hand side is more flowing and sweeps out with the excavated levels radiating from the pond side. Soil from the pond excavations was used to create a low mound as a screen to the swimming pool. The effect is a gentle visual curve down to the pond from the most important viewing position – the kitchen table.

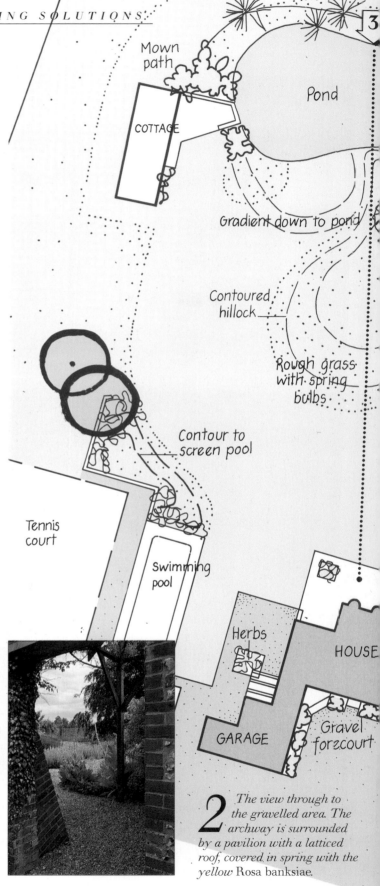

1 The area near the well (on the left) needed plants chosen to hold their own against the dramatic copper beech, and to spread into the gravel. Yellows predominate. The plants include Hypericum *'Hidcote'*, Cornus alba *'Spaethii'*, Verbascum olympicum, *and, in the foreground, clumps of* Sisyrinchium striatum.

2 The view through to the gravelled area. The archway is surrounded by a pavilion with a latticed roof, covered in spring with the yellow Rosa banksiae.

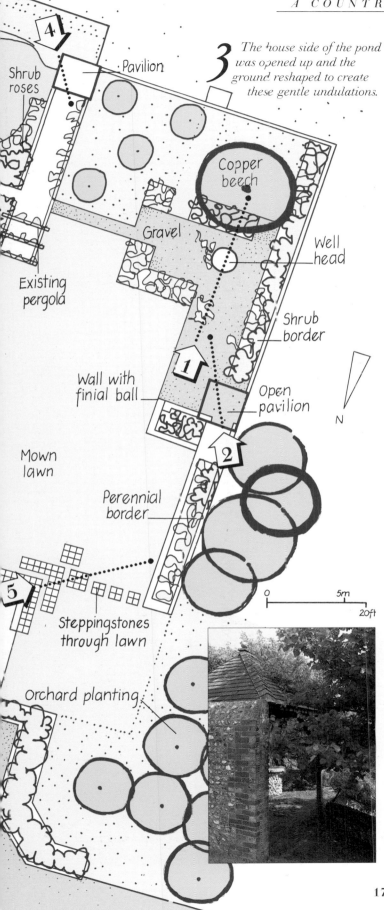

Shrub roses

Pavilion

3 The house side of the pond was opened up and the ground reshaped to create these gentle undulations.

Copper beech

Gravel

Well head

Existing pergola

Shrub border

Wall with finial ball

1

Open pavilion

N

Mown lawn

2

Perennial border

0   5m

20ft

5

Steppingstones through lawn

Orchard planting

4 Left: *The second wooden pavilion marks the end of the pergola. In winter the view from the house reveals the two bare pavilion roofs rising above the walls.*

5 Above: *Broad paving slabs make steppingstones out from the terrace towards the wall border, the lawn appearing to flow around and through them.*

177

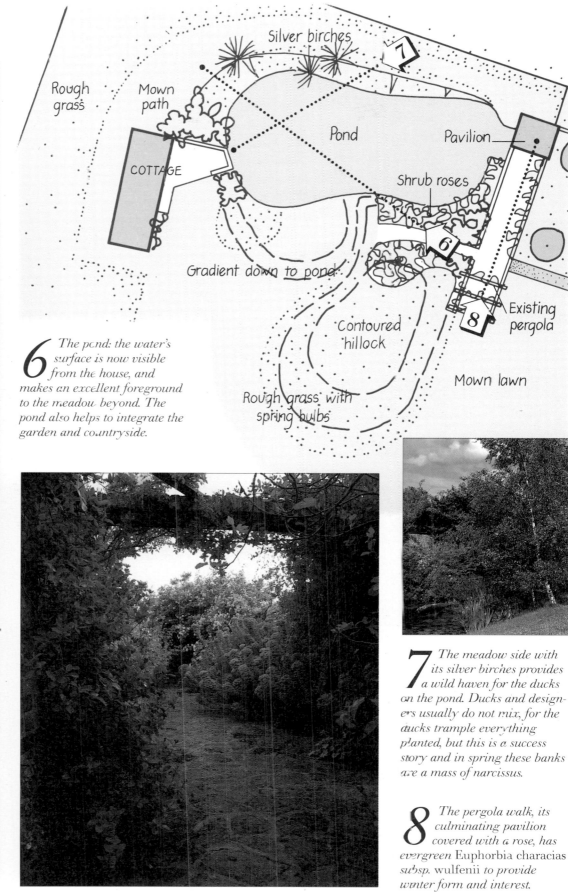

Rough grass

Mown path

Silver birches

7

Pond

Pavilion

COTTAGE

Shrub roses

6

Gradient down to pond

Contoured hillock

8

Existing pergola

Mown lawn

Rough grass with spring bulbs

6 The pond: the water's surface is now visible from the house, and makes an excellent foreground to the meadow beyond. The pond also helps to integrate the garden and countryside.

7 The meadow side with its silver birches provides a wild haven for the ducks on the pond. Ducks and designers usually do not mix, for the ducks trample everything planted, but this is a success story and in spring these banks are a mass of narcissus.

8 The pergola walk, its culminating pavilion covered with a rose, has evergreen *Euphorbia characias* subsp. *wulfenii* to provide winter form and interest.

A DESERT GARDEN

In terms of styling, this garden by James Kell-ogg Wheat, an Arizona landscape architect, is pure Southwest. Such a look is comparatively new, a look that has borrowed from Spanish, Navajo, and indigenous desert elements to create a style with an integrity of its own.

In garden terms, adobe walls, terra-cotta tiles, and cacti all seem quintessential. The native Arizona plants have been grown commercially for some time, for newcomers to the area are actually seeking the desert look. Longer-established residents have, by contrast, struggled with East Coast style gardens for decades, all heavily dependent on water. And there's the crunch – water; a diminishing supply has made the desert style, and therefore desert-style planting, the only option. The changes in the region have been of such a dramatic nature that even developers now require landscape plans to preserve the existing natives and reintroduce more. The native saguaro cactus *(Carnegiea gigan-tea)*, featured strongly in the view of the garden shown here, is so protected that now it cannot be moved without a state permit.

This garden has a sympathetic backdrop in the adobe building and paved terra-cotta surround. It is a mixture of carefully composed forms and tex-tures, all growing slowly in the low-maintenance, low-water-use medium of fine gravel.

PLAN ANALYSIS

In the plan for this garden the strong architectural lines of the house are repeated in pathways and a series of stepped low walls enclosing planting areas and sheltering the patio. (*Patio* is not a word I would normally use for a terrace but its Spanish origins make it appropriate in this context.) The rounded corners of the walls reflect the nature of their material, adobe.

What gives contrast to the layout is the landscaping, which is emphasized by the walls of different levels, and the sparse furnishing of rocks and desert plants. Not every inch of ground is planted, and the spaces in between only serve to enhance the plants' particular forms.

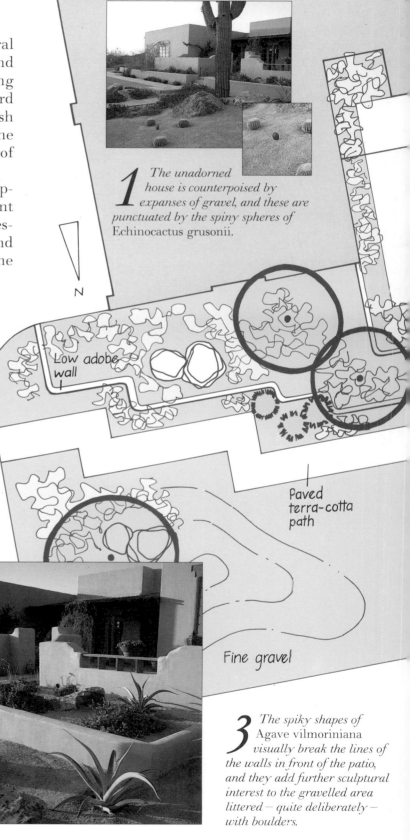

1 The unadorned house is counterpoised by expanses of gravel, and these are punctuated by the spiny spheres of Echinocactus grusonii.

Low adobe wall

Paved terra-cotta path

Fine gravel

2 The house outline is stark and clean, with just the window lintels and glazing bars for detailing; the garden's design helps emphasize those features, while also creating interest of its own. From the path leading to the front door, the eye is led to the windows by the gently curving walls and the balustrade, while the tiles echo the glazing pattern. Adding contrast is the free shape of the tree on the patio.

3 The spiky shapes of Agave vilmoriniana visually break the lines of the walls in front of the patio, and they add further sculptural interest to the gravelled area littered – quite deliberately – with boulders.

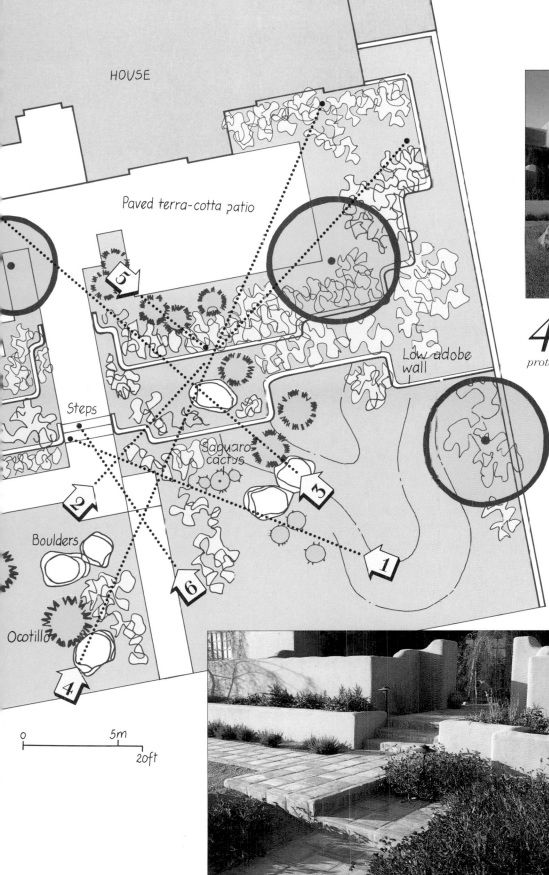

HOUSE

Paved terra-cotta patio

⑤

Low adobe wall

Steps

Saguaro cactus

③

②

Boulders

⑥

①

Ocotillo

④

0   5m

20ft

4   *Two Arizona natives: in the fore-ground the multistemmed ocotillo* (Fouquieria splendens), *behind, the protected saguaro cactus.*

5   Aloe striata *brings plant interest to the area in front of the house win-dows. The plant forms are bold enough to hold up against the stylized balustrade.*

6   *The landscaping is a key feature of this gar-den's design, expressed through low steps and terraced planting areas. In such a frost-free region – although nights can become chilly – terra-cotta tiles are commonplace. Their bold pattern and mottling make a good contrast to the smooth adobe. Sprawling over the path is* Verbena rigida.

AN URBAN WATER GARDEN

Situated in an area of market gardening near Aalsmeer in Holland, this small estate house looks out onto its own magical water garden, at the back of which there is a busy road, screened by a high wooden fence. The rich planting and bold design by Henk Weijers make the garden a haven within its setting, a picture pleasing enough to distract from the ugliness of the road beyond.

Textured precast concrete slabs form a terrace at the rear of the house, and from it a wooden deck crosses the formally shaped pool and leads to a small terrace area. The wooden pathway then follows the boundary back to the house. Near the house and around the edge of the garden are areas of wooden bench seating. There is a small roof garden.

At ground level the garden has a junglelike feel, enhanced by the dragonflies darting about on sunny days and the golden carp swimming in the pool. The selection of plant material is, in summer, the key to the success of the scheme, the vertical plant forms of rushes, grasses, bamboos, and achillea stems making a strong architectural contrast to the linear ground plan. Color combinations are bold and striking, appropriate for a site with no views. In winter, the decking and uncompromising rectangular shapes make the layout sufficiently strong to maintain the interest alone. This is a very small garden behind a small house – but its design is no less imaginative nor less inspiring for it.

PLAN ANALYSIS

From an upstairs window in the house one gains a very clear idea of the plan: strong but simple, holding the eye within the site, and given a huge richness with its planting overlay. The garden is in fact a wonderful example of a semiwild plant grouping held together by a strong ground plan. But what seems formal on plan – a cruciform pattern of interlocking rectangles – is in reality a small planter's paradise. In relation to the whole garden, the pool is quite large; the edges of the pool are entirely lost, and the contrast of water, plants, and bridge is masterly in its simplicity. A more complex ground plan, or indeed any incidental features sited around the garden, would only have confused the issue.

Deck terrace

Wooden bench seating

4

1 *The view of the garden from the roof terrace. The large pool runs expansively across the width, the deck bridge making a strong line to the end.*

2 *Planting between the terrace and the pool includes* Iris germanica *and white* Campanula lactiflora.

3 In the view back to the house the orange hemerocallis and yellow ligularia both read strongly.

4 Growing at the edge of the pool are masses of the bulrush Typha minima, *and behind the yellow achillea there are tall spires of flowering* Lythrum salicaria. *In the background, the boundary fence line is broken up with large clumps of the bamboo Sinarundinaria nitida.*

Deck
bridge

Boundary
fence

Bamboos

Planting

Pool

Terrace of concrete slabs

HOUSE

0   3m

10ft

5 A junglelike feel: near the paved seating area Alchemilla mollis *makes a foaming contrast to the blobs of achillea heads and striped clump of* Arundinaria variegata.

A DIAGONAL DESIGN

Perhaps one of the greatest pleasures of being a garden designer is imbuing clients with a passion for their gardens. This garden is the second I have designed for this particular couple, and they felt inspired to develop the design from my outline plan, adapting my subsequent planting plan by using plants moved from their other garden and including more immediate favorites.

The garden is walled and lies behind a semi-detached period town house. Trees surrounding the site make a green backdrop, and the shade cast by them dictated where the terrace would be, since we wanted it to catch the late afternoon and early evening sun. My intention was to create a view down the garden to the existing apple tree and the terrace couched against the other trees, but at the same time to keep the plan static by binding the garden back to the French windows with an encircling gravel path which opens out into a spacious gravelled area. Diagonal shapes helped me in the first objective by gently leading the eye around the garden, while the lawn helped in the second, sweeping around behind the terrace to hold the eye within the site.

After two years, the garden has taken on a soft, relaxed look, and the owners are to be congratulated on the control of plant masses, which work well with the scale of the structural features.

PLAN ANALYSIS

A site with straight, right-angled boundaries calls for a design that echoes this structure, with the whole effect softened by planting. Whereas layouts of aimless, meandering lines become a visual mishmash once planted, those of straight lines and right angles retain their strength.

The width of the house extension, and the space between this and the boundary, were the bases for the grid squares. I placed the grid at 45° to the house and on this I positioned a series of proportional shapes, starting with the terrace. As the terrace is located away from the house, I sought in my collage of shapes to link it to the paved area outside the French windows by leading the eye through the garden, while keeping attention in the site. By using the shapes on the diagonal I introduced the sort of limited movement needed.

1 The view from the second floor reveals the effect of the diagonals. The design is enhanced by the soft foreground planting.

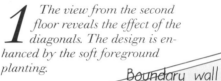

2 Abundant planting is contained within beds of uncompromising geometric shapes. Plants flopping over the edge soften the outline of this large right-angled bed, while the brick retains the overall structure and provides a neat mowing edge.

Boundary wall
Brick paving and step
Planting through gravel
Lawn
Apple tree
HOUSE EXTENSION
CONSERVATORY
Brick edging
Storage shed
HOUSE
Compacted gravel
Pots
Pergola

3 Leaves of similar shape but different sizes make an eye-catching composition. Here large-leaved hostas are grouped with the small-leaved Tiarella cordifolia.

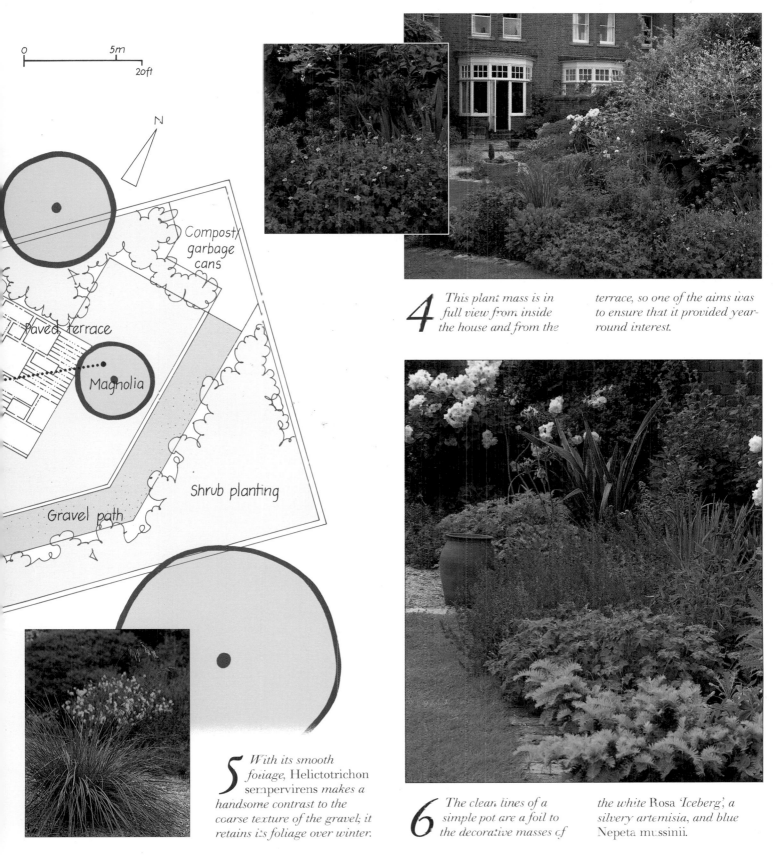

0   5m

20ft

N

Compost/garbage cans

Paved terrace

Magnolia

Shrub planting

Gravel path

4 This plant mass is in full view from inside the house and from the terrace, so one of the aims was to ensure that it provided year-round interest.

5 With its smooth foliage, Helictotrichon sempervirens *makes a handsome contrast to the coarse texture of the gravel; it retains its foliage over winter.*

6 The clean lines of a simple pot are a foil to the decorative masses of the white Rosa 'Iceberg', a silvery artemisia, and blue Nepeta mussinii.

A COURTYARD GARDEN

In recent years, several houses were built within the grounds of a large, old house; this is the new garden of one of them. It includes part of the old walls, the brick potting shed, and a large apple tree, which combine to give the garden a well-established feeling, and have been made the main features of the new design. With its compact size and bricky, almost urban feel, the area did not lend itself to the use of grass; instead, gravel creates the appropriate courtyard atmosphere. Another reason for not using grass was that the garden is designed to be left untended for fairly lengthy periods. In fact, with only occasional correction by thinning out, such a garden improves and softens with neglect.

The modern house with its terrace of concrete pavers is very different in style from the old potting shed facing it, so a series of wide stepping-stones across the gravel is used to provide a visual link between the two. The outline of the paving is softened by plants growing through the gravel.

The points of incidental interest – the statue, font, and tubs – work together visually because they were planned at the design stage and are balanced by the planting. Many times too many random incidents break up a layout to the point it becomes unrestful. This design is strong but simple enough to support a lot of planting material.

PLAN ANALYSIS

The basic grid for this design is generated by the proportions of the house which, being modern, is built in a modular way. A visual rhythm emerges from the rear elements of the house: conservatory to extension, the extension itself, the pergola-covered recess, and the double unit of space between the pergola and the boundary wall. I began the design by fitting the main elements of the garden into grid squares based on these house dimensions, running lines off the house at 90° and 45°. At the front of the house, the grid is halved in size to provide large paved slabs leading from the front door through a gravel area to the garden entrance.

1 The old apple tree is a strong feature, surrounded by a brick-edged bed planted with evergreen Hypericum calycinum.

2 Below: *A lavender bush and a small herb garden at the end of the paved terrace are easily accessible from the house. Beyond, a mixed planting tumbles onto a gravel path.*

3 The gravel area wraps around the side of the house and culminates in a feature: I had planned a bench, but the owners chose a stone font. The composition is enhanced by the repeated use of Alchemilla mollis.

GARAGE

Existing concrete path

N

4 Alchemilla mollis *self-seeds, but has been planted deliberately here to add textural contrast to the paved slabs. The yucca and* Cotoneaster horizontalis *will grow quickly, but in the meantime a stone pot adds interest.*

Boundary wall

0   5m

20ft

Shrub screen

Water tank

POTTING SHED

Stone terrace

Tubs for color

Fruit trees

Apple tree

1

Mown grass

Herb bed

4

Bog plants

Compacted gravel

6

Stone sinks

2

Raised pond

Steppingstones

CONSERVATORY

Terrace

3

5

HOUSE EXTENSION

Pergola

statue

HOUSE

Shade planting in compacted gravel

Wall planting

Seat

Precast concrete slabs

Hedge

Beech trees with planting below

5 *Though the use of color is restrained throughout the garden, the planned succession of incidents prevents dullness in the arrangement.*

6 *Shade-tolerant* Hosta decorata *and* Hypericum *'Hidcote' grow well below the boundary wall.*

7 *An area of mixed planting, including* Rosa *'Rosemary Rose' and* Geranium endressii *'Wargrave Pink', runs alongside a path from the courtyard area. The tumbling mass provides color as well as a contrast to the open expanses of gravel and stone paving.*

A CLASSICAL GARDEN

A happy mix of old and new, traditional and modern characterizes this large country garden. It was originally laid out in the early nineteenth century, reputedly by the English landscape gardener Humphrey Repton, and in my design I tried to keep the feel of his original while seeking a new look overall.

When the owners and I started working on the garden about twenty years ago, it had been badly neglected and was very overgrown. The main feature was a meandering watercourse that needed restoring to its rightful importance in the design. Many of the older trees were cleared and rampant groves of bamboo dug out to open views to the grazing meadows beyond. Some new trees have been planted. The watercourse (left) had to be cleaned and the existing shallow stone waterfall reconstructed.

Horticultural input is limited to one perennial border, so the garden is easy to maintain – but there is, nevertheless, interest throughout the year. For spring, there are great drifts of bulbs, and in winter, yew and box, which thrive on the chalky soil and provide a rich backdrop to the bare gray trunks of the many old beech trees. Running water, swaths of grass, sculpture, and the movement of cattle and horses in the fields beyond give contrast and a series of incidents all year round.

PLAN ANALYSIS

In this garden I was adapting and redefining many existing features – the watercourse, swimming pool, pool house, and canal among them.

An unusual feature of the site was the change of elevation across it. I made this more obvious in my treatment of the waterfall, and in the design of the area around the pool house.

The sweeping curves of the watercourse form the core of the design, but its entry into the garden, through a pipe from a lake at the far end, lacked impact. I introduced some punctuation to the site by contouring the ground to create a gentle hill over the pipe, and placing a temple on the top. The owner has further helped by positioning various dramatic pieces of modern sculpture.

1 Beyond a sculpture by Henry Moore, a temple marks the source of the watercourse – a happy combination of classical and modern.

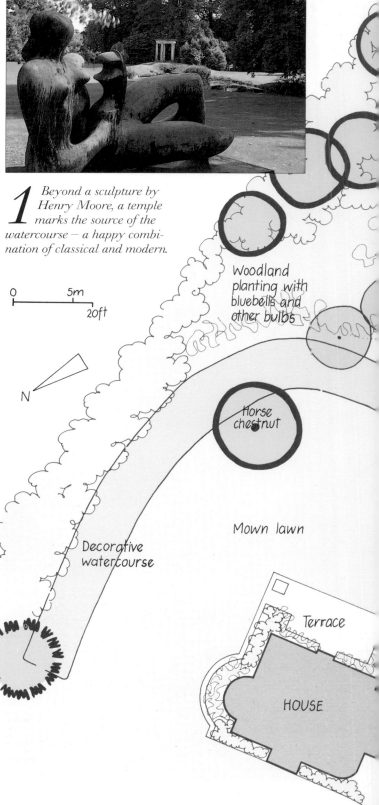

Woodland planting with bluebells and other bulbs

Horse chestnut

Mown lawn

Decorative watercourse

Terrace

HOUSE

2 The cleaned and reconstructed stone waterfall announces the change of elevation across the garden, and is a focal point in the view from the house.

3 Left: Pale pink astilbes provide summer interest and are backed by native yellow flag iris. The naturalized plants growing by the stream need little maintenance.

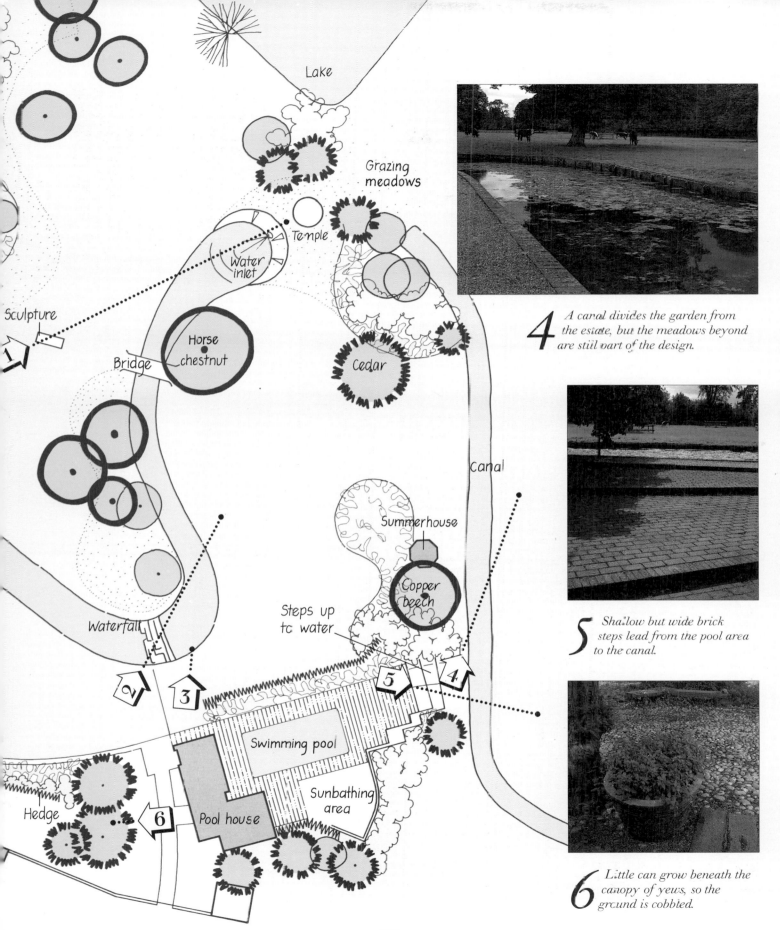

Lake

Grazing
meadows

Temple

Water
inlet

Sculpture

1

Bridge

Horse
chestnut

Cedar

Waterfall

Canal

Summerhouse

Steps up
to water

Copper
beech

2

3

5

4

Swimming pool

Hedge

6

Pool house

Sunbathing
area

4 *A canal divides the garden from the estate, but the meadows beyond are still part of the design.*

5 *Shallow but wide brick steps lead from the pool area to the canal.*

6 *Little can grow beneath the canopy of yews, so the ground is cobbled.*

THE GRASSY LOOK

The view from this garden north of Baltimore, Maryland, was almost too overwhelming; to help shield themselves from it, the owners had tried to create their own world near the house by planting an evergreen screen. In front of this, they proposed to site a swimming pool.

The landscape architects Wolfgang Oehme and James van Sweden saw that this position would have been wrong for the pool. Instead, they reshaped and regraded the site to create a new series of terraced areas running down the south-facing side of the house. The pool is now sited with a surrounding terrace to integrate with the farm view beyond, the stepped levels creating privacy from the house. The ground shaping around the terrace acts as a sort of ha-ha, so a boundary line is not visible, although elsewhere fencing is called for, and is in a simple vernacular style.

The real strength of this design is its dramatic planting of grasses that makes a foreground to the view beyond. Huge textural drifts, with perennials for summer color, match the scale of the field patterns surrounding the garden, visually drawing the two together. Away from the immediate pool surround, a certain amount of shrubby material has been retained from the previous garden, and this helps to bulk up the garden's planting — but what a planting. It is unique to this firm of landscape architects. Colorful and frothing in late summer through to autumn, it retains its interest throughout the winter months, for the swaths of dead seed and flower heads look spectacular in snow, also providing food for birds.

PLAN ANALYSIS

The swimming pool terrace is set into the slope, with a meadow above it protecting swimmers from the winds; below it is a new lawn, surrounded by established planting interspersed with new. The pool is linked to the house by a strong design of overlapping and interlocking rectangles, with a right-angled flight of steps at the change of level that gives the layout a strong directional pull; on plan, the steps are echoed in those that continue below the water level. Steppingstones help to break up the dividing line between terrace and garden.

1 The washed aggregate concrete terrace surrounding the pool provides a wonderfully simple foil to the rich planting around it. The surfacing does not jar with its setting; even the blue stone edging adds only a subtle contrast.

2 Tucked into a gentle swell of ground, the pool and its planting are perfectly integrated into the surrounding panorama.

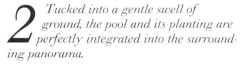

Fence

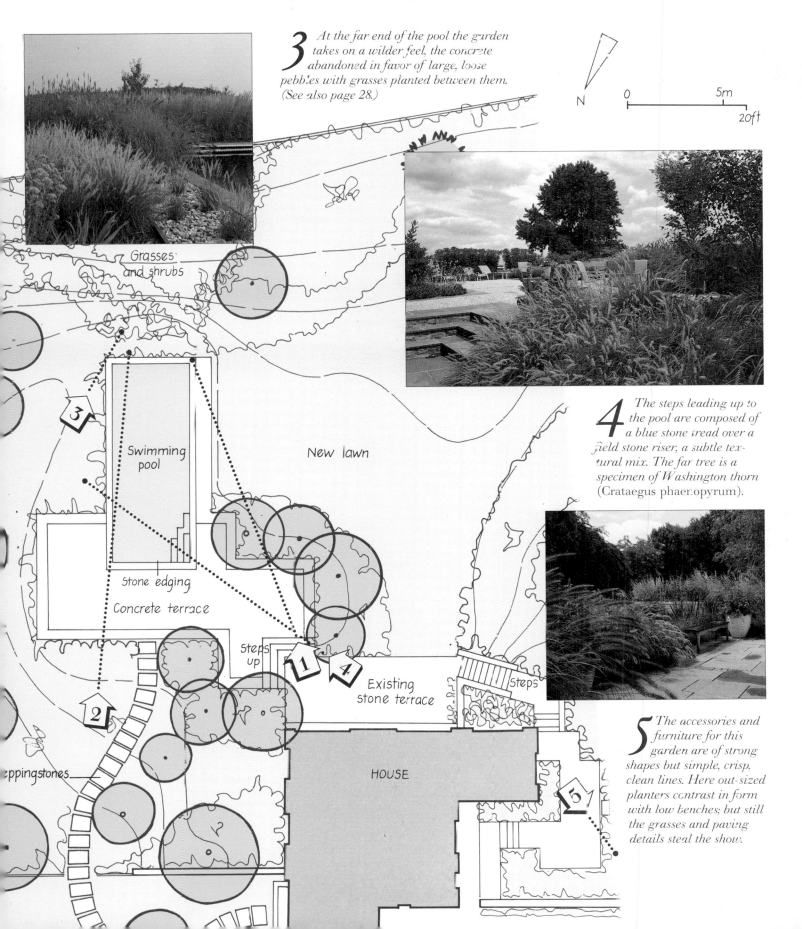

3 *At the far end of the pool the garden takes on a wilder feel, the concrete abandoned in favor of large, loose pebbles with grasses planted between them. (See also page 28.)*

4 *The steps leading up to the pool are composed of a blue stone tread over a field stone riser, a subtle textural mix. The far tree is a specimen of Washington thorn (Crataegus phaenopyrum).*

5 *The accessories and furniture for this garden are of strong shapes but simple, crisp, clean lines. Here out-sized planters contrast in form with low benches; but still the grasses and paving details steal the show.*

N

0   5m

20ft

Grasses and shrubs

Swimming pool

New lawn

Stone edging

Concrete terrace

Steps up

Existing stone terrace

Steps

Steppingstones

HOUSE

3

2

1   4

5

A MODERN DESIGN

Designed by Henk Weijers, the front garden of this site in Haarlem, Holland, runs parallel to the street and has a Japanese quality with clean architectural lines. In plan form its uncompromising blocks of planting, interspersed with gravel surfacing, show how an urban setting can be subtly echoed in a garden's design; the gravel walkways continue on to a paved area used as a car park.

In the partially shaded rear garden, abundant growth is contrasted with a simple, formal though asymmetric design, and some mature trees provide both shade and shelter. Wooden decking walkways surround areas of water, repeating the timber cladding infills of the two-story house (left).

The rich planting overlay only softens the effect of the clean lines, but note how many of the plant forms are architectural as well: green spire leaves contrasted with rounded forms; arrowhead leaf shapes with circular pads of lilies, and so on. The use of grasses and bamboo also reflects a much stronger preference for form in garden planting than one might find in a British garden. When comparing this garden with that by Oehme, van Sweden on pages 198-9, one can see definite parallels in planting design, and indeed it is no coincidence, for both American designers have a strong European background training.

PLAN ANALYSIS

There are various ways to style a house to its garden: in some instances the use of similar materials works; in others, climbers might link the two. Sometimes contrast is effective, perhaps treating the house as a piece of sculpture rising from a garden setting. That is the case here, where garden and structure seem quite at odds with each other – until you study the ground plan. For then, the right angles and the proportions of paths, paving, planting areas, and water make a collage of forms that have a proportional relationship to the structural elements of the house. The shapes are realized in a range of materials and exuberant plantings.

1 *A sentinel pine, set in a raised bed by the front door, is seen to advantage against pale brickwork.*

2 *The horizontal lines of the house and the road alongside are repeated in alternating strips of planting and gravel. The height of the planting blocks is in proportion to their width; dark alleys are not the designer's intention.*

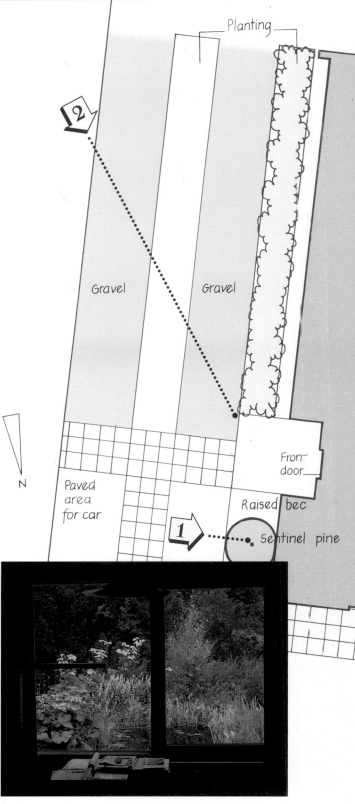

3 *From the office, the water garden is a wonderful blend of strong forms and bold color partnerships, the water's surface enlivened with waterlilies.*

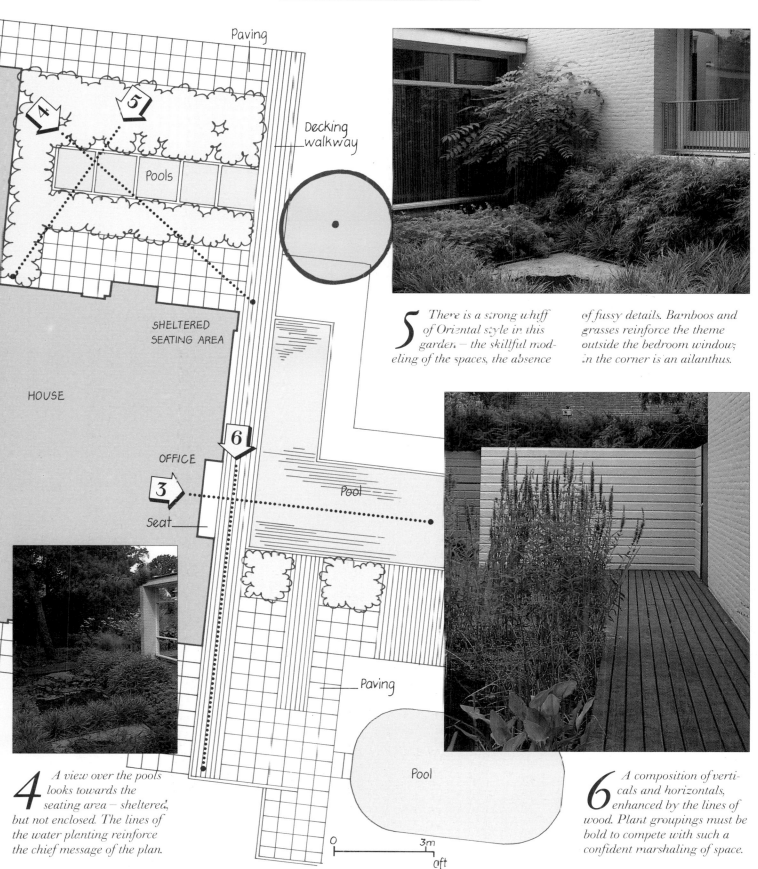

Paving

Decking
walkway

Pools

SHELTERED
SEATING AREA

HOUSE

OFFICE

Seat

Pool

Paving

Pool

0   3m

0ft

5 There is a strong whiff
of Oriental style in this
garden – the skillful mod-
eling of the spaces, the absence
of fussy details. Bamboos and
grasses reinforce the theme
outside the bedroom window;
in the corner is an ailanthus.

4 A view over the pools
looks towards the
seating area – sheltered,
but not enclosed. The lines of
the water planting reinforce
the chief message of the plan.

6 A composition of verticals and horizontals,
enhanced by the lines of
wood. Plant groupings must be
bold to compete with such a
confident marshaling of space.

A GARDEN OF ROOMS

Once a piecemeal collection of unrelated areas, this garden now gives the impression of consisting of a series of "rooms." Each room is distinctive – a sunny lawn, a water garden, an enclosure devoted to plants with red foliage and flowers, a small winter garden, and so on – yet the air of rural charm pervading the whole garden binds them into a cohesive whole.

The garden surrounds a sixteenth-century cottage, with a smaller cottage, several old barns, and an octagonal summerhouse (left) on the grounds. All of these become dominating focal points for the new garden. The entrance is through an arch in the walls of an old barn, which leads to a gravelled area surrounding a raised pool. From here, large paved steppingstones cross a small lawn to the house.

Views open up as one wanders through the garden: from a gate in the wall linking the main house to the guest house, a lawn stretches away, stepping up to a swimming pool backed by a pool house; from an open barn in a corner of the garden – an ideal space for summer outdoor entertaining – there is a view of the water garden and beyond to a clematis-covered pergola walk.

Despite the many different areas, the garden works as a whole, for it is constructed to a very high standard and is wonderfully cared for by the owners themselves.

PLAN ANALYSIS

With a brief to create a series of roomlike areas, my main concern was to ensure some sort of continuity through the garden, so that each room, while being unique, was not discordant with other areas.

The existing buildings provide anchor points within the garden, each determining the style, proportions, and function of the immediate surrounding area – a paved breakfast area beside the house, a brick terrace next to the brick summerhouse, the terrace sited to catch the late afternoon sun. With so much going on – for all the planting is bold and rich as well – the overall proportions of each area had to be as simple and generous as possible.

1 The view over the neatly-edged vegetable garden is enlivened with tubs of annuals. A statue sited to lead the visitor into the next area of the garden stands in the background.

Swimming pool

Pool house

Stone terrace

Ola beech hedge

Red garden

Pergola

Brick paving

Existing beech

Water garden

Winter garden

Vegetable

OPEN BARN

2 Late evening sun catches a random planting in a gravelled area adjacent to the guest house. The same plants recur in a free, self-sown tapestry of small shrubs and annuals.

3 Right: The brick pillars and paving of the pergola echo the pool house at the end of the walk. Even in winter, the generous proportions of the pergola, its oak beams taken from a nearby cottage, make this an inviting walk.

0   5m
20ft

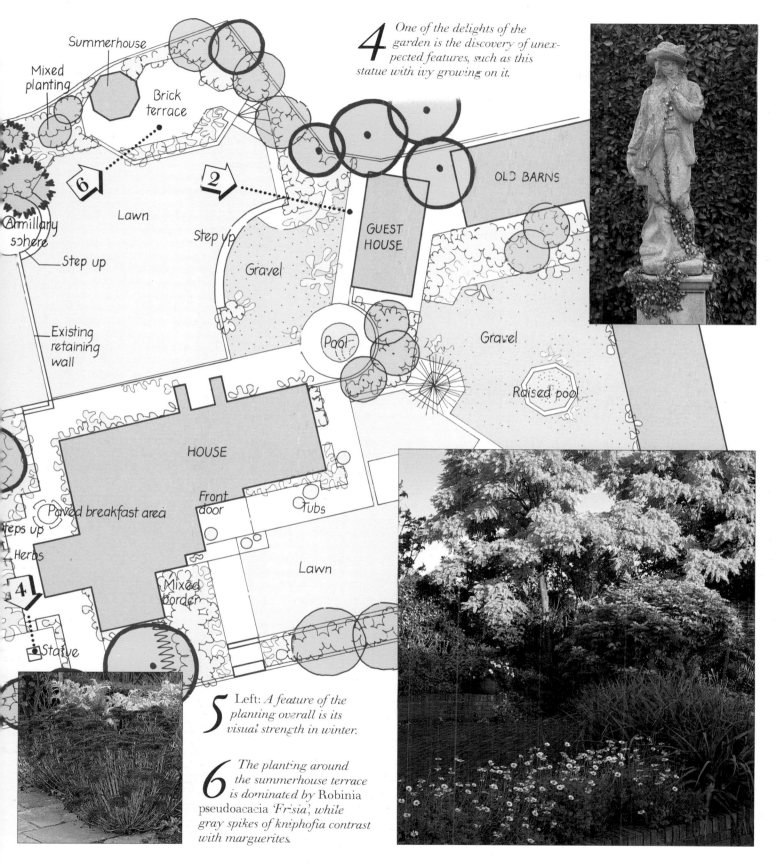

Summerhouse

Mixed planting

Brick terrace

Armillary sphere

Step up

Lawn

6

2

Step up

Gravel

Existing retaining wall

Pool

GUEST HOUSE

OLD BARNS

Gravel

Raised pool

HOUSE

Paved breakfast area

Front door

Tubs

Steps up

Herbs

4

Statue

Lawn

Mixed border

4 *One of the delights of the garden is the discovery of unexpected features, such as this statue with ivy growing on it.*

5 Left: *A feature of the planting overall is its visual strength in winter.*

6 *The planting around the summerhouse terrace is dominated by* Robinia pseudoacacia *'Frisia', while gray spikes of kniphofia contrast with marguerites.*

7 *Foliage forms are enlivened by vibrant scarlet roses in this mixed border. All four main foliage colors are represented in this small area of planting:* cotinus *and* Lonicera nitida *'Baggesen's Gold' provide purple and yellow foliage all year round, with the gray stachys and glossy rose leaves to add summer contrasts.*

8 Right: *Flint cobbles surrounding a young fig tree echo the materials of the main house. The cottagey mixture of plants includes white lychnis, tree peony, foxgloves, and* Eucalyptus gunnii *which is kept pruned down for its young gray foliage. In the foreground* eschscholzia *has self-seeded in the gravel.*

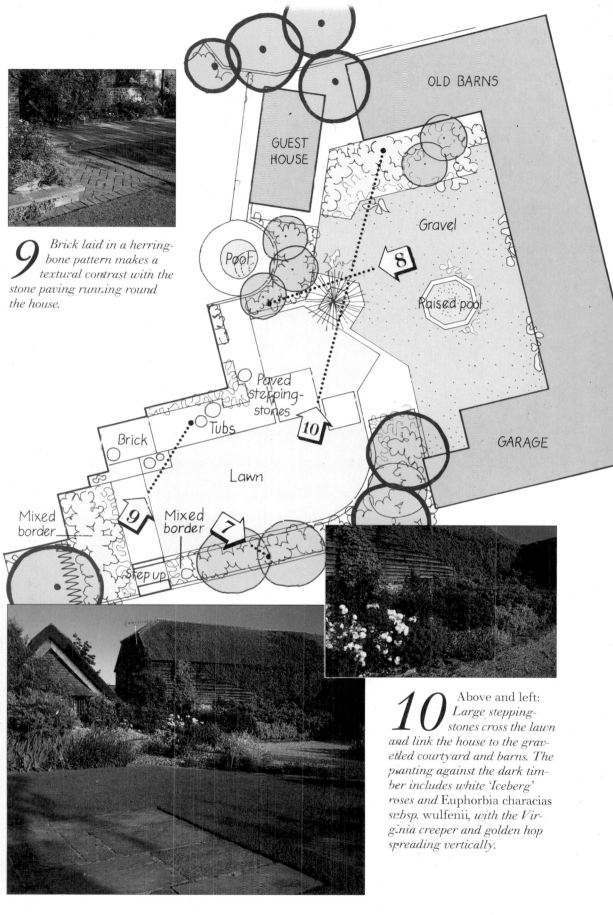

9 Brick laid in a herring-bone pattern makes a textural contrast with the stone paving running round the house.

10 Above and left: Large stepping-stones cross the lawn and link the house to the gravelled courtyard and barns. The planting against the dark timber includes white 'Iceberg' roses and Euphorbia characias subsp. wulfenii, *with the Virginia creeper and golden hop spreading vertically.*

Labels on plan: OLD BARNS · GUEST HOUSE · Gravel · Pool · Raised pool · Paved stepping-stones · Tubs · Brick · Lawn · Mixed border · Mixed border · Step up · GARAGE · 8 · 10 · 9 · 7

7

THE INGREDIENTS OF A GARDEN

This is not a book on how to construct a garden, rather it shows some of the hard elements you might use in the finished design, and the selection can only be partial at that. I have listed these ingredients more or less in the order in which you should be thinking about them when building up your garden detail. Explanatory information on the construction of some of the most common hard elements and garden features can be found on pages 334-41.

PREPARING THE SITE

With the design of your future garden complete, you are ready to enter the next phase, the realization of your plan in hard and soft materials. Choosing from the vast range of materials available, you will see your plan and your style objective coming to life on site.

Not all the work at the drawing board is over, of course, for from your schematic plan you need to produce a series of technical drawings. These are explained more fully on page 344, but in brief you may need a setting out plan – which shows the dimensions on site of all the planned shapes, including such details as the radius of any circular shape – and a structural plan (see page 50). You may be hiring a contractor to carry out much of the work, who will need detailed plans of all new features, supplemented with written specifications.

The aim of these four pages is to outline the groundworks, that is, the work that may be necessary on your site before construction of the garden can begin.

Site Clearance

The degree of site clearance necessary depends on the state of the site and the work that is proposed. Garden construction often follows work on the house, so the site clearance may just be picking up the builder's discarded trash; in rural areas, trees and scrub may need to be removed, or you may find that weeds waist-high appear in the spring. Clearance might be machine work, it might be possible by hand, or it might require the application of a weed or brush killer (before going ahead with this last, check surrounding areas for possible run-off, and keep children and pets away).

In site clearance operations, ensure that the topsoil is removed first, and piled separately from the subsoil, ready to be replaced once construction is complete. Topsoil is a valuable commodity, and must never be mixed with the layers of subsoil beneath it. This may create storage problems in small sites, so think ahead and dump the soil in a convenient area, not one where the future working of the site will be constantly hampered.

Landscaping takes place after the site is cleared. Later work will be the hand finishing of the elevations, but the primary work might include machinery for excavation of pools or ponds, or the creation of hillocks or berms. All landscaping and excavation is carried out in subsoil; only later do you finish the work by returning the topsoil.

Setting Out the Design on Site

Having cleared the decks, you have the perfect opportunity to set out the broad outlines of your proposal to see if your design is working.

With white stakes and string, peg out the design on site, so that it "reads." Mark the straight runs first just with pegs. Establish circles with a makeshift compass: tie one end of a piece of string to a stick, the other to a wooden peg. Adjust the knots to make the length of the string equal to the radius of the planned circular shape. With the peg stuck in the ground at the center of the circle, you can score the shape on the ground with the stick. Peg out the curve you have described, then join all the pegs with string.

Look at your design from all angles – not only from ground level, but from the second floor bedrooms too (always an excellent place for garden contemplation, seemingly). See whether the borders are too wide, too narrow, or in too much shade. Will the terrace or deck be wide enough? Is the swimming pool in the right place? Walk on the paths you have outlined, perhaps push the wheelbarrow along them, for the layout must be practical as well as visually satisfying. If you are contemplating a new driveway and a turnaround for a car, now is the time to try them. Make sure that you can reverse down the driveway and that there is sufficient room for parking, and so on. Perish the thought, but you may find that you want to make some adjustments once you see the design actually laid out.

Pegging out
Peg out your design on the ground before beginning any building work, firstly to ensure that it is practical and making last minute changes where necessary, but also to check that your planned layout will work visually.

Concrete footings
Any construction in your new garden needs the correct foundations, and these details must be specified by you, the designer, or an appropriate expert. Make sure that your plans fulfill the requirements of local building codes.

Understanding the materials,
left and below
You can learn a great deal about detailing and the potential of various materials from closely watching a good builder. To the left is a corner detail of one of the raised brick planters shown below during construction. The shaping of the bricks to achieve the angle is clear.

Site Drainage

Now is the time to consider the installation of a drainage system where necessary. In older gardening books, you will see vast herringbone systems of clay drainage pipes suggested. These systems only worked well below ground that was to be heavily cultivated by an army of gardeners, for while a drainage system removes surplus water, it also takes away the soluble nutrients that are essential for plants, so plenty of organic matter was needed to counteract too heavy drainage.

Where a site needs much drainage, current thinking, at the domestic level, is to go for plantings that flourish in undrained conditions. While this may be appropriate in many gardens where waterlogged soil occurs naturally, some sites do still need to have excess water taken away from them.

New sites often have water standing on the surface. Where this is the result of heavy machinery compacting the soil, aeration may be all that is needed; but where a layer of excavated clay or subsoil has been dumped over perfectly free-draining soil (and disguised by a thin layer of topsoil), removal of the clay and site drainage are called for. An open drain run over a gradient to a ditched outlet will quickly lead surplus water off the site. Where an outlet is not available, lay the drains to a drainage field instead (see page 332).

In a garden, drainage problems are likely to be small-scale and restricted to specific areas that become waterlogged after rain, for example, a frequently trodden lawn laid on clay, or at the foot of a contoured hillock. A simple drain connected to an on-site drainage field should be all that is needed to relieve these areas of excess water. Generally, surplus water run-off from an area of paving is absorbed by a bordering area of earth or grass.

Irrigation

This subject has not received much attention in Britain until recently, although it is taken as the norm in certain areas of the United States and in Australia. There are various irrigation systems for plants and grassed areas. Surface systems providing drip irrigation are used for plants, underground systems, which create a circular spray, for lawns (see page 333). It is the latter type that needs to be considered during the groundwork stage. The specifications of the system will vary according to area, so call in a local irrigation expert. The ethics of the resulting verdant green lawn when naturally it should be brown are another matter, since I personally hate the Palm Springs or Miami Beach year-round plastic look.

Water Spigots

You may need water spigots throughout your garden and if so, now is the time to lay pipes to tapped outlets. If your garden is in colder climes, the pipes must be set below the frost line or they could freeze. The pipes must be pitched away from the house and make sure you have a shut-off valve at the source and a drain at the end to insure proper drainage. Draw the line of the course on a plan – if a water pipe bursts or needs replacing, you will want to know where it is.

Electrical Outlets

At this stage, you need to establish whether you want to light your garden at night, if you need a fridge in the pool house, or a lead to the water pump. The cables for all these power outlets must be laid before the construction of the garden begins. Use three-wire romex direct-burial cables and

Different levels
A newly constructed layout within a small town garden opens out an existing basement *area using a progression of changes of grade. Note the areas of low, brick-built bench seating, top left.*

lay them in a marked or known situation (like beside a path) at the depth mandated by local building codes. Take no risks with electrical wiring; call in an electrician (see also page 333).

Knowing Your Materials

It is a misconception to believe that a good design is one perfect picture; in fact, it is made up of many small parts that should all be perfectly detailed. I think it most important that before contemplating the construction of any garden design, you familiarize yourself with the media in which you are going to work. As you travel about, use a camera as well as your eyes to record any detailing you like.

To detail in brick, you need to know the different types, how bricks are made, and the clays of which they are made. These aspects of the medium, as well as the firing and the way in which the bricks are cut, explain color and texture. Stone, too, needs close examination. See how it is quarried and how it splits. Look at the material used locally or where it appears as rocky outcrops, and examine its detailing carefully.

To work comfortably with wood, visit a lumberyard, look at different woods, see and appreciate their graining, and talk with a carpenter who uses wood sympathetically. This way you get to know the potential of the material, and can with a degree of confidence begin to experiment with your own details. A visit to a mason supplies company or lumberyard is also a useful exercise, to see a selection of materials, and to look at the different types of sand and aggregate, and the varying grades of pebbles or gravel.

Soil Preparation

Once the garden is constructed, the hard work appears to be done; but it will repay you to put as much effort into preparing the planting areas. Replace any excavated sub- and topsoil carefully, then dig in plenty of organic matter: humus will always improve the texture of the soil, and may be necessary to supply nutrients to an impoverished soil. Dig the soil over thoroughly to aerate it and make it crumbly. Conditioning the soil thoroughly before planting enables the plants to establish themselves quickly and so play their part in the design.

A newly constructed garden After construction the areas of paving look dauntingly bare and immense, but green plant material will soon provide softness (see pages 170-3).

SMALL UNIT PAVING

The ingredients with which you create the design of your garden bring it to life, and in doing so they set its distinct style. Selecting the correct hard materials, as well as soft planting elements, makes the styling of your garden suit the house in its midst, your neighbor's house and boundaries, and, in rural situations, the surrounding landscape too. Traditionally, certain materials were available in certain areas only, and there was no choice but to use them. Universal transportation now allows a greater flexibility when choosing materials, to a degree and at a price, but the result is not always the happiest visual solution.

Small paving units, such as bricks, tiles, block paving, and setts, create an attractive, richly textured look, and allow you to pave small or awkward areas more easily. However, the cost of laying a mass of small units will certainly be higher than using larger paving slabs.

Small Pavers for Patterning

Small pavers are perfect for creating surfacing patterns. Whereas with large paving slabs there is the expense of cutting them, small pavers can be combined to interlock in many ways, and different arrangements create distinctive effects that alter the look of a space. Static, densely patterned designs will hold the eye within the site, while dynamic, strong, linear patterns will create movement and lead the eye through the space to a visual conclusion.

Granite pavers may be laid in lines, circles, or fantail patterns. Frost-proof bricks may be laid face down, on edge to reveal a side, or they may be cut to interlock and create a variety of paving patterns. Over wide areas, particularly when using richly colored bricks, remember that simple patterns work best. When laying bricks with larger paving units, avoid a checkerboard design unless it serves a

PAVING BRICKS

Brick pavers, or paviors, are larger, thinner, and considerably cheaper to lay than facing bricks – because of their size and thickness, fewer are needed and less excavation is necessary. Made in a range of clays, with a wide color variation, they are finished in numerous ways to create differing textures and may be shaped to interlock. Pavers made from concrete are similar in appearance to clay paving stones, but have a more precise character. Facing bricks can also be used to pave areas, though they are more expensive.

Red brick
Set out in basket-weave pattern, which has a cottagelike, country flavor, this brick surfacing is hard, non-dusting, and resistant to frost.

Blue bridled pavers
These bricks are laid out in stack bond for a sharp, modern look.

Red multipavers
The color variation of these clay pavers, laid in a longitudinal stretcher bond, creates a mellowed effect. This bonding has a crisp look with strongly defined lines.

Wire-cut pavers, left
The pavers featured in this garden have a dragged finish, and are used both radially and in a circular pattern.

Pressed concrete pavers
Different colored pavers, here dark brown and yellow, make an acceptable and cheaper alternative to clay paving bricks.

Multicolored pavers
The rough, informal look of these clay pavers suits the random feel of the herringbone pattern.

Pressed concrete pavers
Blue in color, these pavers have a champfered edge. While to me concrete pavers lack the earthiness of a clay paver in a domestic setting, they look admirable in larger public spaces.

Plan of terraces

Brick terraces
The bricks used in these stepped terraces are laid in a horizontal stretcher bond, bricks on edge forming the risers. Wide, low steps such as these look gentle and inviting.

formal function within a pronounced layout of buildings. Too strong a pattern dwarfs the user, and you, the human, will feel antlike upon it.

Styling

Consider the texture, color, and style of the paving materials available when selecting them, and choose those that reflect the mood of your garden and its setting. Generally, the finer the finish, the more sophisticated the look. Used bricks, for example, have a rough feel that suits a country setting. In other locations, a mixture of brickwork with stone gives a pleasant rustic effect.

Granite pavers have a strong, urban feel, but as the stone is not native to many regions, give full consideration before laying them. A steely gray color, pavers can be texturally at odds with other natural stones, but they look good both as an edging and at driveway entrances next to dark bitumen surfaces.

Bricks used for paving that adjoins a brick-built construction act as an integrating element. The best kind to use for paving are severe-weathering (SW) facing bricks. Match the pattern of laying to the style of the garden and the overall effect of the bricks themselves. Traditional clay pavers laid in basket-weave or herringbone designs can look good in a country or cottage garden, while in a more modern layout smooth concrete pavers could look appropriate in a simple stack or stretcher bond.

PAVING SHAPES

The range of shapes available in different types of paver offers a rich variety of possible paving patterns. Over large spaces, keep to a simple ground pattern: too much richness soon becomes indigestible. Handmade tiles have a wonderfully earthy feel about them, and are ideal for conservatory use or, in frost-free areas, for terrace surfacing. Although good for balconies, these tiles may be slippery when wet.

Interlocking pavers, right
Pressed concrete interlocking pavers find their place in larger areas such as driveways. I particularly like this dark-colored paver when used with gray granite.

Terra-cotta path, right
Square tiles in two shades of terra-cotta are laid in a cruciform pattern. The decorative central inlay is reminiscent of an Edwardian entrance.

Terra-cotta tiles, above and right
The terra-cotta tile, like brick, is a natural slab made of clay, but dried in the sun. Porous and not frost proof, it is best used in a warm climate or in parts of the garden near the house. The design potential of terra-cotta tiles lies in their mellow coloring – often uneven and mottled – and the shapes available: hexagons could make a tessellated pattern for a smart urban setting, as could simple squares.

GRANITE PAVERS

Where granite was a local material, it was often used to create what was known in the nineteenth century as a "cobbled" road. Granite pavers, of a dimension similar to bricks, were later introduced and laid on industrial roads, the pavers allowing shoed horses pulling heavy drays to get a foothold. In the Low Countries and Germany half pavers create fan patterns in streets and marketplaces. Granite pavers have long been commercially available, either brick-shaped or half this size, and can also be purchased used.

Granite pavers

Granite pavers, above left and above
Pavers come in a variety of sizes since they are hand-hewn. They have a rough, earthy quality, and, being stone, will stand up well to heavy wear. The half-brick size can be laid in circular and fan patterns, as shown in this small European town garden.

Simulated
granite pavers

.**Simulated pavers,** above and right
Often quite convincing, and certainly easier and cheaper to lay than genuine granite because of their regular shapes, simulated pavers can be a good substitute for the real thing. I particularly like the softer colors and shaped edges of Belgian blocks.

Belgian blocks

COBBLES

Kidney-shaped pebbles surface a seating area and corner, above. These cobbles may be spread loose for a beach effect, creating a slight barrier, or be packed together in mortar to provide paved areas. They can also be used to infill sharp corners (which should not be part of your design). Large beach pebbles of cobble size may be laid flat side up to create a smooth surface.

LARGER PAVINGS

According to the location, stone paving slabs, whether the real thing or an imitation cast in concrete, are available in many dimensions and thicknesses, with smooth or textured surfaces. They work well in regions where stone buildings are common, and in other areas, where brick might be unsuitable or unavailable, stone pavers make the ideal choice. The dimensions, finishes, textures, and shapes of precast concrete slabs are endless. The range of colors varies enormously too, and I believe that this is the point from which to start. Consider the tones of your local earth, and look at the shades of brick or stone walls and the color of roof tiles. In Britain, for instance, the stone is gray in the granite regions of the North and the West Country, while in Gloucestershire it is honey colored. Select your paving slabs from an appropriate color palette.

The function of the paving slab within the pattern of your garden design will help you decide which shape to choose. The texture of the slab should relate to its practical use. Use a smooth slab for a terrace that will accommodate furniture, for example, a nonslip one for a pool surround.

CONCRETE PAVERS

I am very fond of this surfacing, which works admirably in many situations, hot or cold. The sizes and colors of the slabs vary greatly. Always wet a slab when making your selection to see how the color changes. Bright colors tend to fade. Jointing between the slabs is usually of the same color, and I prefer it to be slightly recessed on completion.

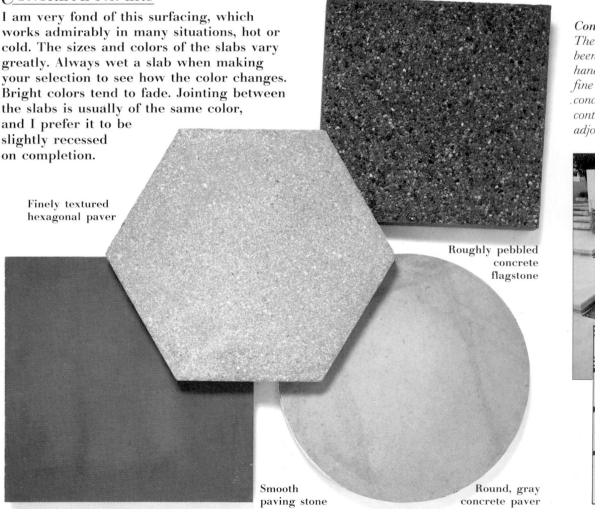

Finely textured hexagonal paver

Roughly pebbled concrete flagstone

Smooth paving stone

Round, gray concrete paver

Concrete steps, below
These areas of concrete have been cast in situ *to create very handsome low, wide steps. The fine texture of this pale-colored concrete makes a good visual contrast to the planting that adjoins it.*

Plan of concrete steps

POURED CONCRETE

Concrete is composed of varying quantities of sand, cement, and gravel aggregate, known as the mix, and quite differing finishes can be achieved by varying the size of the gravel and by exposing it when nearly dry by brushing. If you use local stone as aggregate, the concrete is more likely to blend in well with your location.

This sort of concrete is laid *in situ*, and may need some reinforcement; other materials, such as wood or brick, may be used to contain each concrete slab. This is one of the cheapest ways to lay large areas of hard surfacing.

Textures
Varying degrees of aggregate size create quite different looks when exposed by brushing.

STONE FLAGS

Once a section of stone has been quarried, it is cut and may be given a sawn or rubbed face for use as a surfacing material. When selecting a piece of stone, check on its durability, and find out whether it becomes slippery when wet, or is liable to fracture in frost.

When used for paving, stone flags with their massive scale give a warm, handsome feel to a garden and large, regular pieces of stone work well when laid simply in bold areas. Irregular pieces of stone create a "crazy" effect, which I prefer not to use.

Terrace slabs, above
Squared limestone and sandstone slabs surface this terrace, the open joints planted with thyme which releases its fragrance when crushed.

Plan of Terrace

Artificial stone, above
Slabs of artificial stone are split apart, and textured with a stratified surface and irregular edges to resemble yellow-gray natural stone.

Sandstone paving, below
The slabs of sandstone are cut to form terrace paving. A pattern can be of squares, or the slabs can be laid randomly.

STEPS

The design of steps all too easily appears as an afterthought within a layout – a necessary evil to link two levels. Think instead of a flight of steps as a major garden feature. A flight may sound too grand, but even one or two steps, if they are wide enough, can be an eye-catcher, or act as an invitation to an upper level. Interest is provided not only by their surfacing and construction, but by the way in which you furnish them with features such as handrails or balustrades. Give your steps a practical function too: use them as plinths on which to stand pots and containers filled with annuals, as a base for ground-hugging plants on either side, or even as casual seats.

Go back to design basics – the concept of a garden as a collage of related shapes – and envisage your steps within this pattern. In such a collage, steps are the point where two shapes overlap, so interpret them in a material that links the upper and lower levels.

The look of a flight of steps is influenced firstly by its relationship to any existing architectural features in the garden, and secondly by the ground on either side of them and its detailing. Heavy retaining walls can kill graceful steps, and anyone who has ever attempted to wield a lawn mower in a grassed area abutting a flight of steps will fully understand the importance of taking such garden detailing into account.

The comfort of your steps for climbing depends on your size, but generally, the steeper the step, the quicker you ascend or descend. In a garden, the overall concept is one of relaxation, so keep your steps low and gentle since no one is necessarily going anywhere fast.

In areas colder than my own, the south of England, it is essential to consider the slipperiness of steps in winter frost and snow. Particularly in areas with frost, water should run off the steps after rain, and you should ensure that your steps are constructed with a textured surface and a tread that is wide enough for safe use.

Different forms of steps
You can do more with steps than go straight up or down, for they can become a sculptural garden feature. The simplest variation is to make the steps wider in an irregular way so that plants can grow through them. It is possible to break a flight with a landing, or set the steps moving sideways up a bank to show off their profile on the approach.

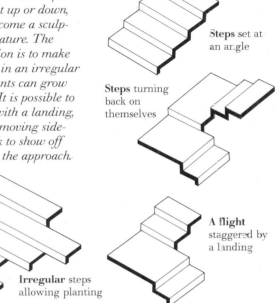

Steps set at an angle

Steps turning back on themselves

A flight staggered by a landing

Irregular steps allowing planting

Winding, weathered steps
A flight of steps, constructed with weathered precast concrete slabs on a riser of the same material, winds its sinuous way uphill. Ivy will slowly creep in from the sides to cover the risers.

Wooden steps
These wooden stairs leading to a bridge have a straightforward simplicity to them which I like.

Wide stone steps

Working on a radius from the center of a terrace, these wide stone steps focus the eye on the feature to which they lead. Note the small shadow recess under each riser which makes the steps visually lighter, giving the impression that they float. A flight of steps such as this may also act as seating for a casual party.

STYLING EFFECTS

The materials you use in the surfacing and construction of your flight of steps will be determined by the look of your garden and its setting, whether urban or rural, as well as by the ultimate practical function of the steps.

The use of the same material, such as dark slate, for both the riser and the tread gives a very tailored effect *(right, below)*.

More ornate steps might be constructed using contrasting or complementary materials in the riser and tread. Wood detailing in the riser, perhaps cedar or a railroad tie, could, for instance, be used in association with an infill of gravel in the tread *(right, center)*. Similarly, a red clay brick riser could be topped with a tread constructed from slabs of natural stone *(right, top)*.

Random cut-stone paving tread

Bricks form the riser

Gravel infill on the tread

Pressure-treated wood detail for the riser

Riven slate tread, matching the riser below

Riser also constructed out of slate

DECKING

Areas of wooden planking, known as decking, are common in the United States and Europe where lumber is relatively cheap and, even if the decking is covered with a dense layer of snow for several months, the long, hot summer months allow it to dry out. In the United Kingdom, decking is a more recent introduction, for the damp climate frequently makes it slippery underfoot, and lumber is expensive.

At ground level, decking can be laid as a surface material and can be an alternative to stone or brick. It also works well in association with water. When used with wooden-frame houses or in conjunction with wooden fencing, it should give a pleasantly unified look – "should," since many decks seem to be only ugly appendages to a home.

When elevated, decking can create a transitional space which is appropriate if built to adjoin a house on a hillside, for the decking creates a level space where there was none before. On a split-level house, extending an upper living level with decking creates extra living space, and the platform can be reached from ground level by steps. Always seek the advice of an architect if you are considering building such a platform.

Decking can also be used to surface an elevated balcony and, being lighter in weight than brick or stone, it makes a good surface for urban roof

DECKING PATTERNS

The pattern of a deck depends on its size and outlook; it should never fight with other features.

Sealing
Most of this selection of decking, constructed in soft-wood, has been clear sealed.

Staining
A colored stain has been applied to the decking above and far right.

gardens. Consult a structural engineer or architect to find out how much load a roof or deck will bear.

When designing a deck, try to work with the lines of the house and, where possible, its proportions. Check that the lumber dimensions are not too massive, and where the deck is very high above the ground, resolve what to do beneath, for this area often becomes dead ground. Consider including within the design of the deck some form of storage, perhaps built-in seating with a lid, useful for toys and last summer's barbecue grill.

Plan of decking

Wooden bridge, above
The horizontal lines of the decking in this Dutch garden contrast beautifully with the vertical forms of the planting adjoining it. The lines of the deck work with the overall intention; they do not try to fight it.

In damp climates, left
As a temporary measure, reduce slipperiness by wire brushing or using special waterproofing compounds. For a longer-lasting solution, try tacking large-hole chicken wire flush to the deck.

Cedar wood
Durable natural cedar wood weathers to a wonderful silver color with time.

Patterning
Some decking designs can be linear, some static, very much like the other lines in a garden.

LOOSE SURFACINGS

Not all surfaces need to be smooth: sometimes a textured or "soft" surface made
up of loose gravel, small pebbles, or wood
chips is much more satisfactory visually. Used as a
contrasting panel within a larger hard-paved layout, it will also help to break up the surface and
add interest.

Gravel, pebbles, and bark used as a surfacing give
a relaxed feel to a garden. They are easy to lay,
cheap, and have an interesting texture. Gravel, in
all its different types and sizes, may be used loose
or compacted for a variety of functions within a
garden – for driveways and paths, for planting and,
when laid loose, for burglar detection, as it crunches
when walked upon.

Plants easily grow through thin layers of gravel
or small pebbles, and these surfaces provide an ideal
place for seeds to germinate. Plants growing in such
soft surfacings should be left to self-seed for a casual, random look that particularly suits country
settings. To prevent unwanted seedlings and keep
the gravel looking fresh, rake it every so often,
avoiding the seedlings you do want. The gravel also
acts as a mulch through the summer (as does a layer
of bark chips on planted areas), and in winter stops
next year's seeds and seedlings from becoming
waterlogged.

Traditionally, gravel is rolled into a subbase
preparation to surface driveways or roads, but when
loosely laid it makes a versatile surfacing for awkward spaces, and areas where few plants will grow,
such as beneath trees.

Smaller-sized gravel, edged with a row of bricks,
is a good replacement for grass. It is easier to
maintain and looks good all year round. Such a surfacing may be raked into abstract patterns or
composed of different colored gravels divided with
bricks to make a geometric design.

When planning loose surfacings, remember that
if they do not abut a hard surface, a retaining edge
is vital to prevent spreading; also, the surface should
be replaced each summer to keep it crisp.

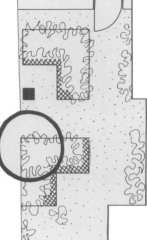

Repeating materials
*Chips of the same stone used in the
rear wall and the bed edging provide
a harmonious setting for the plants in
this Gloucestershire garden.*

Plan of beds and gravel

TYPES OF WOOD

Wood chips, left
*Different types of wood chips may be
used to surface paths in a rural setting. They can, of course, be used
as a surface mulch as well, to keep
down weeds in newly planted
beds. Make sure it is obvious
which is the path!*

Bark chips, right
*Used to create soft
surfacings, these
can work well in a
garden with a wood-
land environment, and
give an organic feel to
the whole garden.*

TYPES OF GRAVEL

Some gravel is obtained by dredging: rounded by the action of water, it is known as bankrun. Pea gravel *(center right)* is larger than fine grit *(right)* and smaller than the coarse aggregate mix of flint stones *(far right)*. All the other gravels shown are chips of a parent rock.

White gravel,
The decorative white chips are from calcinated flint stone. If covering an open area that is often exposed to intense sunlight, avoid pale colors which result in glare.

Granite gravel,
The black gravel derives from black granite, the gray chips from gray granite.

Pink and gray gravel,
Gravel is available in a huge variety of shades and sizes, since each type of parent stone, with its different mineral content, produces chips of a different color and texture. These chips derive from limestone. When selecting gravel, bear in mind that the cheapest form is probably made from the type of stone that is quarried or dredged nearest to you.

Coarse grade gravel,
bottom row
All the examples of gravel shown above are of medium grade size, $^2/_{10}$ to $^4/_{10}$ of an inch, but this gravel made from buff-colored stone is of a coarse grade, $^1/_2$ to $^3/_4$ of an inch.

GRASS

If you choose to incorporate a lawn into your garden plan – or even a rough grass area – let it be part of your overall concept, rather than a filler between the other elements in it. Those living in temperate regions are fortunate in that they consider grass to be a normal medium for the ground. However, it is important to understand that grass is only one layer within an ecological system; unless it is mowed or grazed, herbs and small shrubs generate in it, and, on most soils, trees would eventually grow too. You should start from the assumption, therefore, that if you want a grassed area it will need regular maintenance.

In Europe, grass for sowing is designated as hard wearing for family use, or as a fine lawn mix. Each of these broad types is made up of a combination of grass seeds in varying proportions. There may be slight variations for an acid or alkaline soil, and a further permutation for sun or shade. In the United States, depending on the zone, grass seed mixes vary greatly, according to water availability and winter extremes. Specific seed mixes are also available to suit the tropical regions of the world and Australia. Seek local advice on seed mixes and the rate at which they should be sown.

You can buy wildflower mixes, but if you are considering this, be sure to choose the correct wildflowers for your area. Unless you know what you are doing, or buy a correctly graded mixture, one species will dominate. You need to achieve a good balance of species since an entire insect population depends on what you sow.

Mixing grasses
Decorative rough grass areas have been naturalized by planting spring bulbs in this very English setting. The mix of grasses used will depend on the soil, the climate, and, to a degree, the frequency of cutting.

Cultivated lawn

Wild meadow

Different forms of grass
A pristine lawn needs constant maintenance and, artificial in concept, it all too easily looks ill at ease with its surroundings. With moisture, and without frequent weeding, the velvety lawn naturally becomes a wild meadow. Grass combined with concrete pavers makes an interesting ground pattern.

Combining grass with paving

Achieving Different Looks

The ultimate look you require from a lawn depends on its size and situation, and this also affects your choice of seed mix. Do you seek a close-cropped look, striped after mowing with a reel-type mower, or do you prefer a rougher look, cut higher using a rotary mower? You may desire long sweeps of rough grass interplanted with spring bulbs, for natural-looking grass obscures the dying foliage and eases maintenance – both are mown off together. The hayfield, or even the prairie look, needs different maintenance again, in the form of a front-mounted cutter-bar mower.

To achieve a quick green look, many people use turf or sod. A seeded lawn is usually cheaper and gives, in the long run, a better lawn, since you have greater flexibility in seed selection. It does, however, require more labor and time to establish. A turfed lawn is instant and can be installed at any time of year when there is no frost. I use a little of both for a new lawn. I turf or sod the edge where it meets a planting area or hard surface, then seed to infill behind it. Turf may also be used to prevent erosion on a bank, but make sure that the gradient is maintainable.

EDGINGS

I use edgings not necessarily for decorative effect, but to facilitate the flow of one surface into another. I like simple edgings, hidden by the material they contain. To separate gravel from grass, a fine-cast metal strip, a brick edging, concrete run, or a piece of pressure-treated wood serve well. An upstanding edge usually contains earth in a planted area, but bricks or a flat paver are also suitable: they let plants spread, and do not impede a lawn mower. To lessen the need for an edging, the level of the earth can be reduced. Surfaces that spread with use, such as gravel, or with frost do need containing, but I would set an edging at the same level as the surface.

Decorative edgings for styling effects
Do not overload a garden with fancy edgings: they break up a concept. The simplest edging is a concrete strip. Bricks can be laid lengthwise, haunched to create a zig-zag, or laid side by side to contrast with other textures. The terra-cotta pie-crust tile is often found in nineteenth-century gardens, although it is not one of my favorites.

Plain edging

Pie-crust edging

Clay bricks

Blue wire-cut bricks

COMBINING SURFACES

The various shapes, sizes, and materials of many different paving elements can be successfully mixed to give a garden plan pattern and texture. It may be economic demands as much as visual effect that prompt you into this course: when it proves expensive to pave large areas with brick, for instance, you might prefer to create a brick pattern blended with cheaper gravel or concrete elements. Similarly, if you wish to create a surface by laying small pavers, mixing in a number of large precast concrete slabs helps to bring down the cost.

When mixing different paving materials, keep the areas of each element used as large as possible, and interlock the materials well to ensure a smooth transition from one piece to another. As a general rule, keep the number of types of surface to a minimum, perhaps no more than two or three in any garden. Too many types will look fussy and distract from the strength of your design. Devise a pattern that takes into account the entire garden structure, remembering that the stronger the pattern, the larger the area it covers must be.

Planting between paving elements often softens the effect of hard paving, and looks charming in a country setting. The effect is strongest when just one type of plant is used. Be wary of mixing in plantings that clash with the color palette of the paving. Plant between large, stable elements of paving only, or leave plants to self-seed in the joints between the pavers, bearing in mind that doing so may reduce the potential use of the paved surface.

Concrete and grass, below
Paving slabs with grass between form a handsome path to a pool. Stronger than individual steppingstones, which can seem too small, this bold statement still does not break up the unity of the lawn it crosses.

Stony stream, left
A dry gravel stream of variously sized pebbles makes an interesting feature when mixed with reed-type plants that simulate water subjects.

Heavy ground pattern, left
The railroad ties and paving slabs in this enclosed space contrast with the strong architectural planting.

Hard and soft paving, above
Concrete paving, brick, and gravel all combine to create this garden layout.

Japanese-style feature
Wooden platform steps combine with boulders beneath a cutleaf maple to create a garden with strong Japanese overtones.

WALLS

There are broadly three types of walling material: stone, either random or coursed, brick, and concrete in its various forms. When selecting a material for a wall, consider how the color, size, and texture echo the feel and architectural style of the surrounding buildings and setting, and try to envisage the massed effect.

Walls built of natural stone vary between regions, and the stone local to your area will be most appropriate. Certain types of limestone and sandstone with easily quarried strata allow a wall to be coursed, the stones fitting together like bricks. Other stones smoothed by glacial or water action, or picked up from the field or seashore, are rounded and can be used in a random wall. Traditionally, both types of wall were laid dry, without mortar jointing, while reconstructed stone (a formed stone pressed out of crushed rock and cement) is laid with mortar joints. Stone wall coping varies according to location.

A brick wall can be of various thicknesses with differing bonding – the rhythm of whole to half brick – each bonding, with its own strengths, correct for a particular setting. Some bondings are used because they are traditional to an area or period, others are chosen for their strength, and some are selected purely on account of their appearance.

Bricks gain their distinct color and texture from the clays that compose them, and their manufacture. A facing brick is widely used for completing finishes. Where more strength with greater density and less absorption is required, severe-weathering (SW) facing brick is used. The outer sides of bricks

Dry limestone wall, coping set in mortar

Dry sandstone wall

Flemish cross bonded brick wall

may have a smooth finish or they can be wire-cut, like cheese, for a textured, dragged effect. Since only the outer side is fired for weather protection, and as bricks are laid flat in a wall, the top is capped to protect the soft center (over the generations, the word capping has become "coping"). The same brick laid on edge acts as coping, or paving material is used to make a precise visual connection with the brickwork.

Labor costs, including materials and delivery, for stone or brick walls are high, since walls are made of many small units. Concrete is a cheaper alternative. When a concrete block wall is rendered, painted, and finished with a brick or stone coping, it can be a good substitute for the real thing, and suits urban sites. Solid concrete walling is probably too massive for normal domestic settings, but where such heavy duty walling is necessary, grained wood or even corrugated iron shuttering gives interesting finishes to the concrete.

An organic look
Originally, adobe walling would have been built from local clay, but is now more likely to be clay applied over a concrete block base.

Stones laid in courses with a rough stone coping

Random stone walling with mortar, with a paving stone coping

FENCING

Where a wall would be too solid, blocking a view or impeding a source of light, the huge number of fence types available offers an alternative: animal-proof fences for country situations, peep-proof fences for the suburbs, and urban fences that provide shelter from the winds in exposed roof-top gardens and create internal barriers.

When selecting a fence, first consider the mood and situation of your region, whether urban or rural, and get the local idiom right. A white picket fence, for instance, says something quite different than the three-bar metal railings of a gentleman's park. And the former would be more appropriate in Kentucky than in the nether regions of Kent.

The closer one lives to one's neighbors, the more one seeks some privacy from them. The suburban fence tends to be a solid-wall substitute, created by a woven panel or composed of horizontals (only a physical barrier such as this will keep out the neighbor's dog). These should be made from pressure-treated wood, and, to soften the aggressive appearance of newness, you could always try planting around them.

Fences for urban sites may be fancy in the style of the Japanese fence with its bamboo verticals and tied horizontals, or Gothic, or thoroughly theatrical with a custom design. Lower and less solid, picket fences can be stained or painted in various ways to create different effects.

Within the overall space of a garden, internal divisions may be needed. They look most effective when they form a continuation of the perimeter fence – even if their function is rather different. Make your choice of fence by deciding whether you wish to create definite roomlike enclosures, or prefer to give an inkling of what lies beyond. While I prefer not to use them, double-thickness trellis panels often mark out internal divisions and extend walls. Although internal fences are more decorative than boundary fences, do consider their final use when making a construction plan.

A stark approach
The white-painted verticals on either side of a central frame give this fence an illusion of open paling. The fence does not meet the ground, so rot is prevented and maintenance of a public space eased.

URBAN FENCING

In urban settings, fences give a measure of privacy and close up the boundaries. While acting as a backdrop to vertical plantings, such as climbers, they should also be appropriate in scale and style to the house itself.

Picket fencing
Good where fences do not need to be physically strong, decorative picket fences make a sympathetic background for plantings, although they do not provide a great deal of privacy. Picket with shaped profiling is also available for a crisper, more formal look. Such an unaffected type of fence looks best when left natural or painted white.

Woven fencing
Available in mellow colors, and in horizontal and vertical weaves, this type of fencing is cheap and effective when maximum privacy is required. For added height, woven fences may be set on a wall.

Wrought iron
With a smart look that makes a bold statement at the front of a house, the simple pattern of these fences is not too disturbing when seen in relation to most types of building. If you are not prepared to repaint white fences of any type at least once a year to sustain their crispness, it is better to go for black or green.

COUNTRY FENCING

In rural areas the deterrent aspect of fences has to take precedence over aesthetic preference, although ideally one seeks some compromise. Eighteenth-century ha-ha ditches seemed to work with somnolent cattle, but it is hard to believe that deer did not fly straight over them. Country fencing should provide an open boundary to views and, while being made of materials sympathetic to the setting, must be relatively cheap and need little maintenance, since country gardens tend to be large.

Horizontal bar fencing
In the country I like this fencing, which can be permutated to suit the livestock it contains. A finer form of this fence is available in metal.

British woven willow hurdles
Creating a solid, low fence, these hurdles should be supported with stout oak verticals, since their dense structure does not allow wind to pass through them.

Woven hazel hurdles
More open than willow, hazel hurdles make good country fencing, although their lifespan is limited.

Wooden lattice, below
This soft, rural version of the sharper lattice town fence is much sturdier and more widely available.

Country fencing is often of the wooden horizontal bar type. How many bars the fence has and how high it is depend on the stock to be deterred: horses need a five-bar fence, which is often painted; cattle, four or three; sheep, possibly two bars with a lower area filled with netting to restrain the lambs. Wire fencing, 20 inches in height and buried to almost the same depth, is appropriate in rural situations to deter rabbits and other creatures that could otherwise burrow underneath the fence. The materials used to make fences vary with the location, as, of course, do styles and traditional methods of manufacture. Cedar, locust, and redwood are prevalent in the United States. For longest life, you will want to use direct-burial pressure-treated wood, which is guaranteed by the manufacturer to last for 30 years.

Forming a low, rustic barrier, woven willow hurdles also offer wind protection to young plantings, but for this purpose an open fence is preferable, both because it will stand up better in wind than a closed one, and because it breaks the wind force as opposed to creating turbulence and drafts, which can cause plant damage.

Rustic fencing
Vertical rustic wooden poles on a horizontal frame make a good backdrop to plants, while maintaining a degree of privacy and providing wind shelter too. Here the fence blends into a semi-rural idyll, playing second fiddle – as it should – to the plants and styling elements.

TRELLIS

Unless it is extremely well made and used correctly, I am not fond of trellis. All too often it fights with the architectural detailing of the structure to which it is fixed. Prefabricated panels are rather flimsy, and before long the plant is supporting the trellis instead of the other way around.

Use lattice as an end in itself, not as decoration. Cover the whole façade of the house, for instance, matching the pattern of the trellis to the scale of the window frames. Once applied to a structure and painted, however, trellis is difficult to maintain.

Large-scale trellis, I believe, best fits most situations, since much architectural detailing is either of vertical or horizontal lines. Diamond-effect lattice shapes can be used in their own right to make pyramids to support roses, and a sturdier lattice panel can add height to a boundary wall or fence without blocking the light.

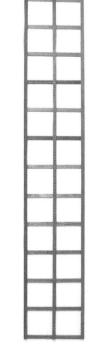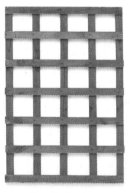

Sturdy lattice panel

Diamond-shaped lattice panel *(far left)* **and large squared trellis** *(left)*

HEDGES

The walls and fences that enclose and divide up a garden are part of the bones of your layout, for they create the rooms in which you work. A hedge has the same function, and although it is slower and ultimately needs more maintenance than its inanimate counterparts, it is often seen as a cheaper alternative at the outset.

In terms of design, hedges not only provide a backdrop for planting, but their dramatic range of color throughout the seasons makes a strong feature in a garden. Structurally, hedges provide good shelter, particularly the evergreen variety in northern climates during the winter months. However, as they take moisture and nutrients out of the soil, hedges may not be a good choice if your planting borders are narrow or the soil is very dry.

When choosing planting material for a hedge, first resolve what the function of the hedge will be: whether it is for privacy, to act as a windbreak, to retain livestock, and so on. Decide, too, on the optimum height necessary to do the job, then take into account that when the hedge reaches this height, you will have to restrain it. A hedge naturally grows upward and outward – in fact, some of the plants we select for hedges, such as beech, hornbeam, and most of the conifers, would grow naturally into forest trees. Lastly, remember that while you conceive your hedge from inside your boundary, the rest of us see it from the other side, within a panorama of the landscape.

Hedges can broadly be divided into wild and domesticated versions. The wild type, appropriate

Box (*Buxus sempervirens*) makes a high solid hedge

Bay (*Laurus nobilis*) makes an evergreen hedge

Beech (*Fagus sylvatica*) retains dead leaves

Sprawling box hedge
The voluptuous curves of an old box hedge line a gravel path in this sumptuous setting. Yew,

which with time creates equally majestic hedges, will take on a similarly rounded form when it matures.

for country gardens, is chosen to suit the type of soil and climate, and includes a good proportion of native plants to help the garden merge into the surrounding countryside. A domesticated hedge of non-native plants, which looks conspicuously unnatural in the countryside, can nevertheless be effective in urban sites.

A hedge may be composed wholly of flowering material; the planting can be mixed to create a loose effect, combining different hedging plants to give winter form while allowing decorative interest in the summer; or it may be made up entirely from plants of one type, so that, if used to any extent, it reads strongly from outside a site. Deciduous hedges have a dramatic sculptural shape in winter, when they reveal the outlying countryside: this is not so appealing in urban areas, for privacy is lost. Crisply formal in mood when clipped, an evergreen hedge forms a major skeletal element in a garden's design, against which other plants look striking.

Laurel (*Prunus laurocerasus*)

Yew (*Taxus baccata*) is visually strong in winter

GATES

As soon as one begins to consider any form of boundary, high or low, open or solid, one must also think about the gate through it. Along with a fence or hedge, gates and entrances are some of the few elements that are more important to the outside world than they are to the garden into which they lead, and if a gate is good, it will hardly be noticed. Making a comfortable transition between street or countryside and garden, a gate should blend visually with your garden, its setting, and the wall or fence.

Entrances and gates set the tone of a space when you step into it, so it is essential to get the styling correct. Where the gate is seen with the house, let the two work together in material, color, and scale, and make sure the gate will suit the architectural features of your home. Linking the gate and door stylistically also unifies the space between them.

The correct choice of gate depends on its function. It may be decorative, acting as a visual break in the boundary; it may be a gate to prevent children from getting out; or it may be designed for general security – if so, it is more likely to be high, robust, and made from metal. For greater security, big double gates are often automated, the sliding mechanism calling for a simple design. Whether a

Painted gate
My favorite gate: play about with the color and it fits most situations. Painted dark blue or pine green, one would be more aware of the view beyond.

gate is functional, decorative, large, or small, it has been my experience that the simpler the gate, the more attractive it is. Avoid the temptation to become pretentious: do not, for instance, use piers that are too large for the gate, or crown them with stone eagles. On the other hand, when some of this theater is called for, do not be shy about it – overscale for maximum effect.

TYPES OF GATE

A stately elegance
Decorative wrought iron is a classic choice for a gate through an old wall or a hedge.

Wrought iron gate
Simple ironwork is visually strong.

Wooden pedestrian gate
A gate of pleasant proportions.

Wooden paling gate
For pedestrian use, this gate suits urban or rural locations.

Rustic double gate

An unpretentious barrier, this double gate of rustic verticals on a three-bar frame would fit many wooded locations around the world. It offers privacy and stylistic nuance for the right setting. Notice the brush-wood fencing on the left-hand side of the gate: the two elements combine to make a pleasing harmony.

Gilded wrought iron gate

I would designate this gate for urban use, although its air of sophistication might limit its use. Gate hardware, the locks and latches, should be carefully selected for much is a finger-trap.

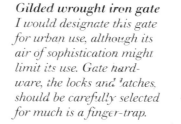

Wooden gate, right

A simple gate such as this may be stained or painted to blend in with the style of the surrounding garden, or to contrast with its location. I consider a wooden see-through gate to be more appropriate for most settings than one of wrought iron.

PERGOLAS

Endless types of small structures can be added to a garden for decoration, yet all too often this is simply gilding the lily – too much lattice or trelliswork comes into this category. The pergola, though, when used correctly, becomes a major garden ingredient, for it has much to do with the way the garden user moves around the overall design, and is an effective binding element for the total garden space.

In order to select the correct pergola form for your garden, first decide whether the structure is directional, that is, leading from one space to another, or whether it defines a wider static place, providing a shelter to sit beneath. A directional pergola has a dynamic visual effect, drawing the eye down its length to a focal point or an entrance, or framing a view. A pergola can also be used visually to extend an interior, creating an outside room.

When designing a pergola, consider the structure in the light of the mood and period of the building near it. Look at the materials your pergola could echo in construction, and pick out details of style and architectural features upon which to hang the design – for example, the height of roof eaves, the tops of windows – to achieve an integrated, well-balanced look.

Pergola proportions are some of the most difficult to get right. It is important to detail correctly the proportion of the horizontal to the width of the vertical against the structure's overall dimension. Sketching many different options is the best way to achieve eventual success.

Consider whether you wish to provide support for plants: the sturdiness of a pergola depends partly on the amount of planting you envisage, and you should add its visual and physical weight into your plans. Ramblers and climbing plants soften the look of a pergola, allow a degree of privacy, and, while providing attractive dappled shade during the summer, let light through in the winter months. Evergreens, though providing privacy in the summer, can create too much shade in winter.

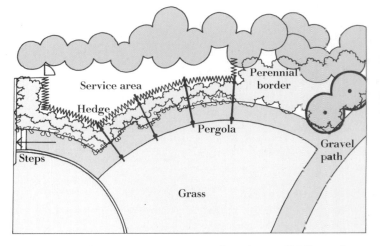

Curved pergola
The pergola in this plan is on a curve, with its wooden horizontals straddling a mixed perennial border and a path. The verticals on one side – perhaps just scaffolding poles to minimize their presence – are concealed in a hedge, and the verticals rising from the path will be classic columns of reconstructed stone.

Pergola for shade
A curving pergola provides dappled shade in the summer for those sitting on the terrace beneath it. The verticals are constructed from light-colored stone, while the two lateral running horizontals are made of steel that is covered with laminated wood.

Wooden arbor
In the pergola style, this white-painted arbor on classic wooden verticals adorns a garden in the United States.

The pergola walk, Kew
In the construction of the rose-covered walk at the Royal Botanic Gardens, oak horizontals sit on brick verticals; wire running between supports the roses.

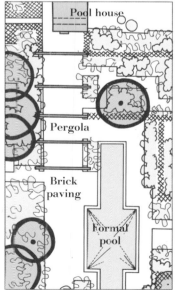

Planning a pergola
The plan of this pergola shows how the structure binds together the other elements of a garden plan (see page 206).

WATER

Water can be incorporated into many spaces. It has a compelling, mesmerizing quality that draws the eye, acts as a foil to planting, and, when still, reflects light and mirrors surrounding features. I do not, however, subscribe to the theory that every garden needs water. In a northern climate particularly, I think water can be very depressing between October and April, with the accompanying dead vegetation, floating leaves, and defense system necessary to keep predators from eating the fish. Perhaps I am just not a water person. Where water is desired by a client, I prefer large, simple sheets of it in the country, and a structured pool, preferably raised, containing a small mass of water in a more urban area.

Because water is a primary force, it calls for simple, practical detailing, not the trivializing of the "fringed pool or ferned grotto" ilk. Water should sit where it would naturally collect so that it looks as natural as possible. Landscaping can help achieve this effect, using soil from any excavations.

Keep the outline and the treatment of the edge as simple and natural-looking as possible. Decide whether you want grass to the edge, a beach, or a boggy margin, then stick to it — so many pools have a fussy edging only compounded by fussy plantings. Pools that imitate naturally occurring water will require a large area. While I am not a great advocate of the Japanese look outside Japan, the way the Japanese deal with water is very instructive, revealing how simplicity and shape are all, and lead to visual strength. A satisfactory alternative to the natural pool is one that fits into the basic geometrical plan of your site. This may work with a terrace area perhaps, or have a direct architectural relationship to the house.

Still Water

An area of still water in a garden adds to the mood of tranquility and relaxation. Informal pools need space to work successfully, and should be thought out in terms of the whole garden design. Formal

A natural look
Fed by a natural spring, this pool was once little more than a duck pond. It still has ducks, but now, opened out to the house and the fields beyond, it has become a focal point of the garden, domestic on one side and wild on the other. Floating algae seem perfectly acceptable here, where they would spoil a more formal stretch of water.

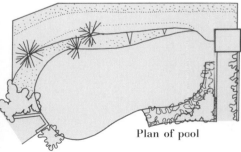

Plan of pool

Formal pool
Backed by a stage of clipped yew, this immaculate formal reflecting pool has great dignity. The concept has not become too pompous, since the placement of the large trees that accompany it is irregular. I am very fond of this deliberate mistake effect.

Small brick pool, above
Filled with random planting, this small, formally shaped pool has a low retaining wall behind, providing casual seating.

Steppingstones, right
Made from wood, these "steppingstones" make an unusual pattern through the water, and provide a crisp contrast to the feathery water plants on either side.

pools of a geometric shape require a crisp edging, and plantings may be used to soften the shape. If you prefer some formally shaped water in a small garden, but the scale of the garden does not allow for it, raise the sides of a pool to create a type of well head. As long as you do not suspend a bucket over the top, it makes a good, simple feature.

The practical aspects of building a pool vary from climate to climate. In temperate zones, a butyl rubber liner has replaced the concrete pool, always subject to cracking. Butyl rubber can be tailored, without folds, to fit a geometrical or free-shaped pool. The secret of its visual success is in the treatment of the edging. The water in all ornamental pools must be sparkling clean, and it is essential to establish a correct plant/fish ratio to achieve it.

Running Water

Visually exciting and pleasing to the ear, running water is a dominating feature that brings life to a garden. The type of moving water introduced depends on the scale and situation of the setting. A suburban garden may be embellished with a small but mesmerizing trickle of water, or a splash over rocks to cool the garden in the summer months; and in a limited space, water may be used vertically instead of horizontally to create a waterfall effect. Even in the smaller-sized garden, running water can still be a viable option: water bubbling up through a millstone and cascading over the surface, for instance, effectively introduces an element of movement to a small space.

In the country garden, running water should always be on a much larger scale and make a bold statement, perhaps in the form of a powerful waterfall, or a rushing stream that, if naturally coursing through your landscape, needs little gilding. To tend the edges of such a powerful natural force too decoratively or formally will only emphasize the artificial feel of the garden, so plantings should consist of a single species growing in a bold mass, as in nature.

Plan of waterfall

Small-scale feature, above
This concept avoids the fussiness of many small features. Water pours onto an old mill wheel and out to a surrounding pool. Bold masses of poolside plants keep the look simple.

Stylized waterfall, left
This newly completed water feature works with steps up to the garden. The concept is of a stylized mountain torrent, which will be softened by integrated planting. Exciting in plan, the water bubbling over rocks is far more spectacular in its finished state.

SWIMMING POOLS

A swimming pool should suit the geometry of the garden, and have an architectural connection with any structure that adjoins it — be it a pool house or a sheltered surround — for although free-shaped pools may sit more sympathetically in a large garden on their own, their servicing needs will foil the effect.

I find that a free-shaped pool seldom works — even when it is custom designed and not of the manufacturer's standard shape. Such pools are difficult to fit into an overall garden plan, leaving awkward angular spaces, are not easy to cover, and furthermore are much more expensive to build, heat, and maintain. Having said that, pools that continue the shape themes of a garden's plan, and even become a crucial link between garden and setting, can have their own drama; see page 23.

A swimming pool should be sited in an open place where it will catch the sun, and it should be built as far away as possible from trees that shed their leaves. In any event, it is best to avoid planting too close to a pool, as plants in general tend to react in an unfavorable way to the chemicals necessary for maintenance.

The setting of your garden and its location will influence the choice of color for the interior of a pool, and the treatment of the coping will relate to any further terrace paving adjoining it. In a northern climate, I find a stone color for the interior is preferable to anything too stark, and I prefer gray to a Mediterranean azure blue.

The paving surrounding a swimming pool should consist of a textured material, for when wet some surfacings become slippery. In more southerly climates, terra-cotta tiling provides a wonderful textured surfacing for a pool surround, and it feels warm underfoot.

Below are examples of two very different pools, one nestling in its setting, the other suggesting the design potential of the pool's interior itself.

Simple pool, left
The variable British climate makes the inclusion of a swimming pool in a garden difficult, for it can look garish. The simple shape and lack of detail in the pool at Kiftsgate Court, Gloucestershire, allow the feature to read as part of its pastoral setting.

Careful detailing, below
Bright colors look good in a warm climate. The detailing of pools and terraces, jacuzzis and levels needs careful consideration, and it would help to make a projection.

LIGHTING

While we react strongly to natural sources of light, such as intense sun- or moonlight, we too often neglect artificial lighting in the garden. Yet the rise of interest in security lighting indicates potential in the subject.

The concept of lighting is extremely subtle, and the choice between one fixture or another is often only one of degree. Furthermore, achieving the correct final effect is largely a case of trial and error, although the planning of a complicated scheme calls for the careful drawing and positioning of outlets for maximum safety. I believe that an electrician should install anything to do with wiring, and where the aesthetics of differing illumination techniques are called for, I would seek the advice of a lighting designer. However, to create the desired effects and to be able to converse with a lighting designer, you need to know about the various types of lighting, which, broadly defined by heights, are safety lighting, uplighting, and downlighting. The scale you work to will determine the type of lamps and fittings needed to create the following effects.

High Light Sources

Moonlighting, a mild, hidden light source set high above the ground, gives a softly lit shadowy effect,

at the same time providing a measure of security.
Area lighting, emanating from almost as high a source, illuminates terraces, lawns, or tennis courts. Even, but not glaring, it should be at least partly concealed by filtering or diffusing.
Diffused light, suitable for outside sitting or eating areas, has a glare-free quality with soft shadows, created by positioning the light source behind a translucent screen or frosted glass.
Cross lighting requires two high light sources, usually broad floodlights rather than spotlights. A stronger beam is used to focus on special features.

Detailed Lighting

Grazing lighting involves positioning the light source close to an object for a detailed and small-scale effect which picks out features such as bark.
Spotlighting is used, conversely, to make a focal point of the important features in a garden.
Accent lighting achieves a similar effect where spotlighting would be too harsh, perhaps in a smaller garden. Using low-voltage fixtures and lamps, it picks out individual elements on areas such as terraces. The fixtures may be decorative.
Silhouetting or shadowing is achieved by concealing the light source, usually down low, to create a

TYPES OF LIGHTING

In general, techniques may be classified as safety lighting, uplighting, and downlighting, the first being the most practical application. Eye-level lighting gives you a further option. Determine which one will suit your purposes, whether strong direct lighting to illuminate paths, or decorative lighting for a more magical effect in an outside eating area.

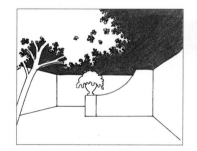

Safety lighting
Extra strong downlighting produces safety lighting, which can be made to shine brightest where it is most needed – on parking areas, for instance. The light source may be set below eye level in order not to dazzle.

Uplighting
Use this ground-level light source, which is not unlike spotlighting, with discretion; too many points of interest detract from a restful garden. Pick out a few features only, and use the technique year round.

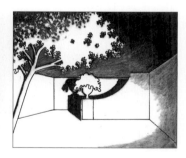

Eye-level lighting
This style of lighting can be used to create a composite of silhouettes and more subtle degrees of shading. It is softer and more diffused than the other types.

shadow effect on a bright wall. This technique works well with strongly architectural groupings. **Fill lighting** gives a dim backdrop to brighter areas. To illuminate a feature you need about ten times more light than fillers supply (see accent lighting). **Contour lighting,** often low voltage, may be used to define a step, highlight the inside of a pool coping, or illuminate the side of a driveway.

Lighting Water

There is increasing interest in lighting decorative ponds or swimming pools. Needless to say, it is essential to install such lighting correctly at the time of construction. Remember that when the water is illuminated, particularly from below, the viewer should not be able to see the light source, and the water must be crystal clear, since light picks up any particles of dirt or algae. Dimmers can be installed on swimming pool lights to create different moods for different occasions. For larger expanses of water, mirror lighting produces reflections in the water of surrounding trees.

Softly lit tropical terrace
None of the light sources here are obvious: the central palm is accented by an uplight, the end wall is silhouetted, and the foreground agave side-lit. Note how well architectural foliages lend themselves to illumination.

Filters and Fittings

I prefer not to use colored light filters as they only vulgarize lighting. By using different types of lamps and wattages and varying intensities, as outlined above, you can create differing color tones, particularly where beams cross and converge, or where they interact with shadows. Start without color filters, and work up to them if necessary.

Choose practical, simple, and robustly designed light fittings, made for use outdoors. All fittings, cables, and outlets should be installed by a professional, and waterproofed and armored where they might get damaged during gardening. Site your lighting system so that it can be turned on from both house and garden, preferably where you can see the magical effect you have created at the flick of a switch.

SCULPTURAL FEATURES

Sculptures and incidents are key moments in a garden's design, for they govern and manipulate the movement of the eye around the site. Careful positioning of a piece of sculpture will bring your layout to life, punctuating your sentences elegantly, perhaps even adding the odd exclamation mark.

Although the positioning of a sculptural feature depends to a large extent on its scale and subject matter, I believe it is more important when siting a sculpture to consider its density and the material from which it is made. External works of art, whether they are classical or modern, need to have both a solidity in order to read against vegetation or landscape, and a simplicity of outline.

Correct Siting

The look of your garden and the effect you desire will help you decide where to place a sculpture, for pieces should never be considered in isolation. They must work within the visual setting, and look pleasing throughout the year and from all angles.

A classic layout with straight views calls for a "period," or a statement at the junction of paths to slow the movement down for a moment. Smaller gardens may need a central feature to hold the eye within the site. If the piece dominates the site too much, however, try moving it to one side, creating a counterpoise to a terrace or plant grouping that strengthens and balances both sides of the garden. This helps to free up the space in the garden and so *include* the statuary rather than *impose* it upon the area. A modern-style layout of asymmetric lines calls for sculpture to be placed as a counterpoise to the ground plan rather than as a conclusion to it. Where the ground plan has a curving flow, sculpture will only disrupt it, although it may be used as the culmination of an overall design.

Choosing Sculpture

Sculptural features may be striking or unobtrusive, traditional or abstract, and the style depends largely

Humorous sculpture
I am very fond of this sculpture, for if there were ever a place to laugh, it is in a garden. To suddenly come across an amusing piece placed among vegetation or by the side of a pool is always a great bonus. This piece in bronze resin, entitled Floating, *is by André Wallace.*

on personal preference and the look of your house and garden. A symmetrical, formal garden needs a strong classical piece, but an informal, asymmetric layout could take something as abstract as a large empty pot. In general, aim for a striking and unexpected blend of classical and modern styles. The broad outlines above for siting a sculpture presuppose that the feature you are using is large. I am all for large pieces, but most people are timid in the scale of the features they buy (finance having much to do with this). Works of art tend to be expensive, and while some people buy for their wall, others buy for their garden.

Smaller eye-catchers — and I believe sculpture or statuary becomes just this when it is not a work of art — can be used fairly often to punctuate a layout. These features act as less demanding incidents along the way, and can contribute that essential element of surprise. But you do not always have to think in terms of art or statuary; a fancy bench can perform exactly the same punctuating role, as can a collection of pots.

Crafted sculpture, above
Reese Ingram's wooden Cat on
a Pole *sits against bamboo. A
number of galleries and
gardens exhibit pieces of
sculpture that are not always
prohibitively priced.*

Formal statuary, left
*The monastic austerity of this
antique piece of statuary looks
good within a formal layout
backed by yew. With time,
much of the reconstructed stone
statuary available mellows to
blend with its surroundings. My
only reservation about such
statuary is the commercial
concentration on "safe," visually
undemanding historical or
nineteenth-century motifs.*

Static design
*One central, generously-scaled
sculpture, balanced by strong
perimeter planting, provides a
static layout.*

Asymmetrical plan
*The siting of the sculpture here
reinforces an asymmetrical
layout. It frees up the central
space for use.*

Incidental sculpture
*Rather than making sculpture
the* raison d'être *of a layout, I
prefer to use it as an incident,
tucked around the corner.*

FURNITURE

One of the high spots of most gardens is a place to sit. I prefer furniture that minimizes style while maximizing comfort, because, whether it consists of loungers to lie on, or a table and chairs at which to sit and eat, furniture can transform a brand new design into a pleasant place to come and relax.

There is a second, sculptural type of garden furniture that should not be confused with the above. Whether placed as a feature at the end of a view, or as an incidental point of interest within a layout, such pieces of furniture are not intended for comfort, but simply to be visually attractive.

Choose garden furniture of the nonsculptural variety as you would select furniture for the home, to suit your needs and by the degree of comfort it offers; and keep it simple, yet tough enough to withstand the elements. Whether it stays *in situ* or is taken inside depends on your climate (the warmer the climate, the better the furniture available). How you treat it and how much you are willing to spend will also be determining factors.

Let the styling suit your setting; you would not use a regency dining suite in a modern house, so why try to do the equivalent outside? Strong colors and patterned upholstery look best in sunlight with the lap of blue water nearby; used out of location in a northern climate, this type of furniture appears garish, even shocking.

Furniture is available in a range of materials. Wooden seating of any form fits, I believe, most situations. It rests easily upon the eye, can be painted for special effect, and lasts for years when seasoned properly. Metal furniture is strong, durable, and surprisingly comfortable: choose sleek, modern lines for urban settings, and avoid fussy, molded-iron chairs and tables. Light, inexpensive, and available in many styles, plastic furniture requires no maintenance, but does not weather well.

Stone furniture is a permanent fixture and therefore should be thought of more as a sculptural addition to a garden.

Comfortable wood, above
The styling of garden furniture must depend on its setting. Any style looks better when couched among greenery – furniture is, after all, something to relax upon. Weathered wood seldom looks out of character, whatever the situation.

Eye-catching feature
To make an attraction of a special tree, "anchor" it to its surround with a circular seat. The pair then work as a feature. This simple, handsome version is made of metal, and for special occasions you could stand pots or baskets of flowers on it.

Theatrical styling, right
The theatrical approach to garden furniture, and very handsome too, if you have the setting. Painted wood can look too dominant, particularly when white, yet this color looks wonderful in front of the dark yew hedging.

POTS & CONTAINERS

Like sculpture, pots should be chosen and positioned to complete the overall collage of shapes and forms that you started in the layout and continued in the planting. I see them not in isolation, but as permanent features providing the culmination of a total look. To this end, I always mark groups of pots on my plans.

I prefer simple containers in many different sizes, for if the container is overflowing with color or vegetation, then the planting is the real eye-catcher and does not need a rivalling attraction in the pot.

On the other hand, some pots are so handsome that they can stand on their own as sculpture. I love the organic shape of the oil jar seen in many Italian, especially Tuscan, gardens, but do the shape and association transfer to another climate? Used carefully, the oil jar can translate well, but do not plant it. When carefully positioned, such a container makes a strong statement, acting as a centerpiece in a space, or punctuating a layout at intervals.

There are, of course, dozens of types of containers, and success ultimately depends on where a pot is used and with what proportion of planting. There is no equation for the height of growing material to pot, and plants are never static anyway. I go for a full look, and do not mix plant types in one pot. My rule is one tub filled with lots of one species. The tub next to it may be planted to harmonize, tumbling plants such as geraniums contrasting with denser, stronger plants, for instance.

Urban-Style Containers

Pots and containers make a strong style statement in an urban setting. Not only in their positioning,

Versailles-type planters, in natural wood and painted

Glazed earthenware container

Unglazed terra-cotta pot

Planted cylinders
Against a colored wall, a handsome architectural feature culminates in terra-cotta pipes. The planting, the pots themselves, and the accompanying gray foliage all become part of the overall arrangement.

Period urns, in concrete or reconstructed stone

Terra-cotta urn

Window box, in terra cotta

but in their shape, size, and color they should relate well to the style and scale of your space. A garden needs to be viewed on a large scale, and its furnishings should work to that scale as well.

Within an urban environment, a bold planting style is effective. Consider using the stark, vigorous shapes of cacti or yuccas. A row of clipped shapes, box balls, or bay pyramids could be a witty update on the standard box hedge in a small formal garden. Square-shaped containers look good in urban settings, especially when filled with clipped plants, but planting is not always necessary for a strong look — by using the correct pot you can achieve the desired effect. A handsome period urn, for instance, is suited to a grand town setting.

Country-Style Containers

Containers that suit traditional country settings may be made from natural products such as stone, slate,

and wood, or, for the more refined, china, earthenware, and terra cotta.

I am particularly fond of half barrels, which seem to suit most situations: there is something robust and wholesome about them, either for permanent plantings or annuals. Baskets are an increasingly popular short-term container, especially in the United States, and they look wonderful filled with flowers, although they must be lined with plastic first and left to dry out in winter; the coarse woven willow basket made in Britain is ideal for the country garden. They also look good in association with terra cotta for a random effect.

Let the choice and arrangement of containers also reflect the mood of your garden. A collection of pots in contrasting colors, shapes, and textures can look charming in a rural setting, and a faded old look works well when combined with delicate planting in soft pastel tones.

Baskets, plain willow or painted

Half barrel
Treat with preservative and never allow to dry out

Terra-cotta pots should be frost proof, and simple in outline

Large, robust containers above and left
If the container is handsome enough, and large enough, it does not need planting, but can act as a sculptural contrast to a fuzz of plants around it.

Handmade pots

PLANT SELECTION

In this chapter we look in detail at plant combinations for particular sites and provide suggestions for plants in a range of key design categories. You will, of course, have your own favorites, but I hope these listings will inspire you to think farther afield.

PLANTING SOLUTIONS

Leaving the cultural elements aside — for of course the right soil, the correct amount of moisture, sun, shade, and warmth will affect your plant selection — there are styles of plant association which create different looks while fulfilling a function, whether that function be shelter, screening, or purely decorative. However, how you mass the plants within those groupings is important, for there are several ways of doing it.

When starting out, perhaps the easiest form of grouping to attempt is that of the massed block. With this technique you create a strongly architectural look, and you can make your plant masses work visually in proportion with your design masses, so that the collage of pattern and shape becomes continuous. This planting pattern is useful for a structured, formal look, too.

Interlocking drifts of plant material create a more informal look which is particularly appropriate in borders. Proportionately, the masses should work in the same way as those of the block technique, but the finished effect will be more fluid and can reinforce an overall flowing design.

Another technique, which I enjoy exploring myself, is to simulate natural plant arrangements — the way in which plants distribute themselves by runner, seed, or other means when left to themselves, and which allows one set of plant forms to interweave with another.

Any of these groupings can work on very different scales. It will depend on the site and the plants chosen. To maintain the concept, repeat certain plants around the garden, and aim for a balance of deciduous and evergreen material.

For the sake of a fuller look in the short term, it usually pays to plant closer than most gardening books suggest, and then divide, or even move, the plants as they spread. The eventual height and spread of any plant are not absolute — so much depends on the conditions in the site and how well

PLANTING PATTERNS

The massed block
For a structured effect, mass the plants in blocks, orchestrating them carefully for contrasts of form and color.

Interlocking informal drifts
For borders, the layered effect of planting in elongated drifts works best, allowing the different groups to blend seamlessly.

Random effect
Produce a junglelike effect by dotting individual larger plants among groups of smaller plants. Use this for a wild look.

they match the plant's needs. On the following pages are solutions for a range of different conditions, each accompanied by a plan showing the likely spread of the plants after five years or so.

Having determined that the plants are suitable for the conditions, the main factors when deciding which plants to choose to create a group are not so much the kind of flowers, but the general shape of the plant, its leaf color, and texture. Loosely termed "form," these characteristics create the permanent framework of the planting; the flowers are but a short-lived bonus. Providing visual interest with contrasting forms and textures is one of the best ways to make a strong design statement in your planting scheme.

An eye for form
Plant groupings that can be
"read" as a composition of

abstract shapes have great
visual strength. Here leaf forms
contrast with color groupings.

A factor often neglected is the light-reflecting or light-absorbing qualities of leaves. Too much dull evergreen foliage can make the garden extremely leaden-looking. The more glossy evergreen leaves, like those of *Choisya ternata*, reflect the light, whereas many of the rhododendrons, for example, simply absorb it, and make the garden lifeless and dull. For the framework of the planting, choose carefully among the evergreens for those that offer good leaf quality, and combine them with plants with sympathetic foliage colors – remember, you can clash foliage colors, as well as flower ones.

SHADY CONDITIONS

Partial shade

For spring-flowering plants, the partial shade of a young leaf canopy is ideal, allowing them to bloom before the shade intensifies. *Fritillaria imperialis*, *Lunaria annua*, *Leucojum vernum*, and *Lamium maculatum* 'Beacon Silver' thrive here under an old tree.

Light shade

Moist soil and very light shade are a good environment for some handsome foliages, including most of the hellebores. Ornamental rhubarb (*Rheum palmatum*) needs plenty of moisture, and in such conditions the forget-me-not (*Myosotis sylvatica*) self-seeds freely.

Lunaria annua

Fritillaria imperialis

Lamium maculatum
'Beacon Silver'

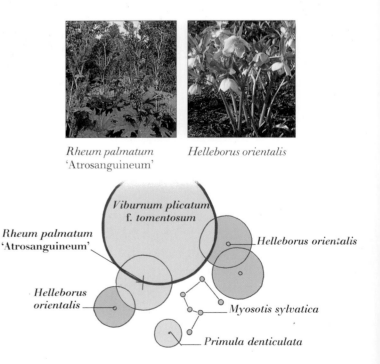

Rheum palmatum
'Atrosanguineum'

Helleborus orientalis

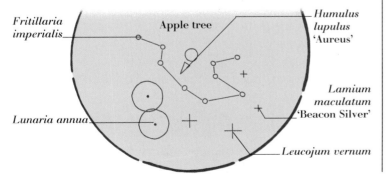

Fritillaria imperialis

Humulus lupulus 'Aureus'

Apple tree

Lamium maculatum 'Beacon Silver'

Lunaria annua

Leucojum vernum

Viburnum plicatum f. *tomentosum*

Rheum palmatum 'Atrosanguineum'

Helleborus orientalis

Helleborus orientalis

Myosotis sylvatica

Primula denticulata

Damp shade

Graded conditions from deep shade to full sun, and very damp to much drier soil, need careful planting. Here, *Iris laevigata* 'Variegata' enjoys having its feet in water in full sun, but hostas and heracleums do best in moist soil and light shade. *Photinia davidsoniae* will cope with either part shade or sun.

Photinia davidsoniae

Iris laevigata

Heracleum mantegazzianum

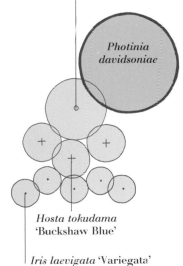

Photinia davidsoniae

Hosta tokudama 'Buckshaw Blue'

Iris laevigata 'Variegata'

Sun and shade

Large, bushy plants, like these euphorbias, create their own shade, so this area needs to be planted with some thought. Here, *Euphorbia characias* subsp. *wulfenii* is underplanted with epimediums and violas, which both like shade. Ligularia will cope with sun provided its roots are kept cool and moist.

Ligularia stenocephala

Epimedium x *versicolor*

Euphorbia characias subsp. *wulfenii*

Ligularia stenocephala

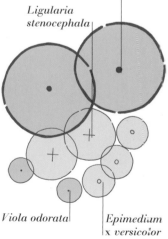

Viola odorata

Epimedium x *versicolor*

Narrow border

With their attractive foliage, trilliums, hostas, and thalictrums are all excellent for a border that gets relatively little sun. In fairly deep shade, where flower color is not really an option, create interest using exciting foliage contrasts.

Dramatic foliage

Contrast has been achieved in the part shade of a town garden using the spiky leaves of *Phormium tenax* next to feathery fronds of the fern *Athyrium filix-femina*. The aucuba tolerates most conditions, even salty winds and atmospheric pollution.

Saxifraga hirsuta   *Trillium grandiflorum*   *Viburnum tinus*

Phormium tenax
'Purpureum'   *Aucuba japonica*

Rhododendron ponticum
'Variegatum'   *Thalictrum rochebrunianum*

Saxifraga hirsuta

Viburnum tinus
'Variegatum'

Trillium grandiflorum

Hosta crispula

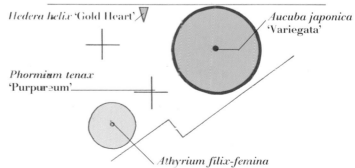

Hedera helix 'Gold Heart'   *Aucuba japonica*
'Variegata'

Phormium tenax
'Purpureum'

Athyrium filix-femina

BRIGHT CONDITIONS

Warm shelter

A sunny, dry, walled border is a good place to grow climbers, including most clematis (if the root run is shaded). The verbascum and euonymus make good foliage contrasts, enlivened by the purple clematis.

Sunny border

Cottage-garden planting of herbaceous perennials works well in a sunny border, where many plants self-seed. Here the straplike leaves of *Iris sibirica* contrast with the softer poppies and geraniums.

Foliage forms

Plants with straplike or feathery foliage look good when set off by strong evergreen forms. Colorado spruce contrasts here with the sisyrinchiums (which self-seed in gravelly soil), and gladiolus.

Euonymus fortunei 'Emerald and Gold'

Papaver orientale 'Allegro'

Geranium psilostemon

Picea pungens 'Glauca Globosa'

Sisyrinchium striatum

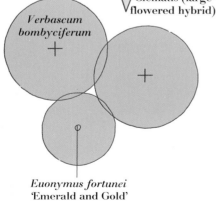

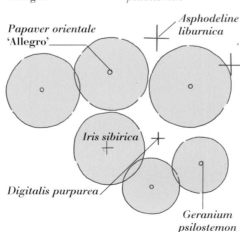

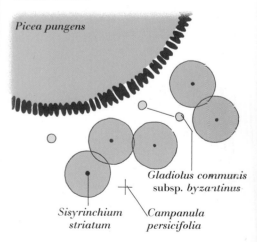

Clematis (large-flowered hybrid)

Verbascum bombyciferum

Euonymus fortunei 'Emerald and Gold'

Papaver orientale 'Allegro'

Asphodeline liburnica

Iris sibirica

Digitalis purpurea

Geranium psilostemon

Picea pungens

Gladiolus communis subsp. *byzantinus*

Sisyrinchium striatum

Campanula persicifolia

Planting for sun and rich soil

Larger herbaceous perennials like acanthus and phlox thrive in these conditions. They spread to make large clumps for an architectural feel to summer plantings, as do the tall spires of certain verbascum species. The birches beyond give structure in winter.

Phlox paniculata
'Brigadier'

Acanthus spinosus

Betula pendula
'Youngii'

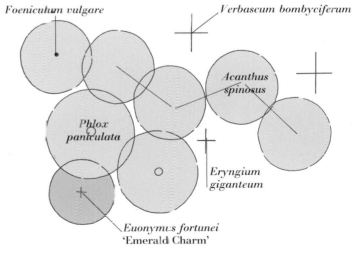

Foeniculum vulgare

Verbascum bombyciferum

Acanthus spinosus

Phlox paniculata

Eryngium giganteum

Euonymus fortunei 'Emerald Charm'

267

Dry, sunny site

Most of the silver-leaved plants prefer these conditions, including santolina, stachys, and senecio, which feature in this gold, silver, and green planting scheme. The strong sculptural feeling is created by using massed clumps of mound-forming plants.

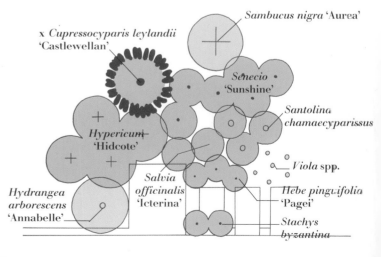

x *Cupressocyparis leylandii* 'Castlewellan'

Sambucus nigra 'Aurea'

Senecio 'Sunshine'

Santolina chamaecyparissus

Hypericum 'Hidcote'

Viola spp.

Hydrangea arborescens 'Annabelle'

Salvia officinalis 'Icterina'

Hebe pinguifolia 'Pagei'

Stachys byzantina

Hypericum 'Hidcote'

Santolina chamaecyparissus

Senecio 'Sunshine'

Planting beside a path

Well-drained soil and a reasonably sunny site give the greatest opportunity to grow a wide range of plants. Here the choice has been restrained in a cool-looking green-and-white scheme, dominated by exotic lilies. In the front of the border the variegated foliage of the pelargonium and the felicia softens the brick edge.

Planting in full sun

Dry, well-drained soil in full sun presents the ideal conditions for many different kinds of daisy, or daisylike plants, as well as a wide range of rock plants. Crammed together, cottage style, often because they have self-seeded, they create a tapestry effect, blocks of color made up of hundreds of individual flower heads.

Short-term effects

Some plants, like the young catalpa here with its extravagant golden foliage, need shelter as well as sunshine to thrive. Once the catalpa is at its full height, the underplanting may have to be altered, as the euphorbias are at their best in early summer, when the catalpa comes into leaf and starts to cast a lot of shade.

Lilium longiflorum

Felicia amelloides 'Santa Anita Variegated'

Helianthemum 'Mrs. Clay'

Othonnopsis cheirifolia

Euphorbia characias subsp. *wulfenii*

Nepeta x *faassenii*

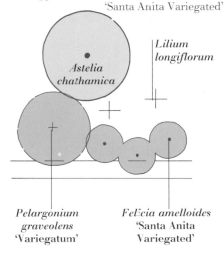

Astelia chathamica

Lilium longiflorum

Pelargonium graveolens 'Variegatum'

Felicia amelloides 'Santa Anita Variegated'

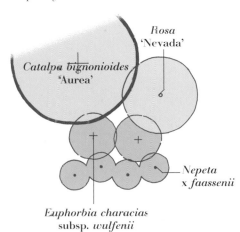

Helianthemum 'Mrs. Clay'

Erigeron karvinskianus

Osteospermum barberiae

Othonnopsis cheirifolia

Carex pendula

Lysimachia nummularia 'Aurea'

Leucanthemum vulgare

Sisyrinchium striatum

Erigeron glaucus

Catalpa bignonioides 'Aurea'

Rosa 'Nevada'

Nepeta x *faassenii*

Euphorbia characias subsp. *wulfenii*

HOT, HUMID CONDITIONS

Architectural planting

One advantage of hot and humid conditions is that they provide
the chance to grow exotic plants, most of them possessing either
dramatic foliage or vibrant flower colors. In these conditions,
ferns flourish, including the tree fern, *Dicksonia antarctica*.

Dicksonia antarctica

Bergenia x *schmidtii*

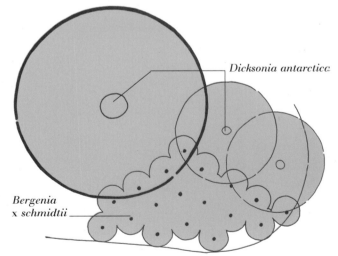

Dicksonia antarctica

Bergenia
x *schmidtii*

Urban tropical

Even a small town garden can turn into a mini-jungle with the right choice of plants. The Abyssinian banana plant (*Ensete ventricosum*), cannas, and melianthus can be grown outside in containers (and brought indoors in winter in cooler areas), but the catalpa simply needs shelter in most climates.

Ensete ventricosum

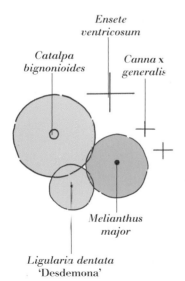

Catalpa bignonioides

Ensete ventricosum

Catalpa bignonioides

Canna x generalis

Melianthus major

Ligularia dentata 'Desdemona'

HOT, DRY CONDITIONS

Vitis coignetiae

Lavatera thuringiaca 'Rosea'

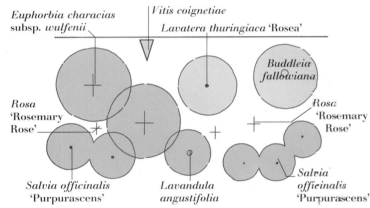

Euphorbia characias subsp. *wulfenii*

Vitis coignetiae

Lavatera thuringiaca 'Rosea'

Buddleia fallowiana

Rosa 'Rosemary Rose'

Rosa 'Rosemary Rose'

Salvia officinalis 'Purpurascens'

Lavandula angustifolia

Salvia officinalis 'Purpurascens'

Sheltered border

Contrasts of foliage color and texture work particularly well in this sheltered border backed by a wall. The sun-loving herbs such as sage and lavender thrive in poor soil.

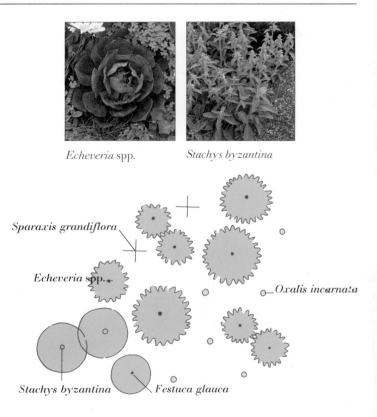

Echeveria spp.

Stachys byzantina

Sparaxis grandiflora

Echeveria spp.

Oxalis incarnata

Stachys byzantina

Festuca glauca

Spreading mats

A good, small-scale example of foliage contrasts beside a dry, sunny path; it would work equally well in a raised bed, as the design is arranged on a horizontal rather than a vertical plane, with the plants packed tight together to create a tapestry effect.

A Mediterranean look

In areas that do not suffer from frost – this grouping is in California – you can grow the attractive evergreen citruses outside, along with palms such as *Chamaerops humilis* and the exotic-looking red-flowered bauhinia. (In other areas grow them in pots and overwinter them indoors.) In dry, gravelly soil, however, even Mediterranean-type plants will stand colder temperatures than in waterlogged conditions. Phormiums, helichrysums and erigerons are all frost-hardy.

Bauhinia punctata

Phormium tenax 'Dazzler'

Chamaerops humilis

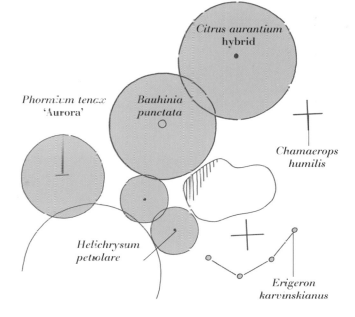

Citrus aurantium hybrid

Phormium tenax 'Aurora'

Bauhinia punctata

Chamaerops humilis

Helichrysum petiolare

Erigeron karvinskianus

SHALLOW SOIL

Gravel planting

Gravel acts as a natural seedbed for many plants, and informal planting schemes are the obvious solution. Verbascum, marjoram — among the many herbs suited to these conditions — and ajuga all enjoy the light, dryish conditions.

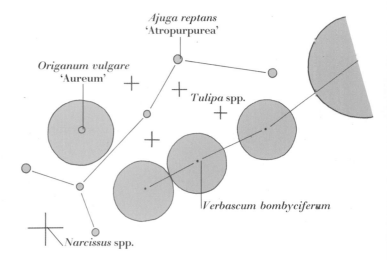

Ajuga reptans 'Atropurpurea'

Origanum vulgare 'Aureum'

Tulipa spp.

Verbascum bombyciferum

Narcissus spp.

Ajuga reptans 'Atropurpurea'

Origanum vulgare 'Aureum'

Verbascum bombyciferum

Planting between steps

Plants for paving need to be tough and, ideally, self-seeding, spreading freely between the cracks – *Alchemilla mollis*, for example. Ferns are also useful for steps, as they enjoy the shade cast by the risers, while vinca makes serviceable ground cover.

Leaf contrasts

Contrasts of foliage form are often most dramatic when kept very simple. Here the sword-shaped leaves of *Phormium tenax* provide a counterpoint to the fleshy leaves of *Sedum* 'Autumn Joy'. Both plants do best in full sun and shallow soil.

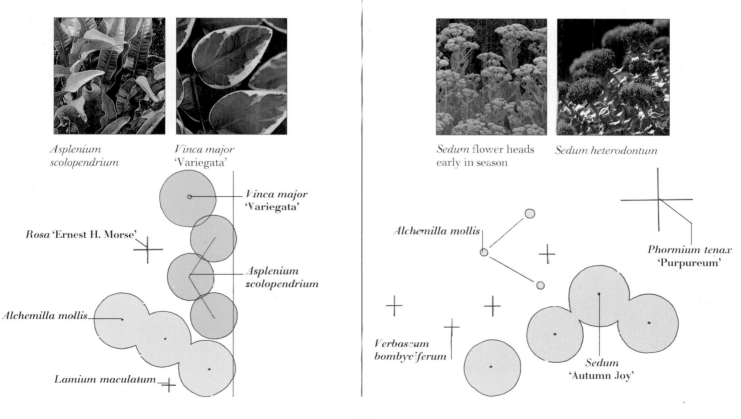

Asplenium scolopendrium

Vinca major 'Variegata'

Sedum flower heads early in season

Sedum heterodontum

Vinca major 'Variegata'

Rosa 'Ernest H. Morse'

Asplenium scolopendrium

Alchemilla mollis

Lamium maculatum

Alchemilla mollis

Phormium tenax 'Purpureum'

Verbascum bombyciferum

Sedum 'Autumn Joy'

PLANTING FOR WALLS

Combining climbers

Clothing walls with an almost continual supply of interest is best achieved by growing climbers through each other. Here a vine and a golden hop, noted for their excellent foliage color, provide a backdrop for two eye-catching, large-flowered clematis. Early- and late-flowering clematis are also useful partners for climbing roses, extending the flowering season from the usual few weeks of summer to late spring through early autumn.

Mild-climate climbers

On a sunny wall in a frost-free climate, you can grow some of the more exotic climbers, of which bougainvillea is undoubtedly one of the best. Bougainvillea produces masses of flowers in summer, in shades ranging from white through orange and scarlet to deep purple. Here it has been successfully combined with the striking festoons of selenicereus, and with hibiscus, which equally demand a frost-free climate.

Vitis vinifera
'Purpurea'

Clematis
'Perle d'Azur'

Clematis
'Ville de Lyon'

Selenicereus
grandiflorus

Bougainvillea
glabra

Bougainvillea glabra
'Snow White'

Year-round interest
Evergreen wall shrubs are
particularly useful, providing
structure all year round. *Carpenteria californica* is one of
the most handsome, with
glossy leaves and scented
white flowers, but it is not
fully hardy. Ceanothus is another good evergreen, and is
covered with cascades of small
blue flowers in early summer.

*Carpenteria
californica*

Euphorbia mellifera

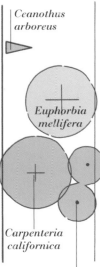

*Ceanothus
arboreus*

*Euphorbia
mellifera*

*Carpenteria
californica*

*Ballota
pseudodictamnus*

EXPOSED SITES

Resilient subjects

On an exposed site, tough grasses and heathers have been grouped together for maximum effect, their massed forms providing a sculptural quality to the planting, which looks as effective in winter as it does in summer. Boulders add to the overall composition. Low-growing plants such as these are also less likely to suffer from wind damage.

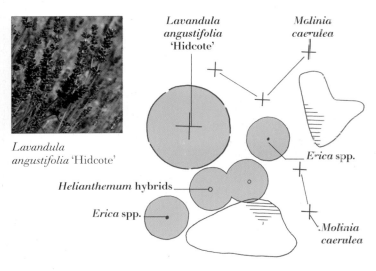

*Lavandula
angustifolia* 'Hidcote'

*Lavandula
angustifolia* 'Hidcote'

*Molinia
caerulea*

Erica spp.

Helianthemum hybrids

Erica spp.

*Molinia
caerulea*

Low-growing island planting

Island beds need careful planting as they are viewed from all sides. Here clump-forming plants are massed together, each chosen for its low-growing nature, for although this exposed site is sheltered by hedges, tall, narrow spikes could still be exposed to high winds. Foliage contrasts are strong, including the spiky, silvery leaves of dianthus and the spotted foliage of pulmonaria.

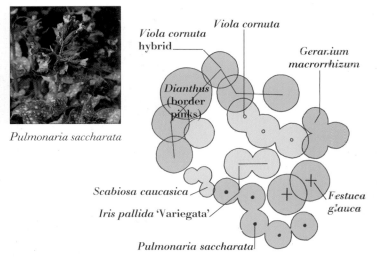

Pulmonaria saccharata

Viola cornuta

Viola cornuta
hybrid

*Geranium
macrorrhizum*

*Dianthus
(border
pinks)*

Scabiosa caucasica

Iris pallida 'Variegata'

*Festuca
glauca*

Pulmonaria saccharata

Providing a shelter belt
The alternative to planting on
an exposed site is to shelter it
with tough shrubs and trees
able to stand the conditions,
and to plant within. This is a
good example of such a wind
belt. The internal interest is
created by the eye-catching
gray foliage of the special
Pyrus salicifolia 'Pendula', by
the purple berberis planted to
its left, and by a collection of
shrub and climbing roses.

Pyrus salicifolia
'Pendula'

THE PLANT CATALOGUE

In this section I show a selection of plant material, organized into the various categories I use when I talk about putting plants together, followed by other categories highlighting particular visual qualities. Indeed, the purpose of the entries is to encourage you to think about a plant's visual potential within a scheme. I am conscious that the groupings are by no means extensive or complete, but I hope they will serve to inspire you to make your own plant listings. I suggest that you work with a good catalogue at hand, because if a plant cannot be obtained commercially there is little point in considering it.

THE PLANT KEY

Siting

- ☀ Prefers sun
- ☀ Prefers partial shade
- ☀ Tolerates full shade
- ◊ Prefers well-drained soil
- ◖ Prefers moist soil
- ● Prefers wet soil
- pH Needs acid soil

PLANT SIZE

Maximum height (H) and spread (S) are given in the captions.

HARDINESS

The USDA hardiness zone ranges are given for all perennial and woody plants. Level of hardiness is indicated for annuals.

Plant type

- ♠ Evergreen tree
- ♀ Deciduous tree
- ♠ Evergreen shrub
- ♡ Deciduous shrub
- ♈ Perennial plant
- ♈ Biennial plant
- ♣ Annual plant
- ♔ Climber

- ♇ Bulb
- ≈ Water plant
- ↓ Grass
- ✳ Bamboo
- ❦ Fern

SPECIALS

I categorize a plant as a special if it has a distinctive quality which is more or less permanent and which allows it to stand out as a sculptural feature within a layout. In a new garden it may be an existing tree by virtue of its sheer size, but more usually the designation depends on good foliage shape or color or on the plant's form. The special can be the pivot in a bed or the major item in a garden; see pages 120-3 for a full description.

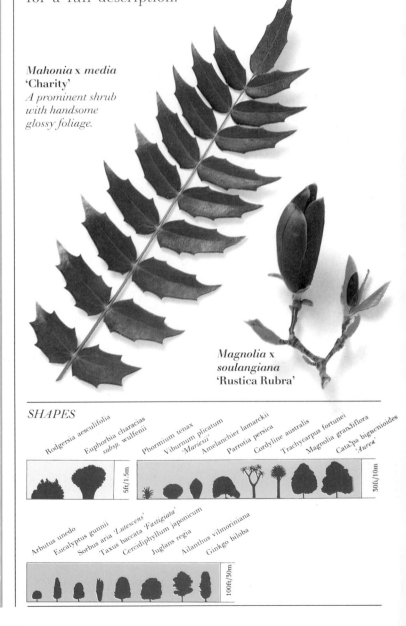

***Mahonia* x *media* 'Charity'**
A prominent shrub with handsome glossy foliage.

***Magnolia* x *soulangiana* 'Rustica Rubra'**

SHAPES

Rodgersia aesculifolia
Euphorbia characias *subsp.* wulfenii
Phormium tenax
Viburnum plicatum 'Mariesii'
Amelanchier lamarckii
Parrotia persica
Cordyline australis
Trachycarpus fortunei
Magnolia grandiflora
Catalpa bignonioides 'Aurea'

5ft/1.5m

30ft/10m

Arbutus unedo
Eucalyptus gunnii
Sorbus aria 'Lutescens'
Taxus baccata 'Fastigiata'
Cercidiphyllum japonicum
Juglans regia
Ailanthus vilmoriniana
Ginkgo biloba

100ft/30m

☀ ◊ Zones 6-9

Ailanthus vilmoriniana

A potentially giant tree with huge jungly leaves, it can be grown as a shrub by cutting it back hard every year. This will also encourage it to produce larger leaves.
H 80ft (25m), S 50ft (15m).

☀ ◊ Zones 8-9

Arbutus unedo

A spreading tree with many virtues: pendant white flowers and strawberrylike fruits in autumn and winter and glossy leaves. A handsome all-rounder.
H and S 25ft (8m).

☀ ◊ Zones 5-9

Catalpa bignonioides 'Aurea'

An imposing small tree with a wide head valued for its large, golden, heart-shaped leaves. Where space is limited, prune it back hard to emphasize this feature. H and S 30ft (10m).

☀ ◊ Zones 4-8

Amelanchier lamarckii

A striking shrub or small tree bearing abundant, pretty white flowers in spring, and apple-green foliage that turns brilliant red and orange in autumn.
H 20ft (5m), S 12ft (4m).

☀ ◊ Zones 5-9

Cercidiphyllum japonicum

A versatile spreading tree that lends itself as a lawn feature and is also useful in large shrub borders as a backdrop. The leaves turn yellow and purple in autumn.
H 50ft (20m), S 30ft (10m).

☀ ◊ Zones 9-11

Cordyline australis

A spiky, symmetrical plant with nuances of the Mediterranean. With its strongly architectural form and striking outline, it makes a good container plant when young.
H 30ft (10m), S 15ft (5m).

☀ ◊ Zones 8-11

Eucalyptus gunnii
The round leaves of silver-blue make eucalyptus a striking border shrub if it is cut back every year. Left to grow tall, however, it will become a shimmering tree.
H 40ft (12m), S 25ft (8m).

☀ ◊ Zones 5-9

Ginkgo biloba
A tall, distinctive feature for large gardens. Its bright green, fan-shaped leaves turn a clear yellow color in autumn. If possible, plant nonfruiting male trees.
H 80ft (25m), S 30ft (10m).

☀ ◊ Zones 5-8

Juglans regia
An attractive tree, the walnut has dense, leathery foliage and distinctive fruits. Mature trees, with their majestic spreading shape, provide a useful shady spot for sitting under.
H 60ft (20m), S 50ft (15m).

☀ ◊ Zones 7-9

Magnolia grandiflora
Grow this exotic-looking tree for its glossy, dark green leaves and large, creamy, fragrant flowers in summer and early autumn.
H 60ft (20m), S 30ft (10m).

☀ ◊ Zones 9-11

Phormium tenax
The upright, straplike leaves of the New Zealand flax are an eye-catching feature all year, and provide a foil to other good leaf shapes, such as those of ferns or hostas.
H 10ft (3m), S 3-6ft (1-2m)

☀ ◊ Zones 7-10

Euphorbia characias
subsp. *wulfenii*
Prized for its distinctive gray-green leaves and curious bottlebrush blooms, this euphorbia has a startling, architectural feel.
H 5ft (1.5m), S 3ft (1m).

☀ ◊ Zones 5-9

Parrotia persica
One of the best choices if you are planting for fall color, as the leaves turn yellow, orange, and then red-purple. It bears small red flowers in early spring.
H 25ft (8m), S 30ft (10m).

☀ ◊ Zones 5-8

Rodgersia aesculifolia
A bold, showy plant with horse-chestnut-shaped leaves and plumes of flowers; it looks effective in poolside groupings with narrow-leaved irises and clumps of hostas.
H and S 3ft (1m).

☀ ◊ Zones 5-8 ♡
Viburnum plicatum 'Mariesii'
An excellent feature shrub
with its tiers of horizontal
branches that bear white
lacecap flowers in spring and
early summer.
H and S 12ft (4m).

☀ ◊ Zones 6-7 ♀
Sorbus aria 'Lutescens'
With its well-defined shape,
the whitebeam mountain ash
is a pretty tree, especially in
windy locations where the
shimmering leaves show their
silver undersides.
H 40ft (13m), S 25ft (8m).

☀ ◊ Zones 6-7 🌳
Taxus baccata 'Fastigiata'
This yew cultivar provides a
strong vertical element and can
be an effective special. Its
pencil shape and dense foliage
grab attention.
H 30-50ft (10-15m),
S 12-15ft (4-5m).

☀ ◊ Zones 8-11 🌳
Trachycarpus fortunei
An utterly exotic but somewhat hardy palm with large,
fan-shaped leaves at the head
of its fibrous trunk. In summer
it bears sprays of creamy
yellow flowers.
H 30ft (10m), S 10ft (3m).

OTHER PLANTS

Aralia elata
Ailanthus altissima
Arbutus x andrachnoides
Eriobotrya japonica
Fatsia japonica
   'Variegata'
Robinia pseudoacacia
   'Frisia'
Rosmarinus officinalis
   'Miss Jessopp's Upright'
Yucca flaccida 'Ivory'

DISTINCTIVELY SHAPED TREES

This category of trees is, in a sense, a continuation of the specials, to the extent that these are plants that can also be used to make arresting focal points or to provide pivotal features within a layout. From this range you can select either an individual tree to make a feature on its own, or, if you are working on a larger scale, you could decide to plant more than one of the same type. Such a planting gives you the opportunity to create a strong character for the overall picture, for while one cypress seldom creates a Mediterranean look, a group of cypresses unmistakably does, while a number of fastigiate hornbeams gives a pronounced spiky effect.

Abies concolor
A large species of fir with blue-green foliage.

KEY

Siting

Prefers sun Prefers partial shade Tolerates full shade Prefers well-drained soil Prefers moist soil Prefers wet soil Needs acid soil

☼ ☼ ☀ ◊ ◐ ● pH

Plant type

Evergreen tree Deciduous tree Evergreen shrub Deciduous shrub Perennial plant Biennial plant Annual plant Climber Bulb Water plant Grass Bamboo Fern

SHAPES

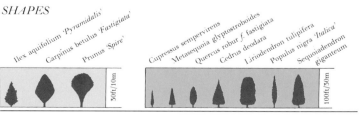

Ilex aquifolium 'Pyramidalis' Carpinus betulus 'Fastigiata' Prunus 'Spire' Cupressus sempervirens Metasequoia glyptostroboides Quercus robur f. fastigiata Cedrus deodara Liriodendron tulipifera Populus nigra 'Italica' Sequoiadendron giganteum

50ft/10m 100ft/50m

☼ ◊ Zones 5-8

Carpinus betulus 'Fastigiata'
A handsome tree for city gardens, the fastigiate hornbeam has a distinctive flame-shaped outline and bears hoplike fruits in autumn.
H 30ft (10m), S 15ft (5m).

☼ ◊ Zones 7-9

Cedrus deodara
A slow-growing conifer for a large garden, characterized by its drooping branches and long leading shoot. *Cedrus deodara* 'Aurea' is much smaller.
H 50-80ft (15-25m),
S 15-30ft (5-10m).

☼ ◊ Zones 8-10

Cupressus sempervirens
A familiar sight in the Mediterranean, this spirelike cypress provides a splendid focal point in large gardens, with its stiffly erect form in darkest green.
H 50ft (15m), S 6ft (2m).

☼ ◊ Zones 6-8 ♤
Prunus x *hilleri* 'Spire'
A pretty flowering cherry with an upright shape, making it ideal for restricted spaces. Its profusion of soft pink flowers is followed by attractive autumn foliage color.
H 30ft (10m), S 20ft (5m).

☼ ◊ Zones 7-9 ♣
Ilex aquifolium '**Pyramidalis**'
English holly is naturally upright and strongly branched, but all its varieties take readily to clipping into formal shapes. As such, they make good focal points. H 20ft (6m), S 15ft (5m).

☼ ● Zones 5-9 ♤
Metasequoia glyptostroboides
A prominent conifer, the dawn redwood looks effective on the lawn or at the pondside; it has blue-green leaves that turn gold before falling.
H 55ft (17m), S 25ft (8m).

☼ ◊ Zones 6-9 ♣
Sequoiadendron giganteum
Giant Sierra redwoods are nature's skyscrapers – commanding conifers that tower above all around. Choose them f you are planting a large estate for posterity.
H 100ft (30m), S 33ft (11m).

☼ ◊ Zones 4-9 ♤
Liriodendron tulipifera
The tulip tree is broadly columnar in shape. Its unusual leaves, and the exotic flowers produced in early summer by mature trees, make it a good choice as a lawn feature.
H 100ft (30m), S 50ft (15m).

☼ ● Zones 3-9 ♤
Populus nigra '**Italica**'
A tall ornamental tree, sometimes used as a windbreak; this is a fast-growing giant, but beware of its spreading roots, which can damage buildings.
H 100ft (30m) S 20ft (6m).

☼ ◊ Zones 5-8 ♤
Quercus robur f. *fastigiata*
This upright form of English oak is a handsome addition to large gardens, particularly when grouped with shrubs having good autumn color, since its leaves turn gold.
H 60ft (20m), S 20ft (6m).

OTHER PLANTS
Acer platanoides 'Columnare'
Cedrus atlantica
Cupressus glabra 'Pyramidalis'
Ginkgo biloba 'Tremonia'
Juniperus communis 'Hibernica'
Juniperus drupacea
Juniperus virginiana 'Skyrocket'
Malus tschonoskii
Nothofagus betuloide

WEEPING SHAPES

The weeping shape or the hanging climber always seems to evoke a cry of exclamation, doubtless on account of its soft and graceful form. Suitably placed and in scale with the surroundings, the weeper can look spectacular – the willow by the lake or the weeping beech by yew hedges. Used carefully and sparingly in a layout, this form becomes an eye-catching feature or a "special" as it is so striking. As an architectural shape the weeper works well, since it picks up the vertical lines of any building with which it is associated and, by the same token, it provides a contrast to the strong horizontal line of water.

Betula pendula
Silver birch: an elegant weeper with yellow spring catkins.

KEY

Siting

Prefers sun   Prefers partial shade   Tolerates full shade   Prefers well-drained soil   Prefers moist soil   Prefers wet soil   Needs acid soil

☀ ☀ ☀ ◌ ◗ ● pH

Plant type

Evergreen tree   Deciduous tree   Evergreen shrub   Deciduous shrub   Perennial plant   Biennial plant   Annual plant   Climber   Bulb   Water plant   Grass   Bamboo   Fern

☀ ◌ Zones 10-11   ♣

Agonis flexuosa
The willow myrtle is an elegant tree with weeping stems of slender, aromatic leaves. It bears attractive, small, white flowers in spring and summer.
H 25ft (8m), S 15ft (5m).

☀ ◌ Zones 3-8   ♀

Betula pendula 'Youngii'
A cultivar of silver birch noted for its markedly weeping habit. It bears gracefully arching stems of small, bright green leaves, and yellow-green catkins in spring.
H 25ft (8m), S 30ft (10m).

☀ ◗ Zones 7-9   ♣

Cedrus deodara 'Aurea'
A dramatic weeping shape, so attention-grabbing that sympathetic partners for it can be hard to find. It has golden foliage only when young.
H 20ft (7m), S 10ft (3m).

☼ ◊ Zones 4-7 ♠

Fagus sylvatica f. **pendula**
Given room and time, this
European beech will become a
monster in maturity, spreading
its tentlike branches of densely
arranged oval leaves right to
the ground.
H 50ft (15m), S 60ft (20m).

☼ ◊ Zones 5-8 ♠

**Prunus subhirtella
'Pendula'**
Clusters of deep pink flowers
appear in spring on leafless
branches; its weeping shape
adds the extra dimension of
form to the ornamental cherry
display. H and S 27ft (9m).

☼ ◊ Zones 5-8 ♠

Pyrus salicifolia 'Pendula'
The weeping pear is a versatile tree; rotund, with silver-
gray leaves and white flowers,
it makes a frothing silver
subject for white schemes or
mixed-color borders.
H 22ft (7m), S 15ft (5m).

☼ ◊ Zones 5-8 ♠

Ulmus glabra f. **atropurpurea 'Camperdownii'**
The branches of this small
tree weep to the ground,
forming in winter a fine
skeletal tracery. In summer
they make a canopy of leaves.
H and S 25ft (8m).

☼ ◊ Zones 5-8 ♠

Salix caprea 'Kilmarnock'
Small and umbrellalike, with
delicate weeping branches, this
willow bears gray, later yellow
catkins in spring, then becomes a dense mound of
summer foliage.
H 5-6ft (1.5-2m), S 6ft (2m).

☼ ◊ Zones 5-9 ♨

Wisteria floribunda 'Alba'
The long tresses of wisteria
can add a decorative weeping
element to a wall or pergola in
spring and summer. Wisterias
can also be trained to grow as
standards.
H to 27ft (9m).

OTHER PLANTS

Caragana arborescens
  'Pendula'
Cedrus atlantica 'Glauca
  Pendula'
Cotoneaster 'Hybridus
  Pendulus'
Dacrydium franklinii
Malus floribunda
Parrotia persica 'Pendula'
Picea breweriana
Prunus 'Cheal's Weeping'
Salix x *sepulchralis*
  'Chrysocoma'
Taxus baccata
  'Dovastoniana'

SKELETONS

I use this range of plant material to put "bones" into a layout. Most good skeleton plants are evergreen for an all-year-round effect. Since the planting is really to provide bulk and winter form, flower interest is a low priority; instead, the importance lies chiefly in the foliage colors and the berrying qualities of a given plant, since these are more enduring characteristics. A good proportion of the evergreen skeleton plants will be used on the perimeter of a site to act as screening material, blocking wind or an unsightly view, or for creating internal spaces within an overall layout. On a smaller scale, the skeletons can provide an evergreen core to a mix of perennial or deciduous shrubs, steadying the overall concept and maintaining a year-round structure. But there is another function for skeletons, and that is winter drama. *Hamamelis mollis*, for instance, could be in my skeleton category for its flowers as well as its evergreen nature. See pages 124-7 for a full description.

☼ ◊ Zones 7-9

Berberis darwinii
This barberry forms an impenetrable mound with orangey flowers in spring. It is a good choice for creating informal hedges and mixed shrub plantings.
H and S 10ft (3m).

☼ ◊ Zones 8-11

Callistemon pallidus
The Tasmanian bottlebrush is an interesting skeleton for dry, Mediterranean-type plantings, with its gray-green foliage and spikes of tufted creamy flowers in early summer.
H and S 10ft (3m).

☼ ◊ Zones 6-9

Buxus sempervirens 'Handsworthiensis'
Trimmed hedges are ideal skeleton features in a garden. This cultivar of box will provide these and also has the advantage of growing tall.
H and S 10ft (3m).

KEY

Siting

Prefers sun	Prefers partial shade	Tolerates full shade	Prefers well-drained soil	Prefers moist soil	Prefers wet soil	Needs acid soil
☼	☼	☼	◊	◓	◆	pH

Plant type

Evergreen tree	Deciduous tree	Evergreen shrub	Deciduous shrub	Perennial plant	Biennial plant	Annual plant	Climber	Bulb	Water plant	Grass	Bamboo	Fern

SHAPES

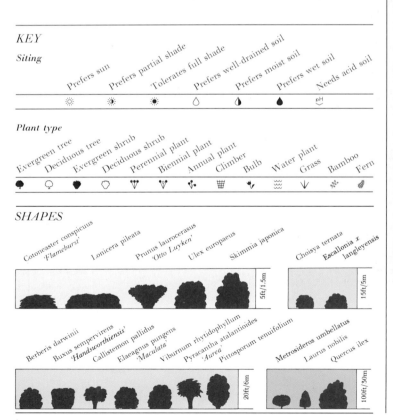

Cotoneaster conspicuus 'Flameburst' Lonicera pileata Prunus laurocerasus 'Otto Luyken' Ulex europaeus Skimmia japonica Choisya ternata Escallonia × langleyensis

5ft/1.5m   15ft/5m

Berberis darwinii Buxus sempervirens 'Handsworthiensis' Callistemon pallidus Elaeagnus pungens 'Maculata' Viburnum rhytidophyllum Pyracantha atalantioides 'Aurea' Pittosporum tenuifolium Metrosideros umbellatus Laurus nobilis Quercus ilex

20ft/6m   100ft/30m

☀ ◊ Zones 8-9 ⬤

Escallonia x langleyensis

A graceful skeleton shrub which has arching stems of dark green leaves and rose-pink flowers in early summer: it can be used as an informal hedging plant
H 6ft (2m), S 10ft (3m).

☀ ◊ Zones 8-10 ⬤

Laurus nobilis

The bay is a distinguished evergreen, with its glossy, dark, aromatic leaves. Clipped into shapes and planted in pots, they make neat skeleton plants; or leave it to grow naturally.
H 36ft (12m), S 30ft (10m).

☀ ◊ Zones 8-11 ⬤

Choisya ternata

This dense, bushy mound is a useful skeleton shrub – as long as it is not exposed to wind – with its shiny leaves and deliciously fragrant, white flowers in spring.
H and S 6ft (2m).

☀ ◊ Zones 7-8 ⬤

Cotoneaster conspicuus 'Flameburst'

A good low-growing evergreen shrub with bright red autumn and winter berries. Grow it in mixed borders, or as an informal hedge.
H 2ft (60cm), S 6-10ft (2-3m).

☀ ◊ Zones 7-9 ⬤

Elaeagnus pungens 'Maculata'

The bright golden foliage of this shrub can be a useful element in skeleton plantings, throwing the more usual greens into relief.
H and S 10ft (3m)

☀ ◊ Zones 9-11 ⬛

Hedera canariensis 'Ravensholst'

A handsome, large-leaved ivy that will provide a permanent green backdrop to showier plants, or give excellent ground cover
H to 20ft (6m), S 15ft (5m).

☼ ◊ Zones 5-9

Lonicera pileata
With its horizontally branching shoots of shiny dark green leaves, this dense, low shrub gives good year-round ground cover, and can be useful underneath trees.
H 18in (50cm), S 8ft (2.5m).

☼ ◊ Zones 9-11

Metrosideros umbellatus
A handsome evergreen tree from the Antipodes, with bottlebrush flowers and reddish shoots. Can be grown as a tender shrub in the mildest areas of temperate climates.
H 30ft (10m), S 25ft (8m).

☼ ◊ Zones 9-11

Pittosporum tenuifolium
A shrub or small tree originally from New Zealand. It has attractive glossy leaves and bears purple flowers in late spring; a good shrub for making into a hedge.
H 15ft (5m), S 12ft (4m).

☼ ◊ Zones 7-9

Prunus laurocerasus 'Otto Luyken'
The laurel is ideal in low-maintenance gardens; this cultivar gives good green cover in dank areas. It is neat and undemanding.
H 3ft (1m), S 5ft (1.5m).

☼ ◊ Zones 6-9

Pyracantha atalantioides 'Aurea'
One of the yellow-fruited firethorns, this evergreen is valued for its ability to flower and fruit well even in a shady position.
H and S 12ft (4m).

☼ ◊ Zones 7-9

Quercus ilex
An excellent shelterbelt plant, the holm oak can be trimmed to give neat hedging. If left to attain its full majestic outline, it makes an attractive evergreen feature tree.
H 80ft (25m), S 60ft (20m).

☼ ◊ Zones 7-9

Skimmia japonica
Male and female types should be grouped to produce the red berries that make this such a desirable shrub. Its evergreen mounded shape contrasts well with upright plants.
H and S 5ft (1.5m).

☼ ◊ Zones 7-9

Ulex europaeus
Gorse, a tough, viciously spiny shrub, is pretty when in flower in spring, and has a complementary effect among heathers and pines, for the heath is its natural habitat.
H and S 4ft (1.2m).

Ilex spp.
Hollies are ideal as skeleton plants, vigorous evergreen shrubs with handsome foliage and berries.

☀ ○ Zones 5-9

Viburnum rhytidophyllum

An invaluable backbone shrub with attractive, deep green, corrugated, slightly drooping leaves. Its creamy white flowers in spring and summer are followed by scarlet berries.
H and S 10ft (3m)

Ilex x
altaclerensis
'Lawsoniana'

Ilex aquifolium
'Argentea Marginata'

OTHER PLANTS

Carpinus betulus
Ilex x *altaclerensis* cvs.
Ligustrum japonicum
Lonicera nitida
Osmanthus delavayi
Prunus lusitanica
Rhododendron ponticum
Telopea truncata
Taxus baccata
Viburnum x *burkwoodii*
Viburnum tinus

PLANTS FOR WINTER INTEREST

I find the winter garden – at least in a temperate climate – extremely attractive. But for it to work, it has to be a garden with an evergreen backbone of dark yew or shiny box foliage, say, against which to appreciate the stems, textures, and soft color of winter plants, as well as the dead russety leaves of beech and hornbeam. Together with these gentle visual delights are the winter fragrances, for most winter-flowering plants have a deep scent, which is enhanced by the gentle warmth of early spring sunshine. Evergreen shrubs are a welcome addition: elaeagnus, various viburnums, and pyracantha. Contrast these with architectural euphorbia, bergenia, and hellebores to provide the basis for a grouping that improves as the season progresses.

KEY

Siting

Prefers sun	Prefers partial shade	Tolerates full shade	Prefers well-drained soil	Prefers moist soil	Prefers wet soil	Needs acid soil
☀	☀	☀	◊	◖	◆	pH

Plant type

Evergreen tree	Deciduous tree	Evergreen shrub	Deciduous shrub	Perennial plant	Biennial plant	Annual plant	Climber	Bulb	Water plant	Grass	Bamboo	Fern

☀ ◊ Zones 7-9

Daphne odora 'Aureo-marginata'
Grow this daphne near your door, where you can best appreciate its deliciously fragrant, pink-and-white flowers in late winter.
H and S 5ft (1.5m).

☀ ◊ Zones 2-8

Cornus alba 'Sibirica'
A cultivar of dogwood that dramatically brightens up the winter garden with its leafless, luminous crimson stems – the new growth produced by hard pruning in the previous spring.
H and S 6ft (2m).

☀ ◖ Zones 4-9

Corylus avellana 'Contorta'
The contorted, corkscrew stems of this hazel give an interesting effect in winter, especially when its long yellow catkins appear in very early spring.
H and S 15ft (5m).

☀ ◊ pH Zones 7-9

Hamamelis mollis
This handsome witch hazel is valued for its sweetly fragrant, rich yellow flowers, produced in tuftlike clusters along bare branches in late winter and early spring.
H and S 12ft (4m) or more.

☀ ◊ Zones 7-9

Mahonia x media 'Buckland'
One of the best mahonias, prized for its year-round sculptural foliage and sprays of yellow flowers that add a touch of color in early winter.
H 12-15ft (4-5m), S 10ft (3m).

☀ ◌ Zones 5-9 ♡

Rubus cockburnianus

An eye-catching plant for wilder parts of the garden, where its chalky white, unruly stems make a dramatic focal point in winter.
H and S 8ft (2.5m).

☀ ◑ Zones 7-9 ◆

Sarcococca confusa

The Christmas box provides useful spreading ground cover, growing freely in dry shade. Its white late-winter flowers are highly fragrant, and are followed by black fruits.
H and S 3ft (1m).

☀ ◌ Zones 7-9 ♧

Viburnum x bodnantense 'Dawn'

A useful winter shrub by virtue of its cheerful display of pale pink, fragrant flowers from late autumn through to early spring.
H 10ft (3m), S 6ft (2m).

OTHER PLANTS

Arum italicum 'Pictum'
Chimonanthus praecox
Clematis cirrhosa 'Balearica'
Cornus alba 'Kesselringii'
Cornus stolonifera 'Flaviramea'
Eranthis hyemalis
Galanthus spp.
Jasminum nudiflorum
Lonicera x purpusii
Prunus subhirtella 'Autumnalis'
Viburnum tinus

Helleborus orientalis hybrids

Helleborus argutifolius

Helleborus spp.
The hellebores are invaluable late-growing, winter-flowering plants, maintaining their foliage form throughout the year.

PLANTS FOR AUTUMN INTEREST

With autumn, foliage matures into a range of spectacular colors, from pale yellows to deepest purples, and the fallen leaves strewn on the ground are part of the season's magic. Where autumn leaves have fallen there are abundant hanging fruits – rose hips, crab apples, and pyracantha, cotoneaster, and viburnum berries. Autumn flower colors tend to be warm: rich reds, golds, lemons, and yellows, while the outlines of the nodding, straw-colored grasses lend a romantic element. Autumn is my favorite season for it is the time to put the garden to bed, to tidy away the summer's dying excesses, and prepare for winter.

Rose hips
Fat, red, and wonderfully redolent of autumn.

☼ ◊ Zones 5-8 ♀

Acer palmatum var. *coreanum*
The Japanese maples give outstanding autumn colors. The leaves of this variety turn brilliant crimson and persist for a long while.
H and S 22ft (7m).

☼ ◊ Zones 6-9

Clematis orientalis
The pendulous, lantern-shaped yellow flowers that appear in late summer turn into silvery, silky seed heads in autumn, making this a worthwhile clematis.
H 10-12ft (3-4m), S 5ft (1.5m).

☼ ◊ pH Zones 5-9

Enkianthus campanulatus
A pretty Japanese shrub that will reward you with a profusion of delicate, bell-like spring flowers, and autumn leaves that turn magnificent shades of yellow to red.
H and S 12ft (4m).

KEY

Siting

Prefers sun	Prefers partial shade	Tolerates full shade	Prefers well-drained soil	Prefers moist soil	Prefers wet soil	Needs acid soil
☼	☼	☼	◊	◑	●	pH

Plant type

Evergreen tree	Deciduous tree	Evergreen shrub	Deciduous shrub	Perennial plant	Biennial plant	Annual plant	Climber	Bulb	Water plant	Grass	Bamboo	Fern
♠	♀	♣	♡	♈	♈	⚘	⊞	⚘	≋	∨	⁂	🌿

☼ ◊ pH Zones 5-9

Nyssa sylvatica
Nyssas have a broad, conical
profile, their lower branches
dipping elegantly to the
ground. A blaze of orange-red
colors contrasts well with
yellow-foliaged subjects.
H 60ft (20m), S 50ft (15m).

☼ ◊ Zones 7-9

Rhus trichocarpa
A sophisticated-looking shrub
or small tree, with splendid
architectural foliage that turns
crimson to orange. The sumacs
look handsome among buildings in town gardens.
H and S 15ft (5m).

☼ ◊ Zones 5-9

Parthenocissus tricuspidata
The familiar Boston ivy
decorates the façades of many
buildings to great effect. It has
markedly ivy-shaped leaves
that turn a spectacular blood
red color in autumn.
H to 60ft (20m).

☼ ◊ Zones 6-9

Pyracantha 'Golden Dome'
The firethorns are valued for
their profuse sprays of bright
autumn berries. This is a
shapely yellow-fruiting variety.
H 5ft (1.5m), S 10ft (3m).

☼ ◊ Zones 6-8

Sorbus 'Joseph Rock'
One of the best decorative
small trees, this mountain ash
is prized for its butter yellow
fruits, which make a distinctive contrast to the fiery red
color of its autumn foliage.
H 30ft (10m), S 22ft (7m).

OTHER PLANTS

Amelanchier lamarckii
Berberis thunbergii
Carpinus betulus
Carya ovata
Cotinus coggygria 'Flame'
Cotoneaster horizontalis
Crataegus persimilis
  'Prunifolia'
Euonymus europaeus
Fothergilla major
Gaultheria procumbens
Liquidambar styraciflua
Nandina domestica
Rhus typhina
Rosa rugosa

A FEW FLOWERING SHRUBS

As I reflect on my favorite flowering shrubs, I realize it is difficult to separate the flower from the foliage; indeed, the best plants are those where the two complement each other. I am very fond of shrub roses, with their soft shapes, their hips, and decorative thorns; potentillas, in shades of white to lemon, yellow, and apricot; and ceratostigma for late summer color. I love, too, the gray-foliaged shrubs and their simple flowers – cistus, ozothamnus, perovskia, sage, and the silky, white-flowering *Convolvulus cneorum*. A useful category of flowering shrubs includes those that can be cut down each autumn, such as buddleias and hydrangeas; interplanted with early perennials and bulbs, they give a satisfying layered effect.

KEY

Siting

Prefers sun	Prefers partial shade	Tolerates full shade	Prefers well-drained soil	Prefers moist soil	Prefers wet soil	Needs acid soil
☼	☼	☀	◌	◔	●	pH

Plant type

Evergreen tree	Deciduous tree	Evergreen shrub	Deciduous shrub	Perennial plant	Biennial plant	Annual plant	Climber	Bulb	Water plant	Grass	Bamboo	Fern
♠	♀	♣	♡	⚐	⚐	⚐	⚐	⚐	≈	⚐	⚛	⚘

☼ ◌ Zones 5-9 ◌

Chaenomeles speciosa 'Moerloosei'
Bushy, many-branched shrub bearing pink and pink-tinged white flowers early in spring. White or blue tulips associate with it well.
H and S 10ft (3m).

☼ ◌ Zones 6-8 ♣

Hypericum 'Hidcote'
A dense, bushy shrub with dark green, evergreen foliage and an abundant display of large golden yellow flowers that lasts from midsummer through to autumn.
H and S 5ft (1.5m).

☼ ◔ Zones 7-9 ◌

Hydrangea aspera subsp. sargentiana
Growing larger than most hydrangeas, this bears downy leaves and large heads of lacecap flowers. It makes a handsome option for shade.
H 8ft (2.5m), S 6ft (2m).

☼ ◌ Zones 5-9 ◌

Buddleia davidii 'Harlequin'
Variegated foliage distinguishes this butterfly bush; its arching stems are topped by waving plumes of purple-red flowers in late summer.
H 15ft (5m), S 10ft (3m).

☼ ◌ Zones 8-10 ♣

Ceanothus impressus
Site this behind elegant lily-flowered tulips which will contrast beautifully with its shower of deep blue flowers; or train *Clematis viticella* through it to prolong its season of interest. H 6ft (2m), S 10ft (3m).

☼ ◊ Zones 5-9

Magnolia quinquepeta
‘Nigra’
A good species for small
gardens, this provides a
dramatic display of color from
spring to summer, with its
waxy, tuliplike flowers of deep
red-purple. H and S 12ft (4m).

☼ ◊ Zones 5-9

Rosa moyesii ‘Geranium’
This large, arching rose brings
a splash of scarlet into a color
scheme. Do not deadhead this
species, as the juicy fat hips
are a wonderful feature during
the autumn.
H 10ft (3m), S 8ft (2.5m).

☼ ◊ Zones 5-9

Rubus ‘Benenden’
A pretty shrub for light woodland or wilder areas, with its
unruly, arching habit. It looks
particularly effective in association with pink-flowering
shrub roses
H and S 10ft (3m).

☼ ◊ Zones 3-8

Syringa vulgaris ‘Madame
Lemoine’
The lilacs bring spring color
and scent. This double flow-
ered cultivar has panicles of
fragrant white flowers in late
spring and early summer.
H 12ft (4m), S 10ft (3m).

Viburnum x *burkwoodii*
Bears rounded white-pink flower
heads in spring.

☼ ◊ Zones 5-8

Philadelphus sp.
Among the most attractive of
the flowering shrubs, philadelphus can be relied on for its
masses of deliciously fragrant
white flowers in late spring
and early summer.
H and S 6ft (2m).

☼ ◊ Zones 2-9

Sorbaria sorbifolia
Fernlike foliage and panicles
of white summer flowers are a
good foil for spiky plants such
as phormiums and yuccas. Its
suckering habit can make it
invasive, so site carefully.
H 6ft (2m), S 10ft (3m).

OTHER PLANTS

Calycanthus occidentalis
Chimonanthus praecox
Choisya ternata
Cytisus spp.
Daphne spp.
Deutzia x *elegantissima*
Forsythia spp.
Fuchsia spp. and hybrids
Hebe spp.
Mahonia spp.
Pyracantha spp.
Skimmia japonica
Viburnum tinus
Weigela florida
    ‘Variegata’

ROUND SHAPES

There is something satisfying about neat plants that maintain their own inherently rounded form. Top of this list are the hebes; sages and lavenders are good, too. Rounded flower heads will always make useful points of emphasis: agapanthus, allium, and mop-head hydrangeas are all superb.

Ruta graveolens '**Jackman's Blue**'
The strong color of the filigree foliage makes this dome-shaped plant a good punctuation mark in a mixed border.

☀ ◊ Zones 5-9

Buxus microphylla 'Green Pillow'
This cultivar of dwarf box forms a neat dome of dark green, ideal as an evergreen punctuating element in a gravel or herb garden.
H and S 18in (50cm).

☀ ◊ Zones 4-9

Euphorbia polychroma
Forming a glowing mound of sulphur yellow in spring, this species of euphorbia is a good early performer, especially attractive among blue-flowering plants.
H and S 18in (50cm).

☀ ◊ Zones 9-10

Hebe 'White Gem'
A hebe that flowers well throughout early summer. Its compact habit and unassuming foliage make it an ideal structural plant in mixed plantings.
H and S 2¹/₂ft (75cm).

☀ ◊ Zones 6-9

Cytisus x praecox
The Warminster broom becomes a tumbling mass of creamy yellow blossom in late spring, and looks effective in combination with the bright blue of ceanothus.
H 4ft (1.2m), S 5ft (1.5m).

☀ ◊ Zones 7-9

Genista hispanica
A good subject for a sunny site or dry bank, making a prickly mound covered with yellow flowers throughout late spring and early summer.
H 2¹/₂ft (75cm), S 5ft (1.5m).

☀ ◊ Zones 7-9

Hydrangea involucrata 'Hortensis'
One of the loveliest hydrangeas, of usefully dwarf habit. In late summer and autumn, its domed profile has a mantle of pinkish white blossoms.
H 2¹/₂ft (75cm), S 3ft (1m).

OTHER PLANTS

Ceanothus 'Cascade'
Cryptomeria japonica 'Vilmoriniana'
Euphorbia characias subsp. *wulfenii*
Lavandula angustifolia 'Hidcote'
Olearia macrodonta
Potentilla fruticosa
Rosmarinus officinalis
Salvia officinalis
Skimmia japonica
Viburnum davidii
Viburnum opulus 'Compactum'

LAYERED SHAPES

The layered forms of many plants can provide striking visual effects in garden groupings, their horizontal line making them stand out. The cedar of Lebanon, for example, is a classic, its limbs sweeping to the ground, while other plants such as *Viburnum plicatum* 'Mariesii' and *Rhus typhina* can also make a linear statement.

Hosta fortunei *and* (top) **H. fortunei 'Aurea Marginata'** *The overlapping leaves of hostas give a layered effect.*

☼ ◊ Zones 5-8

Cornus kousa var. *chinensis*
Conspicuous white flower bracts cover this small tree in horizontal layers in early summer, and fine autumnal color follows.
H 22ft (7m), S 15ft (5m).

☼ ◊ pH Zones 5-9

Hamamelis japonica 'Sulphurea'
A colorful and faintly fragrant addition to the garden during winter, when delicate, spider-like yellow flowers are borne on bare branches.
H 12ft (4m), S 20ft (6m).

☼ ◊ Zones 4-9

Juniperus x *media* 'Gold Coast'
The branches of this hybrid of juniper spread themselves into layered mats: a good horizontal skeleton plant in small gardens or borders.
H 12in (30cm), S 6ft (1.8m).

☼ ◊ Zones 5-9

Cotoneaster horizontalis
This cotoneaster is showiest in late summer, when its fanning stems are clothed in red berries. The leaves turn crimson in autumn.
H 2ft (60cm), S 5ft (1.5m).

☼ ◊ Zones 9-10

Helichrysum petiolare
Throwing out angular shoots of small, hairy gray leaves, this helichrysum gives an excellent layered effect among container plants, or when used as ground cover in sunny borders.
H 12in (30cm), S 5ft (1.5m).

☼ ◊ Zones 4-9

Polygonatum x *hybridum*
The arching stems of this perennial, with their dangling flowers, provide an unusual horizontal element. It looks good in combination with anemones or lacy-leaved ferns.
H 4ft (1.2m), S 3ft (1m).

OTHER PLANTS

Cedrus libani
Hydrangea anomala subsp. *petiolaris*
Juniperus sabina var. ***tamariscifolia***
Mahonia spp.
Parrotia persica
Rhus typhina
Viburnum plicatum 'Mariesii'

FEATHERY EFFECTS

I have recently designated a piece of ground as a "lace" garden, and in it I am planting plants with feathery shapes. Nigella, Japanese maple, and fennel look good, as do the sartorial plumes of astilbe, while the frothing flowers of gypsophila are hard to beat. I find too that ferns are very much underused, surprisingly so since they survive in some of the most adverse sites — often shady, dry locations where little else will grow — and they are a joy when their jungly fronds are unfolding among spring bulbs.

☼ ◐ Zones 5-8   ♡

Acer palmatum 'Dissectum Atropurpureum'

The Japanese maples contribute wonderfully lacy foliage effects; this cultivar becomes a mound of dark purple, turning red and orange in autumn.
H 3ft (1m), S 5ft (1.5m).

☼ ◐ Zones 6-9   ♈

Crambe cordifolia

Crinkly leaves topped by frothing clouds of tiny summer flowers make this an attention-grabbing perennial for mixed border plantings or against dark shrub backgrounds.
H 6ft (2m), S 4ft (1.2m).

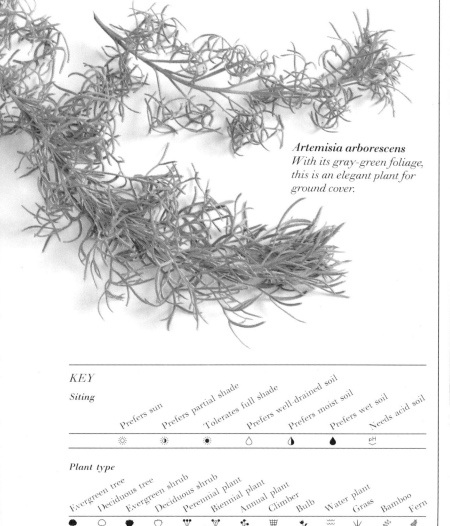

Artemisia arborescens
With its gray-green foliage, this is an elegant plant for ground cover.

☀ ◑ Zones 4-8   ♈

Astilbe x *arendsii* 'Venus'

Classic plants for the pondside or in the dappled shade of semi-woodland conditions, the astilbes bring a soft, feathery note with their plumes of flowers in summer.
H and S 3ft (1m).

KEY

Siting

Prefers sun	Prefers partial shade	Tolerates full shade	Prefers well-drained soil	Prefers moist soil	Prefers wet soil	Needs acid soil
☼	☀	☀	◊	◑	◆	pH

Plant type

Evergreen tree	Deciduous tree	Evergreen shrub	Deciduous shrub	Perennial plant	Biennial plant	Annual plant	Climber	Bulb	Water plant	Grass	Bamboo	Fern
♣	♀	♠	♡	♈	♈	♈	♣	♣	≋	∨	✿	🌿

☼ ◊ Zones 3-8

Dicentra spectabilis 'Alba'
Arched stems bearing heart-shaped flowers bow over delicate, feathery leaves which are elegantly ornamental in themselves.
H 2-2¹/₂ft (60-75cm), S 2ft (60cm).

☼ ◊ Zones 6-9

Perovskia atriplicifolia 'Blue Spire'
A feathery contribution to the sunny border, 'Blue Spire' is a graceful late-summer mass of flower spikes, violet-blue above finely cut gray foliage.
H 4ft (1.2m), S 3ft (1m).

☼ ◊ Zones 4-9

Foeniculum vulgare
With foliage as light and feathery as it is possible to find, fennel has a foaming green presence, contrasting refreshingly with large or coarse-leaved plants.
H 6ft (2m), S 18in (50cm).

☼ ◊ Zones 5-7

Pulsatilla vulgaris 'Rubra'
Feathered seed heads and fern-like leaves give a suggestion of fluffiness close to the soil in well-drained chalky areas. Silken buds and large, glowing red flowers look pretty in spring. H and S 6-9in (15-23cm).

☼ ◊

Nigella damascena 'Miss Jekyll'
'Miss Jekyll' has feathery, bright green leaves and small, pale blue flowers: a frothy annual for filling spaces in dry borders and gravel schemes.
H 18in (50cm), S 8in (20cm).

OTHER PLANTS

Acacia dealbata
Albizia julibrissin
Alchemilla mollis
Filipendula spp.
Gypsophila paniculata
Senecio bicolor spp.
  cineraria
Thalictrum lucidum

FERNS

Adiantum venustum
Asplenium scolopendrium
Matteuccia struthiopteris
Onoclea sensibilis
Polypodium vulgare

FERNS

☼ ◊ Zones 3-8

Asplenium trichomanes
An elegant maidenhair fern for nooks and crannies in damp walls and shady areas, or for containers. H 6in (15cm), S 6-12in (15-30cm).

☼ ◊ Zones 4-8

Dryopteris filix-mas
An excellent fern that blends well with woodland plants and is useful to help create the country garden feel.
H 4ft (1.2m), S 3ft (1m).

☼ ◊ Zones 10-11

Alsophila australis
The Australian tree fern forms a tall umbrella with long, ferny leaves. It adds a stylish "swampy" look to damp areas.
H 22ft (7m), S 15ft (5m).

SPIKES & SPIRES

The particular effect engendered by spiky plants is one I associate mainly with desert plant material – although the phormiums and cordylines from New Zealand also add a note of contrast to otherwise soft groupings. As well as these and other such examples of spiky foliage, there is a range of thistle-headed plants that give a different kind of spiky look: eryngium, echinops, onopordum (the Scotch thistle), and silybum. In addition to spikes, I am always looking for spires – foliage or flower heads to lend a vertical emphasis to a composition. Some perennials and grasses fulfil the need, while there are plenty of admirable spirelike blooms available. On a larger scale, fastigiate forms of deciduous trees and various conifers contribute pencil-like shapes.

KEY

Siting

Prefers sun	Prefers partial shade	Tolerates full shade	Prefers well-drained soil	Prefers moist soil	Prefers wet soil	Needs acid soil
☼	☼	☀	◊	◐	●	pH

Plant type

Evergreen tree	Deciduous tree	Evergreen shrub	Deciduous shrub	Perennial plant	Biennial plant	Annual plant	Climber	Bulb	Water plant	Grass	Bamboo	Fern

☼ ◊ Zones 9-11

Chamaerops humilis
An eye-catching dwarf fan palm, whose tropical-looking features make it a suitable subject in exotic schemes or in association with agaves and yuccas.
H and S 5ft (1.5m).

☼ ◊ Zones 4-9

Digitalis purpurea
Foxgloves are excellent in cottage and country garden schemes. The tall flower spikes of pink, red, and white lend a splash of color during the summer months.
H 3-5ft (1-1.5m), S 2ft (60cm).

Eryngium x oliverianum
The purple-blue, thistlelike heads of this perennial have a distinctly prickly effect.

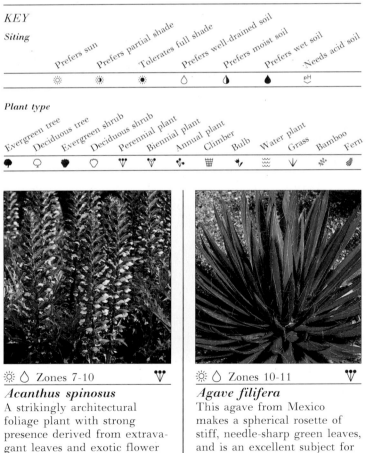

☼ ◊ Zones 7-10

Acanthus spinosus
A strikingly architectural foliage plant with strong presence derived from extravagant leaves and exotic flower stems. Looks good on its own and in a container.
H 4ft (1.2m), S 2ft (60cm).

☼ ◊ Zones 10-11

Agave filifera
This agave from Mexico makes a spherical rosette of stiff, needle-sharp green leaves, and is an excellent subject for arid Mediterranean or desert planting schemes.
H 3ft (1m), S 6ft (2m).

☀ ◊ Zones 10-11

Dracaena draco
Striking, pointed foliage makes this a good focal-point plant. The exotic-looking dragon tree thrives in hot, dry climates where it will grow into a tree of no small proportions. H and S 20ft (6m).

☀ ◊ Zones 5-9

Kniphofia uvaria
Red-hot pokers offer striking contrasts among shrubs in a mixed border, where their stiffly erect flower spikes are an eye-catching feature during the summer. H 4ft (1.2m), S 2ft (60cm).

☀ ◊ Zones 5-8

Lupinus 'Inverewe Red'
The majestic, densely packed heads of lupines are common favorites in country style mixed borders. Plant them in a mass for a striking display of color in early summer. H 3-4ft (1-1.2m), S 2ft (60cm).

☀ ◊ Zones 7-11

Yucca aloifolia 'Marginata'
The statuesque yuccas are excellent for sharpening up softer plant groupings. This variety is useful as a special in small gardens and as a container plant. H and S 5ft (1.5m).

☀ ◊ Zones 7-9

Eremurus robustus
The perennial foxtail lily will give a dramatic emphasis to flower borders in summer with its tall, pointed, spirelike racemes of tiny pink flowers. Straplike leaves precede the flowers. H 7ft (2.2m), S 3ft (1m).

☀ ◊ Zones 3-9

Lysimachia punctata
The bright yellow spires of this prolific perennial look especially effective in semi-wild plantings or anywhere a small-scale vertical emphasis is required.
H 2-2½ft (60-75cm), S 2ft (60cm).

OTHER PLANTS

SPIKES
Aciphylla squarrosa
Agave americana
Cordyline australis
Phormium tenax
Trachycarpus fortunei

SPIRES
Aconitum spp.
Beschorneria yuccoides
Carpinus betulus
  'Fastigiata'
Crataegus monogyna
  'Stricta'
Cupressus sempervirens
Delphinium spp.
Fagus sylvatica 'Dawyck'
Lythrum virgatum 'The
  Rocket'
Quercus robur
  f. *fastigiata*
Taxus baccata
  'Fastigiata'
Verbascum olympicum

LARGE LEAVES

Generously foliaged plants, whatever their scale, are invaluable in mixed plantings. Indeed a good clump of hosta or bergenia is just as useful a contrast as the massive *Gunnera manicata*. Large-leaved climbers, especially *Vitis coignetiae* and some of the ivies, have a powerful presence and make a bold contrast to the fluffy foliages of other climbing subjects, while other large-leaved plants – boggy rheums, ligularia, and rodgersia – look good positioned close to water.

KEY

Siting

Prefers sun	Prefers partial shade	Tolerates full shade	Prefers well-drained soil	Prefers moist soil	Prefers wet soil	Needs acid soil
☼	☀	☀	◇	◍	◆	pH

Plant type

Evergreen tree	Deciduous tree	Evergreen shrub	Deciduous shrub	Perennial plant	Biennial plant	Annual plant	Climber	Bulb	Water plant	Grass	Bamboo	Fern

☼ ◇   ♈
Brassica oleracea
Most often grown as annuals, cabbages, with their globes of huge, leathery leaves splashed with extravagant colors, can make an arresting sight in decorative plantings.
H and S 12-18in (30-50cm).

☼ ◇ Zones 7-9   ♧
Arum italicum 'Pictum'
With glossy, dark, flecked leaves that unroll through winter, when most perennials have died down, this is a useful addition to any garden.
H 6-10in (15-25cm),
S 8-12in (20-30cm).

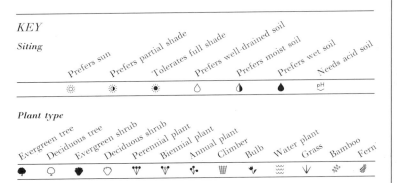

☼ ◇ Zones 3-8   ♈
Bergenia cordifolia
An excellent choice for ground cover in shady beds, bergenia has large, crinkly, leathery leaves which the winter frost burnishes to a handsome purple-red.
H 18in (50cm), S 2ft (60cm).

☼ ◇ Zones 8-11   ♣
Fatsia japonica
A statuesque plant with big, palmlike, glossy leaves, fatsia is useful as lush shade planting near the house, but has too tropical a feel for cottage or country style schemes.
H and S 10ft (3m).

☼ ◇ Zones 7-10   ♈
Gunnera manicata
A marshy monster of vast proportions that adds drama to large ponds and streams. Grow drifts of primulas and astilbes nearby to provide color in the spring and summer.
H 6ft (2m), S 7ft (2.2m).

☀ ◐ Zones 3-9 ♈

Hosta sieboldiana

The larger-leaved hostas are important plants for this category, with their strongly architectural forms and quilted leaf textures. The bluish green *sieboldiana* is one of the best. H 3ft (1m), S 5ft (1.5m).

☀ ◐ Zones 4-7 ♈

Veratrum album

The clumps of deeply pleated leaves can combine successfully with variegated hostas or spring bulbs. White flowers are borne on tall stems in late summer. H 6ft (2m), S 2ft (60cm).

Ligularia dentata 'Desdemona'
A large-foliaged perennial with crinkly, deeply veined leaves that have a strong tactile quality.

☀ ◌ Zones 5-9 ♈

Rheum palmatum

The ornamental rhubarbs are highly decorative with their deeply cut leaves and tall, branching flower spikes. They are good plants for wild areas and pondside groupings. H and S 6ft (2m).

☀ ◐ Zones 5-9 🗑

Vitis coignetiae

This spectacular and vigorous vine produces huge, textured leaves which overlap in dense layers and turn a magnificent crimson in autumn. Summer flowers are followed by purple fruits. H to 50ft (15m).

OTHER PLANTS

Catalpa bignonioides
Cynara cardunculus
Ficus carica
Hedera canariensis
Hedera colchica
Lysichiton camtschatcensis
Macleaya cordata
Paulownia tomentosa
Peltiphyllum peltatum
Rodgersia aesculifolia
Rodgersia tabularis
Trachycarpus fortunei

GRASSY EFFECTS

With an increasing concern for a more natural look, grasses are becoming very popular and you can see the effect of them *en masse* on pages 198-9. After their full flowering in autumn, the seed heads remain until cut down in spring, providing a great addition to the winter garden; to avoid a dull patch in early summer, combine grasses with bulbs and early-flowering perennials. Another way to prolong interest is to include the less invasive forms of bamboo, which retain their foliage when grown out of the wind. Select bamboos with care: overuse can convey too strong a Japanese flavor.

KEY

Siting

Prefers sun	Prefers partial shade	Tolerates full shade	Prefers well-drained soil	Prefers moist soil	Prefers wet soil	Needs acid soil
☼	☼	☀	◊	◖	●	pH

Plant type

Evergreen tree	Deciduous tree	Evergreen shrub	Deciduous shrub	Perennial plant	Biennial plant	Annual plant	Climber	Bulb	Water plant	Grass	Bamboo	Fern
●	♀	●	◇	❦	❦	❧	⊎	❦	≋	↓	❊	⫶

☼ ◊ Zones 7-11   ↓

Arundo donax var. **variegata**
A rampant spreading grass with broad leaves striped creamy white. Effective among bold, round-leaved plants and dark-foliaged shrubs.
H 8-10ft (2.5-3m), S 2ft (60cm).

☼ ◊ Zones 5-9   ↓

Carex pendula
This is an attractive sedge for planting among more colorful border plants, or in the company of variegated grasses. It bears graceful, pendant flowers in summer.
H 3ft (1m), S 12in (30cm).

☼ ◊ Zones 7-9   ❧

Dierama pulcherrimum
While technically a corm, this plant contributes a grassy look to a mixed planting, with its elegant, pendulous stems, bearing pink flowers in late summer.
H 5ft (1.5m), S 12in (30cm).

Phalaris
arundinacea var. *picta*
A spreading grass with broad, white-striped leaves and narrow spikes of flowers in summer.

☼ ◊ Zones 4-8 ⋁

Festuca glauca

The conspicuous gray-blue leaves of this small, tufted grass make it a striking plant for garden use and low ground cover. Good on dry soil. H and S 4in (10cm).

☼ ◊ ⋁

Lagurus ovatus

One of the prettiest hardy annual grasses, with its egg-shaped, soft white flower spikes in summer and long, flat leaves. H 18in (45cm), S 6in (15cm).

☼ ◊ Zones 5-11 ⋁

Miscanthus sinensis 'Zebrinus'

An excellent background grass in summer borders, with broad, yellow, irregularly spaced marks across its leaves, and white flower sprays. H 4ft (1.2m), S 18in (45cm).

☼ ◊ Zones 6-9 ⋁

Stipa gigantea

A graceful grass with tall stems of elegant, oatlike, silvery flowers that shimmer and shine through the summer months, making a striking clump in the border. H 8ft (2.5m), S 3ft (1m).

OTHER PLANTS

SEDGES

Carex elata 'Aurea'

GRASSES

Glyceria maxima 'Variegata'
Helictotrichon sempervirens
Molinia litoralis

BAMBOOS

Phyllostachys flexuosa
Shibataea kumasasa

BAMBOOS

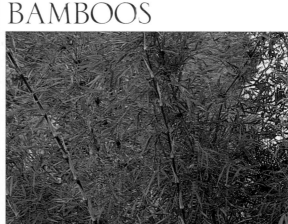

☼ ◊ Zones 6-9 ✻

Chusquea culeou

An evergreen, ornamental, clump-forming bamboo from Chile; it is slow-growing, and produces tall, leafy canes. H 12ft (4m). S 8ft (2.5m) or more.

☼ ◊ Zones 8-11 ✻

Arundinaria viridistriatus

The loveliest dwarf bamboo, with brilliant, refreshingly golden foliage, occasionally pencilled with thin, green stripes. H to 3ft (1m). S indefinite.

☼ ● Zones 6-11 ✻

Sasa veitchii

A handsome spreading bamboo, particularly effective by the pondside; its bladelike leaves develop creamy margins as the season progresses. H to 5ft (1.5m). S indefinite.

CREEPING & SPRAWLING SHAPES

I am very fond of this range of plant material, for these are the plants that overlay the plan's outline, generally loosening up and softening the look of the layout. I use this material at the edge of my planting areas, and if they adjoin gravel or paving, I will put a few plants in the prepared bed and one or two in the gravel or between the pavings to "speed up" the natural spreading process. If the plants are evergreen, all the better, as then I have the effect all year round. Many sprawling plants provide ideal ground cover, but before planting them, clear the ground of all weeds, since once they grow through they are difficult to remove.

☀ ◊ Zones 5-9

Epimedium x *versicolor*
This epimedium spreads its lovely fresh green and red-flecked foliage even through dry shade. Its delicate, yellow spring flowers make it an ideal partner for spring bulbs.
H and S 12in (30cm).

☀ ◊ Zones 4-10

Hebe 'Purple Queen'
A bushy shrub that looks effective in sunny borders. Plant *Lonicera nitida* 'Baggesen's Gold' (see page 317) behind to illuminate its deep purple flowers and dark green leaves. H and S 2½ft (75cm)

KEY

Siting

Prefers sun	Prefers partial shade	Tolerates full shade	Prefers well-drained soil	Prefers moist soil	Prefers wet soil	Needs acid soil
☀	☀	☀	◊	◊	●	pH

Plant type

Evergreen tree	Deciduous tree	Evergreen shrub	Deciduous shrub	Perennial plant	Biennial plant	Annual plant	Climber	Bulb	Water plant	Grass	Bamboo	Fern

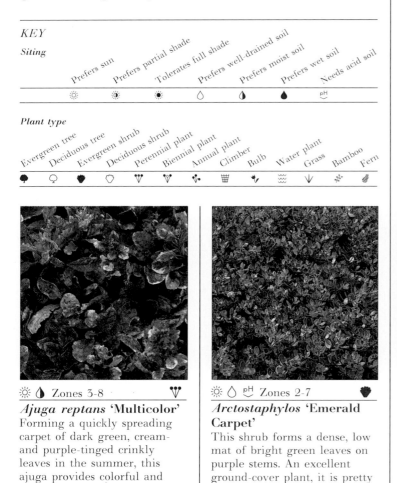

☀ ◊ Zones 3-8

Ajuga reptans 'Multicolor'
Forming a quickly spreading carpet of dark green, cream- and purple-tinged crinkly leaves in the summer, this ajuga provides colorful and effective ground cover.
H 5in (12cm), S 18in (50cm).

☀ ◊ pH Zones 2-7

Arctostaphylos 'Emerald Carpet'
This shrub forms a dense, low mat of bright green leaves on purple stems. An excellent ground-cover plant, it is pretty among heaths and azaleas.
H 12in (30cm), S 5ft (1.5m).

☀ ◊ Zones 4-8

Geranium 'Johnson's Blue'
The cranesbill geraniums flop gently from their crowns, making sprawling mounds of nodding leaves. This desirable hybrid has abundant, luminous purple-blue summer flowers.
H 12in (30cm), S 2ft (60cm).

☼ ⬤ Zones 4-8 ♨

Lamium maculatum 'Album'
The white-flecked form of deadnettle creeps in spreading mats, ideal for border edges and between pavings. Little white flowers appear in spring. H 8in (20cm), S 3ft (1m).

☼ ⬤ Zones 4-9 ♡

Rosa 'Rosy Cushion'
The ground-cover roses make good flower-decked sprawlers; this pink cultivar has glossy leaves and looks good among the blues and silvers of perovskia and echinops. H 3ft (1m), S 4ft (1.2m).

☼ ⬤ Zones 4-9 ♨

Stachys byzantina
Grow the soft lambs' ears for their large, tactile, felty leaves. The woolly, silver-gray, light-reflective foliage makes them good front-of-border plants. H 12-15in (30-38cm), S 2ft (60cm).

☼ ⬤ Zones 5-7 ♣

Taxus cuspidata 'Aurescens'
The Japanese yew is a useful, spreading background evergreen. Its needlelike foliage is golden yellow when young, maturing to dark green. H 12in (30cm), S 3ft (1m).

Sedum spectabile

Sedum alboroseum **'Medio-variegatus'**

☼ ⬤ Zones 6-9 ♣

Lavandula angustifolia 'Hidcote'
Lavender is a useful sprawler for softening the edges of paths and cottage style borders. 'Hidcote' has violet flowers and a reasonably compact form. H and S 2ft (60cm).

CLIMBERS & WALL PLANTS

Structures softened visually by climbers are an enduring feature of European gardens, with roses a common first choice, especially in association with clematis. I prefer the small-flowered species of clematis as I find them less blowzy. Evergreen wall subjects always have a place and among my favorites is ivy. Vines are good too, especially with the light shining through their leaves, and there is a whole range of undervalued wall shrubs — ceanothus, carpenteria, solanum, and azara.

Parthenocissus quinquefolia
Virginia creeper has a good leaf color for walls or buildings.

Vitis coignetiae
A vigorous vine with leaves that turn crimson in autumn.

☼ ◊ Zones 4-9　　　🗑

Actinidia kolomikta
An attention-grabbing deciduous climber with tricolor, heart-shaped leaves, so vividly and strikingly colored that on a warm wall this plant will make a feature on its own.
H 12ft (4m).

☼ ◊ Zones 8-11　　🖤

Azara microphylla
With deliciously vanilla-scented yellow flowers in early spring, dark glossy foliage and elegantly branching stems, this shrub or small tree is effective against a white wall.
H 20ft (6m), S to 15ft (5m).

☼ ◊ Zones 7-9　　🖤

Carpenteria californica
A handsome wall shrub, carpenteria has long, dark green leaves and during the summer bears lovely, large, fragrant white flowers with yellow centers.
H and S 6ft (2m).

KEY

Siting

Prefers sun　Prefers partial shade　Tolerates full shade　Prefers well-drained soil　Prefers moist soil　Prefers wet soil　Needs acid soil

☼　☼　☀　◊　◗　●　pH

Plant type

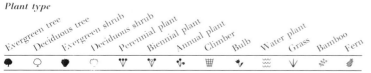

Evergreen tree　Deciduous tree　Evergreen shrub　Deciduous shrub　Perennial plant　Biennial plant　Annual plant　Climber　Bulb　Water plant　Grass　Bamboo　Fern

☀ ◊ Zones 6-9   ♛

Clematis montana
An early-flowering deciduous
clematis with profuse quantities of small, single flowers. It
is a vigorous climber for large
areas of wall or for scrambling
over fruit trees. H 22-36ft
(7-12m), S 6-10ft (2-3m).

☀ ◊ Zones 7-10   ♛

Pileostegia viburnoides
With its flower heads of tiny
white flowers, this is an
excellent evergreen woody-
stemmed climber that gives
good, dense, year-round cover
for concealing eyesores and
ugly views. H to 20ft (6m).

☀ ◊ Zones 7-9   ♠

Pyracantha rogersiana
The pyracanthas give a year-
round wall display. Pruning
can make them dramatically
two-dimensional; they seem to
hug the wall with their flower-
and berry-laden branches.
H and S 10ft (3m).

☀ ◊ Zones 8-11   ♛

**Trachelospermum
asiaticum**
Given time and a sunny position, this twining evergreen
climber will cover ugly fences
and structures with its creamy
summer flowers and glossy
foliage. H to 20ft (6m).

☀ ◊ Zones 7-9   ♛

Tropaeolum speciosum
The herbaceous flame creeper
bears exotic scarlet flowers in
summer. Its light-colored
foliage will enliven dark
evergreens, and these, in turn,
will enhance its bright colors.
H to 10ft (3m).

☀ ◊ Zones 7-9   ♠

**Jasminum humile
'Revolutum'**
A useful evergreen wall subject
with glossy, bushy foliage and
large, fragrant, bright yellow
flowers from early spring to
late autumn.
H 8ft (2.5m), S 10ft (3m).

☀ ◊ Zones 5-9   ♛

Lonicera periclymenum
Relaxed and scrambling, this
honeysuckle is a lovely deciduous climber for cottagey
gardens. Its fragrant, dark red
and yellow-white flowers
appear in summer.
H to 22ft (7m).

☀ ◊ Zones 4-9   ♛

Rosa 'New Dawn'
A climbing rose that is a great
performer: vigorous, fast-
growing, and a prolific flower-
er, bearing pearly pink blooms
over a long season. Lovely
with pale blue clematis.
H and S 15ft (5m).

OTHER PLANTS

Berberidopsis corallina
Campsis grandiflora
Ceanothus spp.
Cobaea scandens
**Fremontodendron
  californicum**
Hedera spp.
Humulus lupulus 'Aureus'
Hydrangea anomala
  subsp. **petiolaris**
Jasminum officinale
**Solanum jasminoides
  'Album'**
Wisteria floribunda 'Alba'

INFILLERS

By infillers I mean the bulbs and self-seeders that can be used as stopgaps between permanent shrubs and trees (see also pages 132-3). A newly planted garden can have a whole range of infillers in its first year to bulk up the still-young shrub material and provide points of interest within the overall scheme. Position infillers randomly, planting bulbs such as tulips and daffodils in groups as they fall and scattering seeds about to create a pleasantly ragged look, a sort of organized disarray. Alliums are excellent around the base of a new shrub and clumps of forget-me-nots, planted in drifts, make ideal infill in the spaces between shrubs. For a wonderful cottagey abundance, sow poppies, nasturtiums, alchemillas, and sunflowers.

KEY

Siting

	Prefers sun	Prefers partial shade	Tolerates full shade	Prefers well drained soil	Prefers moist soil	Prefers wet soil	Needs acid soil
	☀	☀	☀	◐	◑	●	pH

Plant type

Evergreen tree	Deciduous tree	Evergreen shrub	Deciduous shrub	Perennial plant	Biennial plant	Annual plant	Climber	Bulb	Water plant	Grass	Bamboo	Fern
●	♀	♣	♡	♈	♈	❦	⊞	❦	≈	↓	✿	✾

☀ ◐ Zones 3-9   ❦

Erythronium dens-canis
When naturalized under trees and shrubs, the dog's-tooth violet, with its dainty spring flowers and speckled leaves, makes a charming infill plant. H 6-10in (15-25cm), S 3-4in (8-10cm).

☀ ◑ Zones 4-9   ♈

Euphorbia cyparissias
This euphorbia has fresh green, feathery foliage, and quiet lime green flowers in late spring. It will spread itself around, providing a good degree of ground cover. H and S 12in (30cm).

☀ ◐ Zones 4-8   ♈

Alchemilla mollis
The felty leaves and frothing summer flowers of lady's-mantle make excellent infill in virtually any garden. It also seeds itself prolifically, providing good ground cover. H and S 18in (50cm).

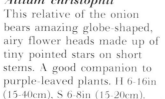

☀ ◐ Zones 4-10   ❦

Allium christophii
This relative of the onion bears amazing globe-shaped, airy flower heads made up of tiny pointed stars on short stems. A good companion to purple-leaved plants. H 6-16in (15-40cm), S 6-8in (15-20cm).

☀ ◐   ❦

Eschscholzia californica
Infillers can be striking in themselves: hardy California poppies with their vibrant orange summer flowers could make a bold contrast to blue cornflowers and delphiniums. H 12in (30cm), S 6in (15cm).

☀ ◌   ❦

Felicia bergeriana
Use in gaps in sunny borders for a frothing mass of blue-and-yellow daisylike flowers. Good when grown in containers, too, in association with *Helichrysum petiolare* 'Limelight'. H and S 6in (15cm).

☀ ◌ Zones 8-10   ❦

Nerine bowdenii f. *alba*
In its white and pink forms, this bulb gives a showy display of flowers through autumn. It is a fine companion to the silver-colored *Artemisia arborescens*. H 18in-2ft (50-60cm), S 5-6in (12-15cm).

☀ ◌   ❦

Nicotiana Domingo Series
The tender tobacco plant's advantages as infill are its long flowering season, its fragrant flowers, its tolerance of sun or shade, and its tenacious ability to self-seed. H and S 12in (30cm).

☀ Zones 3-9   ❦

Narcissus 'Sun Chariot'
Narcissus is always an ideal infill choice for early spring. 'Sun Chariot' is good in short grass and gravel, or planted to precede perennial foliage. H 6in (15cm).

Verbascum nigrum 'Album'

Verbascum bombyciferum

☀ ◌ Zones 4-9   ❦

Papaver orientale
The oriental poppies are useful self-seeding infillers, with their exciting colors, dramatic seed heads, and rosettes of toothy leaves. H 3ft (1m), S 12in-3ft (30cm-1m).

OTHER PLANTS

Alstroemeria, Ligtu Hybrids
Anemone blanda
Arisaema sikokianum
Arum italicum 'Pictum'
Crocus spp.
Cyclamen spp.
Digitalis purpurea
Felicia amelloides 'Santa Anita'
Lilium regale
Lunaria annua
Moluccella laevis
Sisyrinchium spp.
Tropaeolum majus

SILVER LEAVES

Silver- and gray-leaved plants can play a strong role: they lighten a green grouping and introduce texture to an otherwise smooth mass of vegetation with their often hairy or woolly leaves. *En masse* in winter they can look strikingly in keeping with the colors of the season, while some of the taller gray plants make useful focal points during the summer.

Cynara scolymus
The statuesque, frondlike leaf of the globe artichoke.

☼ ◊ Zones 8-10

Hebe recurva

Open and lax in habit, with slender white flowers and narrow, bluish silver leaves, this hebe complements sun-loving cistus and helianth-emums.
H 2ft (60cm), S 2½ft (75cm).

☼ ◊ Zones 5-8

Artemisia ludoviciana
var. *incompta*

Forming a low mass of foaming, feathery leaves, this is perfect for a dry, sunny spot, and an ideal partner for magenta-colored roses and pink cistus. H and S 2½ft (75cm).

☼ ◊ Zones 7-9

Cytisus battandieri

Its shimmering, silvery green leaves joined in summer by large, bright yellow pineapple-scented flowers, the pineapple broom is an interesting feature shrub for any garden.
H and S 13-14ft (4.5m).

☼ ◊ Zones 8-11

Convolvulus cneorum

A plant that sprawls and romps about. Its silky, silvery leaves shimmer in sunlight and from late spring to late summer it has white flowers with yellow centers.
H and S 2½ft (75cm).

☼ ◊ Zones 5-8

Eryngium giganteum

The metallic, silvery sheen and spiny character of this thistle make it an excellent plant for sunny borders and gravel schemes, complementing pinks, blues, or yellows. H 3-4ft (1-1.2m), S 2½ft (75cm).

☼ ◊ Zones 7-9

Verbascum olympicum

With its tall, woolly spikes and bold rosettes of fleshy, silver leaves, this verbascum seeds itself freely, making eye-catching punctuation marks in sunny gardens.
H 6ft (2m), S 3ft (1m).

PURPLE LEAVES

Used sparingly and in relation to silver or gray plants, purple- and bronze-leaved subjects can make an emphatic color statement. It is during autumn, however, that these plants – the deeply colored Japanese maples and the glossy purple-bronze of pittosporum, for example – really come into their own against the oranges and reds of the season.

Foeniculum vulgare
'Purpureum'
Bronze fennel

☼ ◊ Zones 5-9

Acer palmatum 'Bloodgood'
The deeper-colored Japanese maples can be somber and dark, but bright green bamboos and grasses will enliven them and sound the right stylistic note. H and S 10ft (3m)

☼ ◊ Zones 5-9

Cotinus coggygria 'Purpureus'
The rich wine-purple foliage of this smokebush can be dramatically enhanced by airy allium flower heads, as here, or silvery eryngiums.
H and S 15ft (5m).

☼ ◊ Zones 6-9

Salvia officinalis 'Purpurascens'
A purple cultivar of the culinary sage. The roughly textured leaves and purple flowers are at their best among silvers.
H 2ft (60cm), S 3ft (1m).

☼ ◊ Zones 5-9

Berberis thunbergii 'Atropurpurea'
Phormium tenax or glaucous yuccas set off the dusky, ruddy foliage of this berberis. Or try it beside *Rosa glauca* with its purple-gray leaves and delicate flowers. H and S 6ft (2m).

☼ ◊ Zones 9-10

Pittosporum tenuifolium 'Tom Thumb'
One of the most eye-catching of the purple/bronze-leaved shrubs. Its high-gloss leaves with their undulating edges reflect the sunlight dramatically.
H and S 2¹/₂ft (75cm).

☼ ◊ Zones 5-9

Weigela florida 'Foliis Purpureis'
This shrub has subtle purplish bronze leaves and funnel-shaped, pale pink flowers. Associates well with silver-variegated ajugas at its feet.
H and S 5ft (1.5m).

OTHER PLANTS

Acer platanoides 'Royal Red'
Atriplex hortensis 'Rubra'
Canna x *generalis*
Euphorbia amygdaloides 'Purpurea'
Phormium tenax 'Purpureum' and 'Bronze Baby'
Rheum palmatum 'Atrosanguineum'
Sedum telephium subsp. *maximum* 'Atropurpureum'
Viola labradorica

GOLDEN LEAVES

Golden-foliaged plants are always uplifting, always bright and sunny-looking; in real sunlight they positively glow with well-being. Planted in moderation, the odd gold-leaved plant will visually lift a flat green grouping; the combination of gold with gray or purple I find too strong an accent altogether, though. The golden hop, *Humulus lupulus* 'Aureus', is an excellent rampant herbaceous gold climber, and I like the ever-popular *Robinia pseudoacacia* 'Frisia'. Golden foliage mixes well with yellow and lemon flowers, and looks good, too, in combination with blues.

☀ ◊ Zones 6-8   ♀

Acer shirasawanum f. *aureum*
A slow-growing tree or shrub with lobed leaves of handsome yellow. This maple looks particularly pretty when grown on the edge of light woodland. H and S 20ft (6m).

***Philadelphus coronarius* 'Aureus'**
The foliage has a lovely golden freshness in spring.

☀ ◊ Zones 2-8   ♡

Cornus alba 'Spaethii'
The leaves of this vigorous and undemanding dogwood are conspicuously edged with gold. Good in mixed borders, it will also brighten up somber evergreens.
H 6ft (2m), S 5ft (1.5m).

☀ ◊ Zones 5-9   ♀

Gleditsia triacanthos 'Sunburst'
A graceful, proud tree: the golden yellow foliage of early summer is seen to best effect against a dark background of evergreen shrubs.
H 36ft (12m), S 22ft (7m).

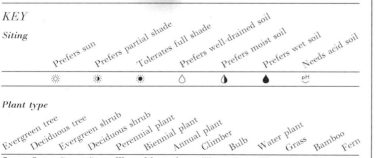

KEY

Siting

Prefers sun	Prefers partial shade	Tolerates full shade	Prefers well-drained soil	Prefers moist soil	Prefers wet soil	Needs acid soil
☀	☼	☀	◊	◑	◆	pH

Plant type

Evergreen tree	Deciduous tree	Evergreen shrub	Deciduous shrub	Perennial plant	Biennial plant	Annual plant	Climber	Bulb	Water plant	Grass	Bamboo	Fern
●	♀	❀	♡	❦	❦	❧	❦	⊞	❦	≈≈	∨	❦	❧

☼ ◊ Zones 8-9 ⊞

Hedera helix 'Buttercup'

This aptly named ivy with bright, buttery leaves is useful for lighting up dull walls and shady corners and is effective among darker ivies and other nonvariegated foliage plants. H 6ft (2m), S 8ft (2.5m).

☼ ◊ Zones 7-9 🍂

Lonicera nitida 'Baggesen's Gold'

A bright, versatile shrub covered in small, golden, light-reflecting leaves. Its spreading branches give it a loose but bulky outline; clip it for a neat shape. H and S to 5ft (1.5m).

☼ ◊ Zones 4-8 ☷

Origanum vulgare 'Aureum'

The pale gold mound of wild marjoram looks most effective when allowed to ramble over stones and gravel; its color and flavor develop best in sun. H 3in (8cm), S indefinite.

☼ ◊ Zones 4-7 ⬡

Sambucus racemosa 'Plumosa Aurea'

Golden yellow, deeply cut, feathery leaves give this elder an airy appearance. Deep purples and blues show off its handsome foliage to best effect. H and S 10ft (3m).

☼ ◊ Zones 6-9 ⊞

Humulus lupulus 'Aureus'

Rampant and bright, scrambling over everything nearby, this herbaceous climber forms dense layers of overlapping, greenish yellow leaves. H to 20ft (6m).

☼ ◊ Zones 4-9 ⬥

Robinia pseudoacacia 'Frisia'

The golden, layered foliage of the false acacia lights up any garden. An elegant feature on its own, it is also effective against a dark background. H 50ft (15m), S 22ft (7m).

☼ ◊ Zones 4-7 ⬡

Spiraea japonica 'Goldflame'

The early leaves emerge fiery orange, yellowing and greening as they age. The heads of pink summer flowers make this a useful shrub for flower borders. H and S 3ft (1m)

OTHER PLANTS

Catalpa bignonioides 'Aurea'

Euonymus fortunei 'Emerald and Gold'

Filipendula ulmaria 'Aurea'

Hypericum x *inodorum* 'Summergold'

Iris pallida 'Variegata'

Philadelphus coronarius 'Aureus'

Taxus baccata f. *aurea*

BOG & WATER PLANTS

Garden pools and water gardens can be beautiful as long as they are not simply an artificial, scaled-down version of what occurs in the wild. Natural areas of water are usually quite open and uncluttered and the way in which a limited range of reeds and marginals group themselves in drifts, becoming thinner where the water is deeper, should be a model for the way you use your water plants: for maximum effect use more plants of fewer varieties. Many water plants are interesting architecturally, since through lack of oxygen at the root they have adapted themselves to having a greater leaf area above water. Bog plant selection has to be governed by the seasonal variation in water levels; each plant must be suitable for the depths of water available.

:☼: ◐ Zones 4-9 〰

Caltha palustris

Grow this pretty plant in shallow water or moist soil at the pondside, where its glorious, golden yellow flowers can be seen to their best advantage reflected in the water.
H 2ft (60cm), S 18in (45cm).

:☼: ◐ Zones 4-8 ⚚

Ligularia stenocephala

A distinguished feature plant for the pondside or bog garden, bearing spires of bright yellow flowers above its mound of round, jagged-edged leaves.
H 4ft (1.2m), S 2ft (60cm).

KEY

Siting

Prefers sun	Prefers partial shade	Tolerates full shade	Prefers well-drained soil	Prefers moist soil	Prefers wet soil	Needs acid soil
☼	◑	☀	◇	◐	◆	pH

Plant type

Evergreen tree	Deciduous tree	Evergreen shrub	Deciduous shrub	Perennial plant	Biennial plant	Annual plant	Climber	Bulb	Water plant	Grass	Bamboo	Fern
♣	♤	♠	♡	⚘	⚚	⚛	⚶	⚭	〰	⌄	⁂	❦

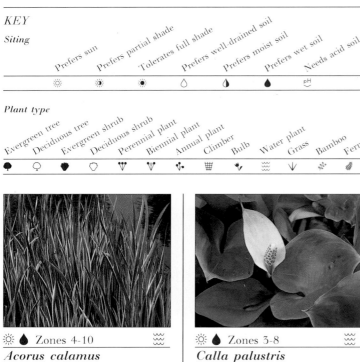

:☼: ◆ Zones 4-10 〰

Acorus calamus 'Variegatus'

With its swordlike, striped leaves, this plant complements large-leaved plants, such as rheum and rodgersia. It thrives in boggy ground.
H 2½ft (75cm), S 2ft (60cm).

:☼: ◆ Zones 3-8 〰

Calla palustris

This marginal water plant has broad, glossy leaves which contrast well with variegated irises and sedges. Red fruits follow the large white flowers that emerge in spring.
H 10in (25cm), S 12in (30cm).

:☼: ◆ Zones 5-9 ⚚

Iris pseudacorus

The flag iris, with its cheerful, bright yellow flowers and tall, upright, straplike leaves, looks lovely in spring, growing among bog primulas at the water's edge.
H to 6ft (2m), S indefinite.

☀ ● Zones 7-9 〰

Lysichiton americanus x camtschatcensis

This bog arum needs deep mud, from which dramatic pale yellow spathes emerge in spring. Huge leaves follow, particularly striking in summer. H and S 2½ft (75cm).

☀ ● Zones 5-9 〰

Nymphaea odorata 'Firecrest'

The serene and classic beauty of a waterlily will enhance any water garden. 'Firecrest' has green-purple leaves and pink flowers.
S to 4ft (1.4m).

☀ ● Zones 6-8 〰

Primula florindae

An ideal poolside primula with elegant yellow flowers borne on tall stems in summer. It is particularly pretty among irises, white astilbe, and yellow lysimachia.
H 2ft (60cm), S 12in (30cm).

☀ ● Zones 6-9 〰

Typha minima

This marginal water plant is grown for its fine, grassy leaves and cylindrical seed heads. It is not too invasive, so is suitable for smaller ponds.
H 2ft (60cm), S 12in (30cm).

Persicaria milletii
Spikes of crimson flowers and green straplike leaves look admirable rising above water.

9

FURTHER
WORKING
INFORMATION

*In this section I have included some techniques of
drafting to supplement your drawing skills further, and
to encourage you to move from a simple plan to
more complex drawings based upon it. Also included
are various items of practical information intended
to enable you, at the very least, to hold your own
in discussions with a client or contractor. I have always
supposed that knowing what you need to know is
halfway to learning, so I make no apology for saying
that most of what appears on the following pages should
be supplemented with further specialized reading.
I hope you will feel inspired to go on to expand your
skills and your understanding of design.*

LANDSCAPE SYMBOLS

H ere is a visual glossary of the symbols I use on plans. The symbols for structures cover primarily the hard garden surfaces such as walls, steps, and different types of paving; those for planting indicate the various types of trees, shrubs, perennials, and other plants. On plan the symbols are drawn to scale wherever possible, and make the transition from the broad outline plan to the detailed structural and planting plans. There are no hard and fast rules governing the symbols that you use; the important thing is that you can distinguish between the different elements. When drawing a symbol, I keep it simple and generally try to make it look as much as possible like the shape of the plant or structure it is representing – so, for instance, a spiky architectural symbol is good for a yucca. On plans, I also draw symbols with a different weight of line, depending on how dominant the feature is. So the tallest trees, the highest walls, and the house, for example, would be shown by a bold line, and paving slabs a fine line. Templates of symbols are available.

STRUCTURAL

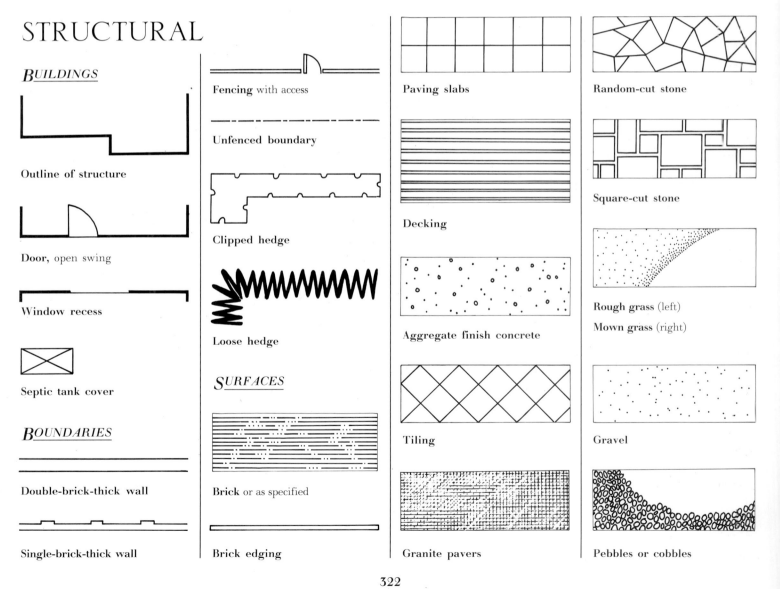

BUILDINGS

Outline of structure

Door, open swing

Window recess

Septic tank cover

BOUNDARIES

Double-brick-thick wall

Single-brick-thick wall

Fencing with access

Unfenced boundary

Clipped hedge

Loose hedge

SURFACES

Brick or as specified

Brick edging

Paving slabs

Decking

Aggregate finish concrete

Tiling

Granite pavers

Random-cut stone

Square-cut stone

Rough grass (left)

Mown grass (right)

Gravel

Pebbles or cobbles

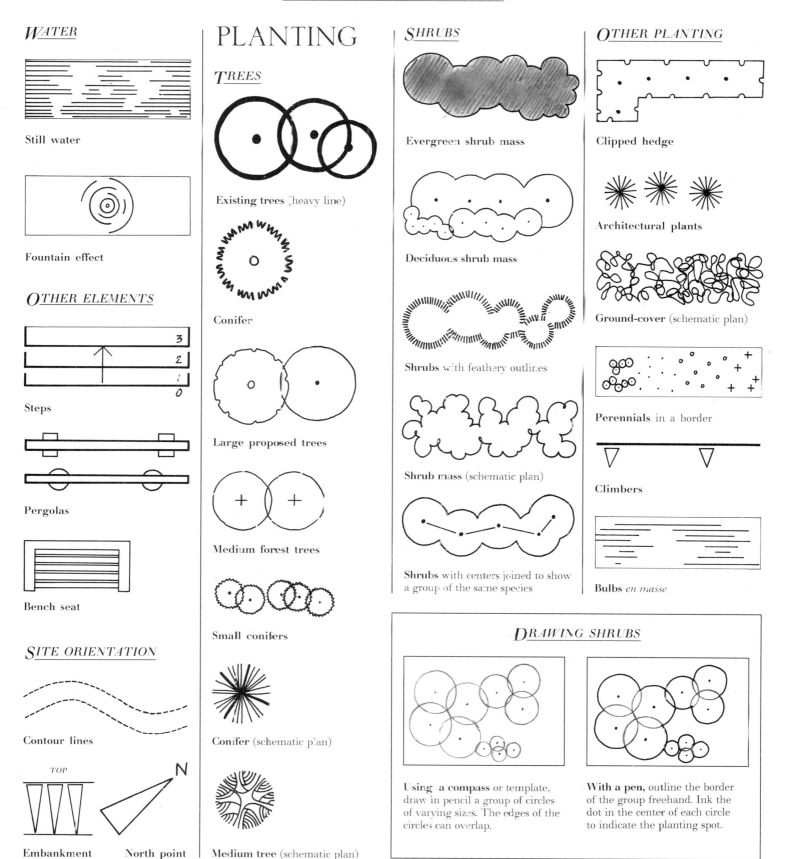

WATER

Still water

Fountain effect

OTHER ELEMENTS

3
2
1
0

Steps

Pergolas

Bench seat

SITE ORIENTATION

Contour lines

TOP
N

Embankment   *North point*

PLANTING

TREES

Existing trees (heavy line)

Conifer

Large proposed trees

Medium forest trees

Small conifers

Conifer (schematic plan)

Medium tree (schematic plan)

SHRUBS

Evergreen shrub mass

Deciduous shrub mass

Shrubs with feathery outlines

Shrub mass (schematic plan)

Shrubs with centers joined to show a group of the same species

OTHER PLANTING

Clipped hedge

Architectural plants

Ground-cover (schematic plan)

Perennials in a border

Climbers

Bulbs en masse

DRAWING SHRUBS

Using a compass or template, draw in pencil a group of circles of varying sizes. The edges of the circles can overlap.

With a pen, outline the border of the group freehand. Ink the dot in the center of each circle to indicate the planting spot.

DRAWING TECHNIQUES

As you are preparing a design, you should be carrying in your mind's eye not only the ultimate styling of it, but the height of the walls and the type of steps that you are planning two-dimensionally. Projections, elevations, and possibly a perspective drawing are all useful techniques for helping you to refine your concept and resolve its problems more fully.

A projection is three-dimensional. It brings height into your design, and also allows you to see how the scale of the plan is working overall, how the component parts of the garden relate to the structures surrounding it – the fence, the wall, and above all the house. With a projection, you can resolve the look of any steps, retaining walls, or tricky small details that you have included in your design. If you are designing for others, a projection explains your structural concepts and it will eventually help whoever has to build the garden too. Remember that the vertical dimensions will be to the same scale as the horizontal ones.

An elevation is a scale drawing of the external face of a structure, without any perspective. It is different from a section, which shows a slice through the structure. A good way of understanding the difference between the two is to think of an orange: a slice of the orange, such as might be used to garnish a drink, is a section; a side view, showing just the skin, an elevation. When drawing an elevation from a garden plan you may in the process show some parts of it, such as a boundary wall, in section, as in the example on page 326.

A perspective drawing is another way of representing an aspect of your future garden three-dimensionally. I have always found the need to produce a perspective drawing fairly limited, even though it is rather more realistic than a projection. Nevertheless, it is useful to know the method for producing a one-point perspective.

A SIMPLE PROJECTION

A projection gives the impression of a third dimension of depth, but without perspective. To produce a projection, you will need a T-square and either a 90° x 45° x 45° triangle or a 90° x 60° x 30° one. This simple exercise for projecting a house demonstrates the basic projection techniques.

1 Using a 90° x 45° x 45° triangle and a T-square, draw a plan of a square box. Turn the plan 45° so that the box sits on a point.

2 Move your triangle along to project the box corners vertically upwards; make the lines the same length as the base plan sides.

3 Using the 45° edge of your triangle, join up the sides of the box to form a cube. Imagine the cube as a house with a flat roof.

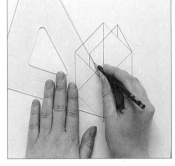

4 Now add a pitched roof. At the top of the cube, project a vertical line up from the midpoint of one of the sides forming the flat roof. Repeat on the opposite side and join the two lines together at the top. Lastly, join the ends of the lines you have just drawn to the corners of the cube on each side.

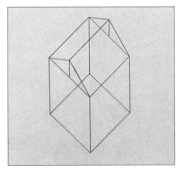

5 You now have a simple projection of a house. Its angle looks slightly strange – as if you are looking down from your neighbor's roof – but this does not matter.

PROJECTING A PLAN

This sequence follows on logically from the house projection and shows you how to apply the same basic principles to a working drawing. I have taken as my example the plan for the walled town garden on pages 170-3. In the exercise, a 90° x 45° x 45° triangle is used. For any plan that already incorporates shapes at 45°, project using the 30° or 60° edge of the other triangle.

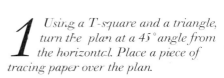

1 Using a T-square and a triangle, turn the plan at a 45° angle from the horizontal. Place a piece of tracing paper over the plan.

2 With the 90° edge of the triangle, project the verticals of the perimeter wall. Draw in the top of the wall with the 45° edge.

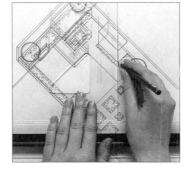

3 Now draw in the other verticals and 45° lines on the plan. You will need to turn the triangle around for some of the 45° lines.

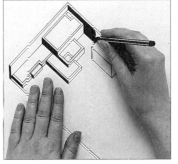

4 Roughly shade in some of the projected faces with a felt-tip pen to give the drawings depth and form.

Intermediate stage

The plan is now three-dimensional and you are starting to see how the garden spaces relate to the surrounding structures.

Finished projection

By now you should have the feeling that you are looking in on the garden. Adding in existing trees shows how the planting relates to the structures.

ELEVATION

In this simple exercise, a section has been taken through the plan for the walled town garden on pages 170-3 to show the end of the garden – the different levels of walls, the built-in bench seat, and trees – in elevation. The exercise illustrates how you can use an elevation to establish the heights of the structures, making any modifications as you go along, although if you have already done a projection, you can take the heights from this.

Walled garden, right
The view of the garden seen in elevation below.

The section line, right
This is the line from which the elevation is taken. Here it is drawn along the foot of one of the overlapping rectangular walls.

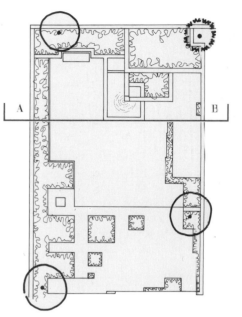

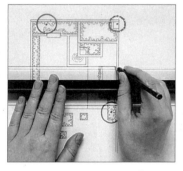

1 Choose the part of the plan that you want to see in elevation. Then place a piece of tracing paper over the plan and, with the T-square, draw a horizontal line – the section line – across the plan.

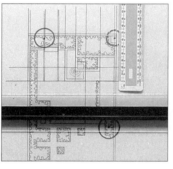

2 Project a vertical line up from the section line through each line that is at right angles to it. Next, add the horizontals, working to scale and establishing heights for the structures.

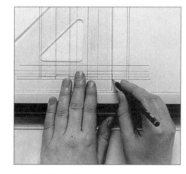

3 You have created a framework of horizontal and vertical lines and, by referring back to your original plan, you can now accurately draw in the shapes of the structures.

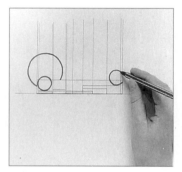

4 Erase any grid lines that you have not used, and draw in the outline shapes of trees with a felt-tip pen. Add in any trees outside the boundary that would appear in the view, too.

The finished elevation
Notice that foreground structures have been emphasized with a thicker line. As structures become more distant, they have been drawn with a progressively finer line.

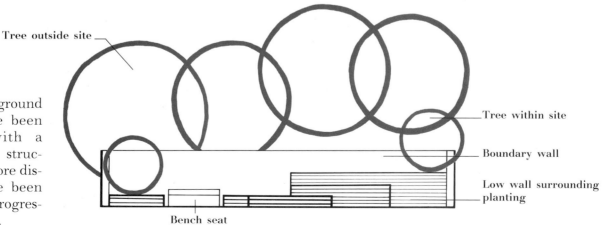

Tree outside site

Tree within site

Boundary wall

Low wall surrounding planting

Bench seat

ENLARGING THE SCALE

There are various ways to enlarge the scale of a drawing. You can use scaled dimensions, going from ⅛"–1' 0" to ¼"–1' 0", for instance. For accurate angles, place your enlarged version over the original and trace the angles from it. You may also use a pair of compasses to double the scale, by doubling the original widths. For greater accuracy, place a grid over your plan at, say, an equivalent to a fifteen-foot interval on site, and draw the grid at its enlarged scale, taking dimensions from the original plan and transposing them to the new size. In more difficult areas, use scaled dimensions within individual squares. A small plan can be enlarged on a photocopier: check it carefully.

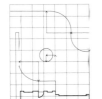

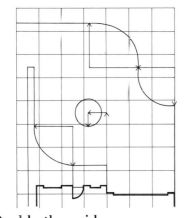

Double the grid

This plan has been enlarged to twice its size by doubling the dimensions of the grid square.

PERSPECTIVE

The simplest type of perspective is one-point perspective, and it is on this that I will focus. However, it is also useful to look at two-point perspective so that you know the difference between the two.

I have chosen to produce a one-point perspective of the walled town garden featured on pages 172-3. Do not be deterred by the drawings on these pages; this type of construction looks much more complicated than it really is.

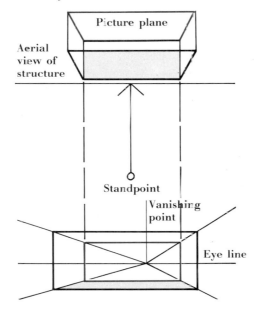

One-point perspective

This occurs when a structure is looked at straight on from a fixed standpoint. When this is drawn on the plan, all the parallel lines from the standpoint to the object appear to converge into the object in the perspective drawing to meet at an imaginary point at eye level, called the vanishing point.

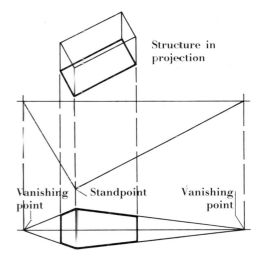

Two-point perspective

When a structure is viewed at an angle, each visible side seems to disappear into its own vanishing point.

A PERSPECTIVE DRAWING

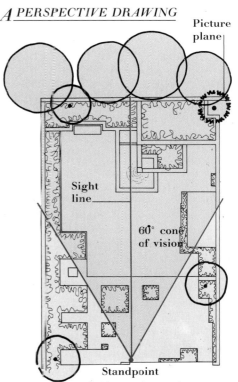

1 *Using the schematic plan, choose the view that you wish to realize and your standpoint. Draw a line on the plan from the standpoint to the picture plane. The line will be central to what is known as the cone of vision, a splay no more than 60° wide. (Continues overleaf)*

A PERSPECTIVE DRAWING *continued*

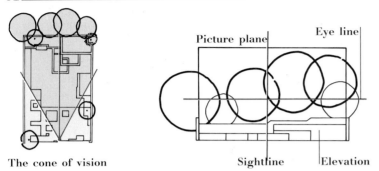

The cone of vision

Picture plane — Eye line

Sightline | Elevation

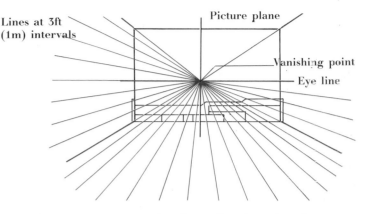

Lines at 3ft (1m) intervals

Picture plane

Vanishing point
Eye line

2 *Using an elevation of the view, draw a horizontal line across at eye level. You can choose where this eye line goes: mine is 13ft (4m) high as the garden is viewed from a balcony. The junction of the eye line and the sightline is the vanishing point.*

3 *From the vanishing point, draw a line through each corner of the picture plane. Mark off its sides – I have taken a 3ft (1m) interval – and draw lines from the vanishing point through each of the 3ft (1m) marks, making a radiating pattern.*

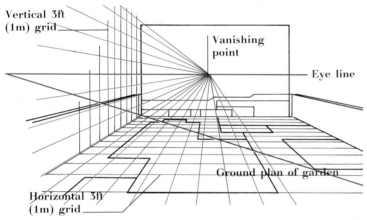

Vertical 3ft (1m) grid

Vanishing point

Eye line

Ground plan of garden

Horizontal 3ft (1m) grid

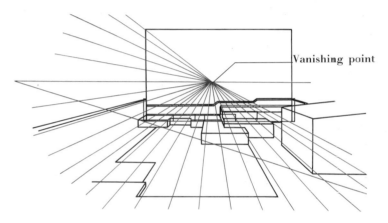

Vanishing point

4 *Measure the distance on the plan in step 1 between the standpoint and the picture plane. Mark this dimension on the eye line to either left or right of the vanishing point. From the mark describe a line through the nearest bottom corner of the picture plane, and continue it across your 3ft (1m) lines. Where the diagonal meets a 3ft (1m) line at the base of your pro-jection area, draw a horizontal line. You have established a grid in perspective onto which you can transfer your layout from the plan. Draw verticals at 90° to the horizontals for a vertical 3ft (1m) grid as well.*

5 *You can now project the elevational drawing in your picture plane forwards, for the elevation gives you the height of each feature. Take a line from the vanishing point through each point in your elevation, and start to construct a series of boxes, linking up all the sides. At any one horizontal point, check your vertical dimensions using the vertical grid. Slowly your one-point perspective will come to life as you add more and more details.*

Distorted perspective Outside the 60° cone of vision, your one-point perspective quickly becomes distorted.

Cone of vision

6 *Instead of erasing the network of grid lines, it is easier to place a piece of tracing paper over your one-point perspective and trace over the shapes of the structures. Add in any large trees that are in the view, too.*

ERGONOMICS

How broad should the terrace be, or how high a pergola? What is the right width for a path or a car turnaround? These are questions to which there really is no stock answer. The designer evolves a solution to each situation; the common denominator, however, is the human form and, to a degree, the machines that we use.

As a general rule, everyone seems to function more or less in the same way: our bulk, either singly or *en masse*, our adult height, and the length of our pace are relatively standard. A clue to the ergonomics of a garden is the proportions of the living quarters of the house. Most of us live in fairly small spaces: 14 x 20 feet for a living room is average. Moved outside, these dimensions would not be generous, given that furniture for summer living is often bulkier than that inside, so proportions for garden spaces generally need to be larger.

TERRACE SPACE

When working on plans, I always think of a person lying down – approximately 6ft (2m) in length – and I use this measurement of scale to check the size of a terrace for a chaise longue. You can measure your own or proposed garden furniture for lounging or dining and then allow at least three feet all around for access and for moving the furniture about easily.

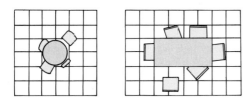

Tables and chairs on an 18in (500mm) grid

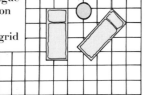

Chaise longue and table on an 18in (500mm) grid

Minimum dimensions

These diagrams show the minimum practical space for accommodating different furniture combinations on a terrace so it does not feel cramped.

PERGOLA HEIGHT

I would also relate pergola height to human form, making the verticals at least 7½ft (2.5m) high. The appearance of this height, however, will vary according to the spacing of the verticals, and the dimension of the material of which they are made or the bulk of plant growth upon them. A pergola that is to be used only for sitting and not as a pathway can of course be lower.

DRIVEWAYS AND FORECOURTS

Skimping on the space that you allow for a driveway or a forecourt in front of the house or garage can prove disastrous to neighboring areas of grass or planting, for a definite amount of room is needed to park a car and to drive it in and out. A good width for a driveway is 12ft (3.5m); where this becomes a forecourt to a garage, it must noticeably broaden, allowing a car to approach and reverse into the garage. Allow space for visiting cars to park, too.

Turning arc, right

Because only the front wheels of a car turn, a driveway curve must be at least one third wider than the vehicle itself.

PATH WIDTH

It is usually said that a path should be wide enough for two people to walk easily side by side, and the dimension of 3ft (1m) is quoted. I personally like a width of at least 5ft (1.5m), to allow for the invasion of plants on either side of the path. Therefore, let your dimensions be as generous as possible.

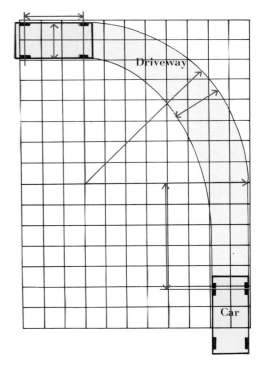

Driveway

Car

LANDSCAPING

Before any surfacing or utilities are laid, it is essential to get the grading of the site correct. The landscaping necessary will depend on the site and your proposed design. You may be incorporating a swimming pool, a tennis court, or a parking space, all of which will require significant earthworks at an early stage during the construction of the garden. There may be other elements on the plan, too, that will require using machinery for excavation.

It is useful to look at how contours work and what grading is all about. On page 151, I discussed small changes of elevation and how to calculate them; now it is the turn of the whole site.

CONTOURS & ELEVATIONS

Generally, there is no site that is perfectly flat, for theoretically all ground is quantified by an elevation calculated from sea level as the mean or zero. On plans, elevations are described by flowing lines known as contours. When you change the grading within your site, for example to put in a new driveway, you adjust the contours, although they will be the same where they enter and exit the site — otherwise you would be adjusting the grades of your next door neighbor's garden.

TAKING ELEVATIONS

Before adjusting contours, you need to know what the existing elevations in your site are; the steeper the site, the more there will be. If you are working with an architect, you may well find that your elevations have been taken already. Failing this, ask a surveyor to provide you with spot elevations across your site, expressed as plus or minus readings from a fixed point that you decide on, such as the front door step. You can then interpolate between those spot elevations to build up your own contours.

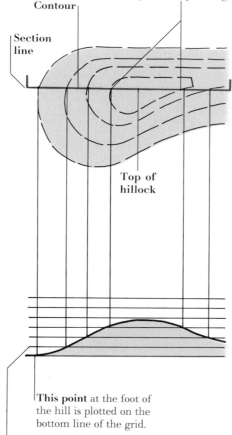

Points on the same contour are plotted on the same grid line as they are at equal height.

Contour

Section line

Top of hillock

This point at the foot of the hill is plotted on the bottom line of the grid.

The distance between the horizontal lines represents to scale the contour intervals.

A SIMPLE EXERCISE

As a general rule, the closer together your elevations are, the steeper the bank that they represent. To understand this concept, try the hillock exercise below.

Contours in plan

Draw a plan of a hillock, putting in contours which you conceive of as 18in (500mm), or any other convenient measurement, apart. Draw a line across the center of the hillock from which you can drop a section.

Contours in section

Below the plan, draw a series of horizontal lines at the same scaled intervals as the contours. Then, plot the points on the plan where the contours and section line meet by dropping vertical lines down to the horizontals. If you join the points up where the bottom of your vertical lines meet the horizontal lines, you have a hillock section. You will see that by opening out your contours you reduce the gradient of a bank; a mower is not supposed to be used on a gradient of more than 30° from the horizontal. Thought of in this way, you are beginning to infuse theory with practicality.

ADJUSTING CONTOURS

You should now be able to conceive of your garden as being covered with contours, particularly if it is on a steep site. You should see how you would adjust the contours to put in a driveway or a path, for example, so that it is level; and how in a limited space, it is easy to get too many contours too close together, and you therefore need a retaining wall to hold the steep bank.

By checking your adjusted contours with regular sections, you can see the amount of earth that you are theoretically moving, and you can check that what you excavate or cut equals what you spread or fill. This way you are using all your soil on site and not having to remove anything or import soil or fill. At this stage, only adjust contours in subsoil.

You should work with the contours to adjust a planting area laid over them so that the shape of a bed runs with a contour rather than against it. Geometric shapes placed at random on contoured ground appear unsympathetic; always try to achieve an organic unity.

Changed contours

The existing contours in this site have been adjusted to put in features such as a swimming pool, parking spaces, and level lawns. Soil from excavations has been used to mound up banking Where contours enter or exit the site, they have been left unchanged, so that the grading of the surrounding terrain is not altered.

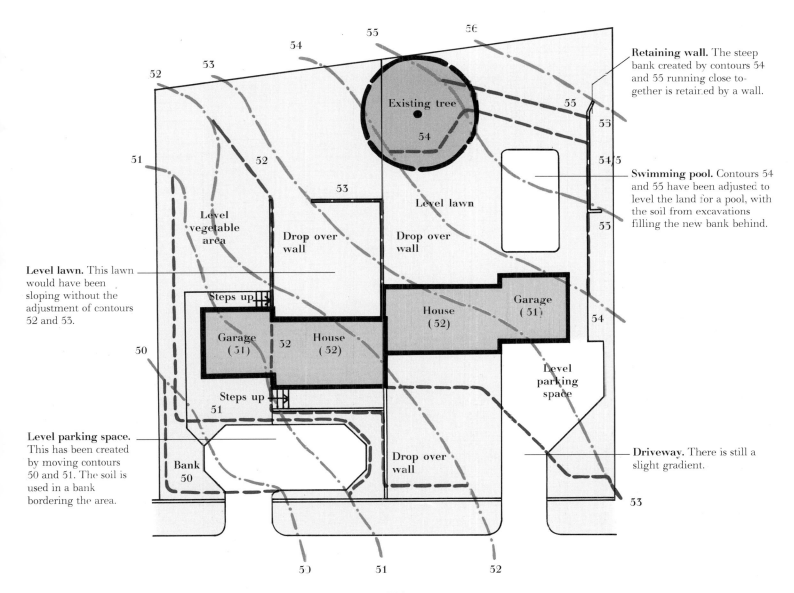

Retaining wall. The steep bank created by contours 54 and 55 running close together is retained by a wall.

Swimming pool. Contours 54 and 55 have been adjusted to level the land for a pool, with the soil from excavations filling the new bank behind.

Level lawn. This lawn would have been sloping without the adjustment of contours 52 and 53.

Level parking space. This has been created by moving contours 50 and 51. The soil is used in a bank bordering the area.

Driveway. There is still a slight gradient.

Existing tree

Level lawn

Level vegetable area

Drop over wall

Drop over wall

Steps up

Garage (51)

House (52)

House (52)

Garage (51)

Level parking space

Steps up

Drop over wall

Bank 50

PLANNING THE UTILITIES

At an early stage, you should consider whether the site needs drainage or irrigation, or cables laid for outside lighting. Any such work must be done before building work begins. The arrangement of pipes or cables will vary according to location: drainage pipes, for example, may have to be laid around rocks or tree roots, and the pattern of electrical cables will depend on where the power is needed. These hidden elements of constructing a garden, or groundworks, need to be costed where they apply and will naturally affect the price of a landscape job. So, include details in the written specifications accompanying the design plans that you give to the landscape contractor.

LAYING OUT THE DRAINAGE SYSTEM

A full underground drainage system is only necessary when the site, or parts of it, has standing water on its surface for long periods. In such a system, flexible plastic pipes will be laid in a pattern and to a depth according to location, with minor runs feeding a main channel, leading to a nearby ditch.

DRAINAGE FIELD

This is a hole, 3ft (1m) square and 3ft (1m) deep, partially filled with rubble, the surface of which will eventually be 3ft (1m) below the finished surface level of the earth above it. A flexible drainpipe is led to the drainage field which, like a reservoir, stores surplus water, allowing it to seep out gradually into the surrounding earth. After the drainage field has been capped with a porous mat and backfilled with earth, it may be planted over, but will probably need to be redug every ten years or so, depending on the soil around it. There may be more than one drainage field on a site, all of which should be sited at a distance from the house.

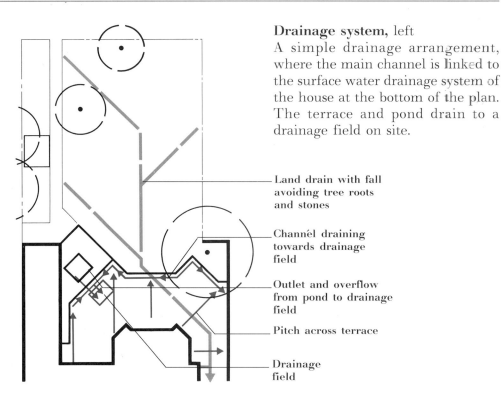

Drainage system, left
A simple drainage arrangement, where the main channel is linked to the surface water drainage system of the house at the bottom of the plan. The terrace and pond drain to a drainage field on site.

Land drain with fall avoiding tree roots and stones

Channel draining towards drainage field

Outlet and overflow from pond to drainage field

Pitch across terrace

Drainage field

Constructing a drainage field, right
Dig a hole to a depth of 6ft (2m), fill to 3ft (1m) with rubble or large gravel, and cap it with a permeable mat, available from garden suppliers, to prevent earth from trickling into the drainage field and eventually "choking" it. Then fill the hole to surface level with 3ft (1m) of topsoil.

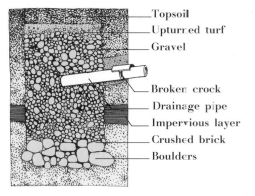

Topsoil
Upturned turf
Gravel

Broken crock
Drainage pipe
Impervious layer
Crushed brick
Boulders

IRRIGATION

There are various forms of irrigation; one general system consists of a grid of underground pipes, which supply a series of sprinklers with pop-up valves. It works on the pressure of the water, which, when turned on, pushes up a retractable valve just above ground level, creating a circular spray of water. The valve sinks down when the system is switched off; this is especially useful on a lawn as it facilitates mowing. Individual water pressures will give differing spray circles, so the distance between valves varies according to location; call in a local irrigation expert. If you are working for a client and propose to do this, ask the expert for an estimate, and submit it to your client. If your client agrees, let him sign the contract with the expert. Do not sign it yourself.

Irrigation system, right
A full irrigation system, joined to the house mains, where the sprinkler heads are positioned so that the garden is soaked evenly.

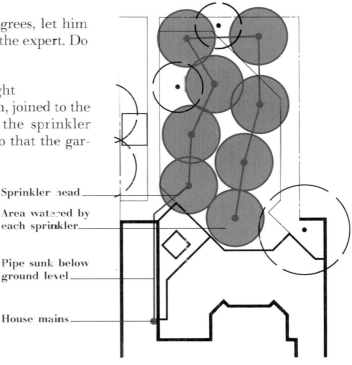

Sprinkler head

Area watered by each sprinkler

Pipe sunk below ground level

House mains

ELECTRICITY

Always engage the help of an experienced electrician before doing any electrical work. Use three-wire romex direct-burial cable and lay it in a marked or known situation, such as along the bottom of a wall or the side of a path, at the depth mandated by local building codes. Where the cable comes above ground, you may be required to run it through a protective conduit of some sort.

Garden circuit
This simple garden circuit, connected to the garage supply, powers a water pump and lighting.

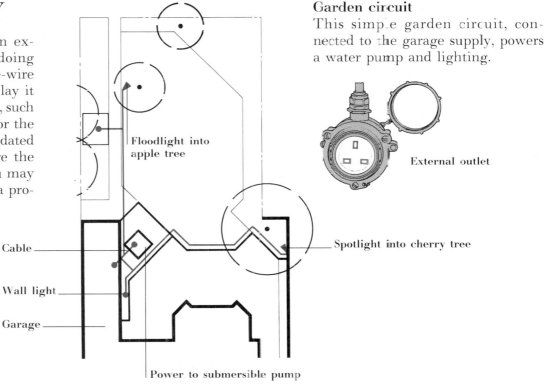

Floodlight into apple tree

External outlet

Cable

Wall light

Garage

Spotlight into cherry tree

Power to submersible pump

CONSTRUCTION DETAILS

The following pages outline the basic construction techniques and considerations to bear in mind if you are designing or building a structure yourself or briefing someone else to do the work for you. Where the depth of the foundations and the amounts of the materials are specified, this is only a guideline; these details will vary from area to area.

If you are at all doubtful about the safety of any structure you have designed, seek specialist advice from either a structural engineer or an architect. Miscalculation on detailing and a resultant collapse of the structure can be dangerous and expensive, so ensure your details are right from the outset. Even if you are employing a building contractor to do the work for you, have your details checked carefully, although few builders will erect an unsound structure knowingly. When briefing them, it is always worth asking their advice on how they would build your structure.

Before erecting a structure, such as a garden building, check that you do not require a building permit and that the proposed building doesn't violate any community building codes.

PAVING

The foundations you use beneath your paving elements depend on the surface's intended function: a driveway, for instance, will take far heavier wear than a terrace. Under the driveway, you will need to lay crushed stone with a covering of concrete, and on this you lay your final surface. Concrete is not always necessary where the surface is only for walking upon. The specifications for the foundations will depend on your location, the amount of frost in winter, and local building codes. In areas of great cold, paving for heavy use must have deep foundations so that the frost does not lift the surfacing; where the paving is only for pedestrian use, a thin sand base is adequate, allowing the frost to lift the paving, which can then be reconsolidated in spring. Lay all paving at a slight pitch to allow for drainage — into nearby planting or gravel, or a specially constructed drainage field (see page 332). It should never be pitched towards a building.

SMALL UNITS

Whether bricks, pavers, or any of the other options, small paving units are likely to shift after laying because of their size and relatively light weight. For normal wear, this can be avoided by setting them in a mortar base over a layer of crushed stone. For heavier wear, a thicker layer of crushed stone will need to be covered with a layer of concrete. Before fixing units, lay them out loose to ensure the pattern works.

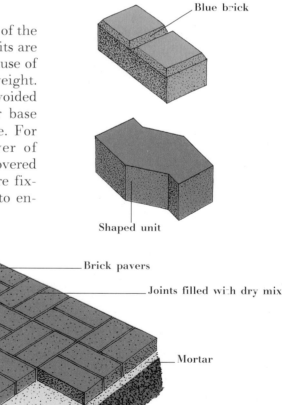

Blue brick

Shaped unit

Brick pavers

Joints filled with dry mix

Mortar

Base of crushed stone

PRECAST SLABS

For normal use, lay a crushed stone base of about 4in (100mm), covered with 2in (50mm) of builder's sand if the slabs are heavy, or a mixture of sand and cement if they are smaller and so need to be held more firmly. Most paving for heavy use will need about 6in (150mm) of crushed stone under 3in (75mm) of concrete

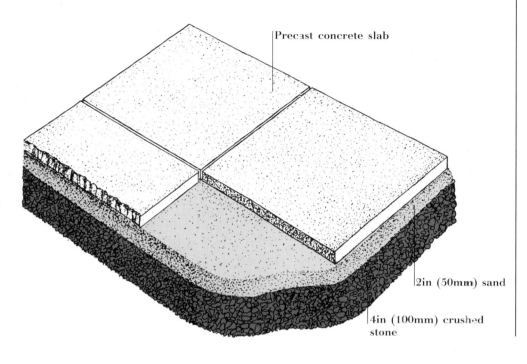

Precast concrete slab

2in (50mm) sand

4in (100mm) crushed stone

JOINTING

The jointing between paving or bricks is a sand and cement mix, known as mortar. This is brushed dry into the joints when the paving units are in position, and gradually hardens as it absorbs moisture from the ground. The mix can be colored to create different effects, although this is usually only applicable for walls, since at ground level a mortar infill always discolors with damp and usage.

Start looking closely at paving stones as you walk around and at the various techniques that are used for jointing: some mortar projects above the paving stone, some is recessed, sometimes there is none and the clean edge of a paving stone is "butt-jointed," or butted up tight against its neighbor.

STEPS

Step construction varies greatly, depending on the materials used to make the steps, which in their turn complement the other architectural features on the site. Broadly, it is similar to laying paving or building a retaining wall (see page 339), as each riser – the vertical part of the step – is a miniature retaining wall. Set each step firmly in mortar over a concrete and crushed stone base, and ensure that there is adequate drainage. To determine the number of steps that you need, measure the change of elevation across the slope (see page 151) and divide it by the riser height. Step dimensions are more or less standard, depending on comfort for the user (see overleaf).

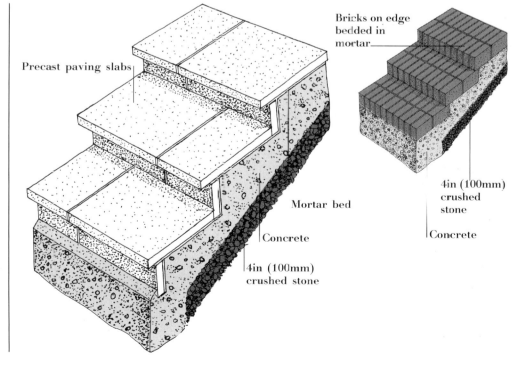

Precast paving slabs

Mortar bed

Concrete

4in (100mm) crushed stone

Bricks on edge bedded in mortar

4in (100mm) crushed stone

Concrete

CALCULATING STEP DIMENSIONS

There are equations for the correct relationship of riser to tread (the horizontal part of the step), but broadly, for ease of use, each riser should be between 5in (125mm) and 9in (230mm) high, with the tread between 12in (305mm) and 18in (460mm) wide. Any more or less than this is disturbing to walk up, since you will have to change your pace. Another useful rule for getting the relationship between the height of the riser and the breadth of tread right is twice the riser plus the tread should equal 26in (660mm). So with a 4in (100mm) riser, you will need a 18in (460mm) tread; allow for a very slight pitch forward on the tread, included in the riser dimension, to drain water off the steps. However, there are probably many steps that do not conform to these dimensions, and you should also consider the height, and consequently the natural step width, of each individual who regularly uses them.

DECKING

Wooden decking needs strong poured concrete footings or foundations below ground level into which are set piers of brick or precast concrete. These in turn provide the base for wooden posts, which support a wooden framework of joists and beams on which the deck sits. The structure is fixed together with galvanized fasteners. Where decking adjoins a different surface, such as paving or concrete, or a door, construct a drainage channel below the junction. Decks need a damp-proof course, and a simple way of doing this is to put a layer of plastic sheeting under the joists in the wooden subframe.

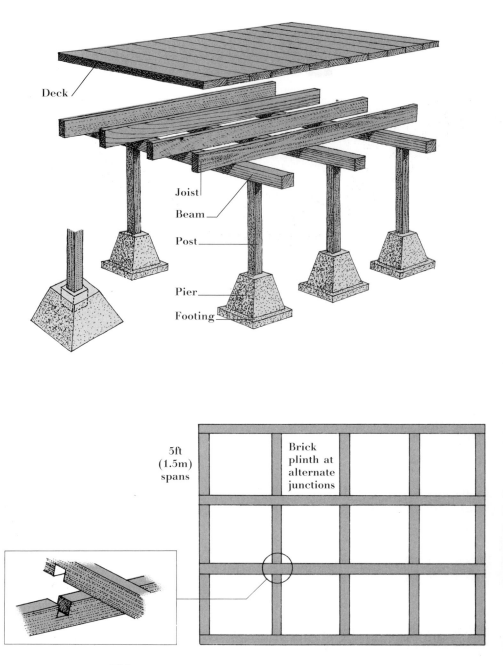

Low-level decking
To avoid weeds growing underneath and through the deck, spread black plastic sheeting between the wooden supporting posts and cover any visible parts of the sheeting with pebbles or gravel.

Wooden frame, right
The decking is nailed to a subframe constructed of pressure-treated wood. The size of the individual planks used will depend on local building code requirements as well as the estimated load that the deck is intended to handle.

GRAVEL

To construct a semihard gravel surface which is easy to walk on and through which plants will grow, excavate to a depth of approximately 6in (150mm) and roll and pack into this a layer of bankrun gravel; since this gravel has clay in it, it will harden when it combines with moisture. Then, roll a thin layer of clean loose gravel chips into the layer of packed down gravel. If your soil is very spongy, dig deeper and stabilize the area with a layer of crushed stone before rolling the bankrun gravel into it. When laying gravel next to grass or an area of planting, you could use wooden, brick, or concrete edging to prevent the areas from merging.

Planting in gravel, below
Create a planting pocket in a gravel surface by using a metal spike to make a hole through the layers, so that the roots of the plant can reach the soil below.

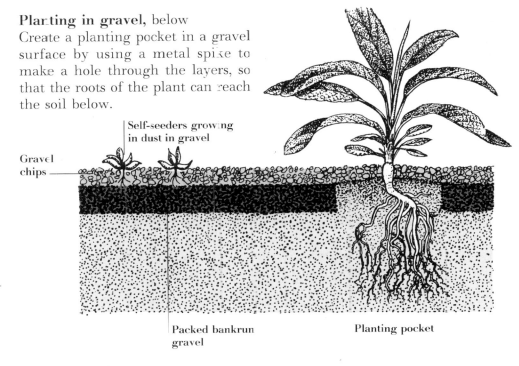

Self-seeders growing in dust in gravel

Gravel chips

Packed bankrun gravel

Planting pocket

ESTABLISHING A LAWN

If you are employing a contractor to do this work for you, make sure that he maintains the lawn until it is established to your satisfaction – whatever the length of the grass – and gives it at least three mowings. When preparing an area of ground to be laid in turf or seeded, cultivate the soil well and level it. Then, after removing any large stones with a rake, firm the surface.

Mowing edge, below
You will facilitate mowing if you construct a brick or concrete mowing edge at the foot of any structures bordering the lawn.

Lawn

Mowing edge

TURF OR SOD LAWN
Before laying a turfed, or sodded, lawn, ask about the source of the turf you propose to use, and even go to see it before it is lifted, if you can. Make sure it is in good condition and free of weeds. If you are laying turf on a steep bank or gradient, you may need to peg each sod so it stays in place. When newly laid, turf must be well watered so that individual sods do not dry out and shrink.

USING TURF & SEEDS
When establishing a new lawn, I use a combination of turf and seeds. Around the edge of the lawn, I lay an outline of turf to make a clean laid edge where the turf meets an area of planting or hard-surfaced area, then I sow seed to infill. The type of seed used will vary according to the soil and location (see pages 228-9).

WALLS

All walls need strong and stable footings. The depth of these varies, depending on the wall's height, its intended function, the type of soil, the level to which frost occurs, and local building codes. I have been amazed when working recently in North America to find how deep the footings have to go to avoid frost for even the smallest wall, so this sort of detail is highly localized.

When designing any wall over 3ft (1m) in height, seek a structural engineer's advice on both the depth of its footings and its manner of construction, for a collapse could endanger life and expose you, if you are working for a client, to substantial financial liability.

BRICK WALLS

A brick wall can be of various thicknesses and of different arrangements of bricks (bonds), each thickness and bond having differing strengths and being right for a particular place. Bricks laid horizontally across the wall are called stretchers, and bricks laid end-on are called headers. The courses of bricks are laid from the poured concrete foundation, and great care should be taken to ensure that the wall is square, both horizontally and vertically. The density of a wall determines the frequency with which supporting piers or buttresses are needed, but it is possible to do without these, for example by building the wall in a zigzag or a serpentine shape.

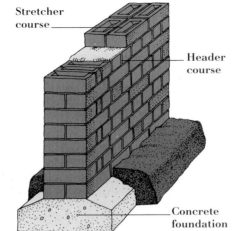

Stretcher course

Header course

Concrete foundation

English bond brick wall
The bonding used in this wall is known as English bond, with the bricks laid in alternate courses of stretchers and headers.

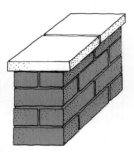

Brick on edge   Concrete slab

Coping
Since only the outer side of a building brick is fired for weather protection, a brick wall needs capping, or coping, along the top, either with the same brick on edge or with some other appropriate material.

CONCRETE BLOCK WALLS

This is the cheapest form of wall construction, since the blocks are usually larger than bricks or stones and so quicker to lay. Solid concrete blocks are half as deep as the hollow blocks and have to be supported by piers, the number of piers that you need for each three feet of wall depending on the structure, height, and function of the wall. Hollow-core blocks are usually kept for strengthening a retaining wall but when they are used in a standard wall, their large size usually obviates the need for piers.

Wall strength
Staggering a wall in a zigzag fashion or stepping it backwards and forwards by the thickness of a brick makes piers unnecessary.

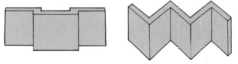

Overlap   Zigzag

STONE WALLS

Most stone walls are made of cut stone, which is either laid coursed, so that the stones line up, or randomly, if rounded fieldstone is used. The gaps between the stones may be filled with mortar or laid dry – without mortar – in the traditional way. Walls of reconstructed stone blocks are always laid with mortar joints. The materials used for capping stone walls vary depending on location, as do the footings for the wall.

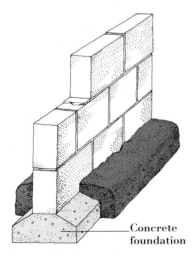

Concrete foundation

Concrete block wall
This is set in a similar concrete foundation to that of a brick wall.

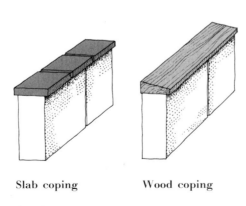

Slab coping   Wood coping

Coping
Finish a concrete block wall with a protective capping. Precast paving slabs work well, as do bricks, stones, or wood.

RETAINING WALLS

Whether made of brick, concrete, or stone, a retaining wall may have to support the full wet weight of the soil behind it, so it is essential that it is strong and has proper drainage. Always seek specialist advice on the construction of a retaining wall over 3ft (1m) high, for the footings and thickness of the wall, and hence the weight of earth that it retains, will vary enormously.

To relieve water buildup from behind a retaining wall, include weep holes at intervals of 6ft (2m) at its base, above ground level. These can take the form of gaps in the jointing, or a better method is a drain set through the wall and angled downwards. Backfill to the weep holes with rubble to facilitate drainage and to stop earth from escaping. A retaining wall will last longer if it is properly damp-proofed at the rear.

Concrete retaining wall, right
Built on concrete foundations, this wall has a coping of paving stones. The brick edge at the foot of the wall makes the mowing operation easier. Hollow concrete blocks inserted with reinforcement rods can be used to construct a stronger wall; fill the hollows with wet concrete before capping.

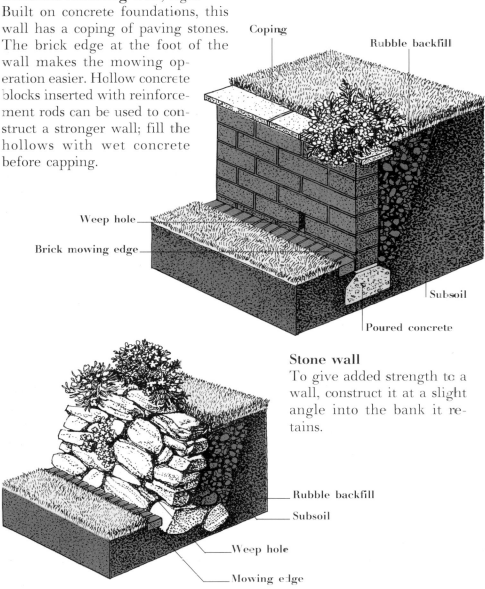

Coping

Rubble backfill

Weep hole

Brick mowing edge

Subsoil

Poured concrete

Stone wall
To give added strength to a wall, construct it at a slight angle into the bank it retains.

Rubble backfill

Subsoil

Weep hole

Mowing edge

FENCING

A fence is only as strong as the vertical posts that support it. The posts should preferably be made of direct-burial pressure-treated wood, which is guaranteed by the manufacturer to last for 30 years. The wood can be driven into the ground, set in stone, with a poured concrete collar, or fixed to one of the varieties of metal shoe, and anchored firmly in concrete; a concrete spur is equally effective. Set metal or concrete posts directly in concrete. Wooden fence posts will last longer if the tops are rounded to repel rainwater. Caps made of wood or sheet metal can also be fitted to the tops.

Metal fixings, bottom left
Fix the fence post to a metal shoe — such as a steel spike — and set this in concrete.

Concrete spur, bottom right
Bolt the post onto a concrete spur set in concrete.

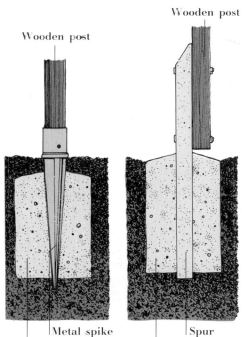

Wooden post

Wooden post

Metal spike

Concrete

Spur

Concrete

PERGOLAS

The construction of a pergola varies, depending on your chosen materials, and whether it is free-standing or supported on one or more sides by a wall. It is important to pay particular attention to detailing – for example, how the horizontals are joined to the verticals – as this influences the total look. A pergola needs strong and stable foundations. Use direct-burial pressure-treated wood, or fix each pergola vertical to a steel foot set in concrete, or a concrete spur (see previous page). Metal or concrete verticals can be set directly in concrete.

A simple pergola, below
This pergola is made from pressure-treated beams and scaffolding poles. The wooden horizontal is joined to the metal vertical by drilling a hole into the beam, to half its thickness, and inserting the pole. A metal joist

GATES

A gate takes heavy wear, so when constructing or buying one, make sure it is built to last. Sturdy piers – or side supports – to bear its weight are essential, as are hinges that are strong enough to prevent sagging; for extra strength always use three hinges instead of two. If large double entrance gates are not automatic, they are often very heavy to open and close. To relieve the load, fix a wheel and metal channel to work with the swing of each gate if your driveway is level.

shoe, attached to the supporting wall, holds the beam at its other end. The run of five beams is strengthened laterally with a metal tie. The vertical poles of the pergola rest in strong poured concrete foundations set below ground level.

Gate strength
The verticals of this tall wooden gate are supported by both horizontal and cross braces.

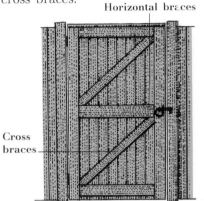

Horizontal braces

Cross braces

Metal joist shoe
The metal L-shaped shoe fits between the bricks and supports the wooden beam.

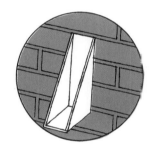

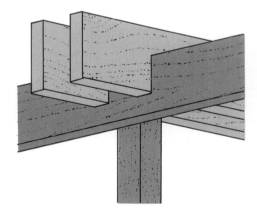

Wood to wood
A section has been cut out of the vertical to house the horizontal and the two are bolted together with corrosion-resistant fasteners.

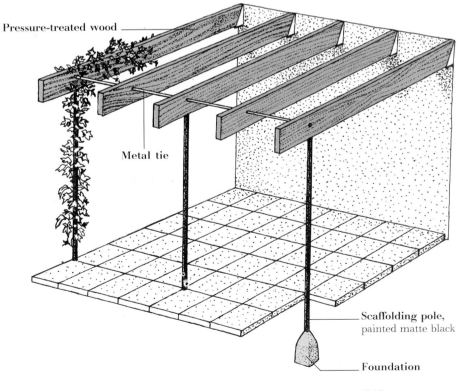

Pressure-treated wood

Metal tie

Scaffolding pole, painted matte black

Foundation

WATER

In small gardens, I prefer to contain water in a formal pool; a natural-looking informal pool just looks contrived where space is at a premium. Always seek expert advice if you are considering installing an electric water pump – unless it is a simple submersible type.

FORMAL WATER FEATURE

Waterproof concrete can be used to construct a formal pool. Include in the design an overflow pipe to prevent flooding and an outlet to a separate drainage field (see page 332) to allow for occasional cleaning. Where frost is light, use reinforced concrete and build the pool with sloping sides so that as the water freezes and turns into ice, it has room to expand. In colder areas you may need to empty the pool entirely to prevent frost damage. Pool copings should overhang the water by at least 2in (50mm) to hide any change in the water level due to evaporation, and conceal the green algae stains that inevitably occur where a surface meets the water.

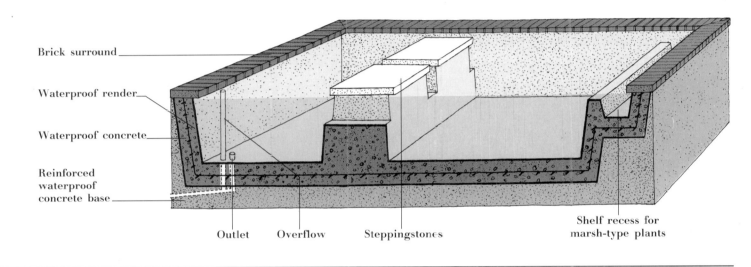

Brick surround

Waterproof render

Waterproof concrete

Reinforced waterproof concrete base

Outlet   Overflow   Steppingstones

Shelf recess for marsh-type plants

INFORMAL WATER FEATURE

Butyl rubber sheeting may be used for lining the larger area of an informal pool or equally can be tailored to fit a smaller formal pool. It will be laid on sand or a cushion sheet, and you will need to finish off the edge of the sheeting carefully. Two ways of doing this are shown below. On the left, the pool side has been dug out to make a shelf, and earth laid over the sheeting to hold it in place and create a boggy effect. At the edge of the shelf, a large stone has been set in mortar on the sheeting to stop the earth from slipping to the bottom of the pool. On the right, the end of the sheet is wrapped over a block retaining wall and covered by a coping.

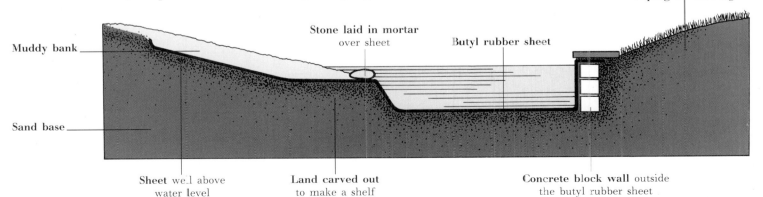

Grass level above coping for mowing

Muddy bank

Stone laid in mortar over sheet

Butyl rubber sheet

Sand base

Sheet well above water level

Land carved out to make a shelf

Concrete block wall outside the butyl rubber sheet

THE GARDEN DESIGN PRACTICE

There is an increasing number of people who feel that they would like to run some sort of garden design practice: a consultancy, a design-and-build firm, or just add design to an established horticultural business, and I would applaud their enthusiasm. Can I lay out some guidelines and point out a few traps along the way?

First of all, are you sufficiently competent to provide a service and charge for it? To a degree, competency has to do with experience, and we all have to start somewhere. But I firmly believe that a design training is important: this not only teaches a technique, but initiates a design philosophy which the individual should enhance by travel, reading, and generally learning to use his eyes.

Training

There are various methods of training, through landscape architectural studies, garden design schools, and practical experience in a landscape design office.

In the United States you have several levels of study open to you if you wish to follow a career in garden design. Several schools offer one- or two-year programs that culminate in a certificate of landscape design, while at certain universities you can earn a bachelor of landscape architecture with four years' study. With an additional three years of study, you may earn a master's of landscape architecture. At that point, in order to be qualified to work on public commissions (and, perhaps more importantly, to give yourself added protection in any possible future liability suits), you must take and pass your particular state's licensing test for landscape architects, much as a lawyer must take and pass the state bar examination in every state in which he or she plans to practice.

Landscape architecture is a profession whose spectrum of studies is very much wider than that of garden design, and it includes studies in geology, ecology, land reclamation, structural engineering, and urban planning, as well as studio practice, of which a tiny part is garden design. Landscape architects are often accused of not knowing their garden plants – why should they? Domestic horticulture has little to do with their concerns. There are, however, landscape architects who do specialize in that subject.

Short-term courses on garden design are given under the auspices of arboretums, botanical gardens, or institutions of continuing education. Indeed this book outlines the contents of my own course of five weeks' duration. But this is a small amount of time, no matter how intensive the course, in which to provide students in any horticultural or design field with enough expertise to start up on their own, without their clients paying for their lack of experience, or their paying for it in the form of liability suits when a retaining wall gives way or a water main is broken during earthworks.

Practical experience gained working with an established designer both in his studio and on site is always invaluable.

Selling Yourself

You may be the most amazing designer in the world, but sitting by the phone waiting for a commission will not get you far. You have to promote yourself. And once you have decided to work on your own, have a card printed stating on it who you are and what service you are offering.

You will discover that at any social occasion, when it is revealed that you have the remotest connection with horticulture, you are avalanched with people talking about the black spot on their roses, or giving you a verbal guide around what sounds like the most boring garden in the world. So, whip out your card and ask whether you might talk about this in the morning. Most people will move away – although probably the occasional one will say that you are just the person he has been seeking.

Always remember that no matter how reticent you feel about offering a design service to potential clients, they probably know less about the process than you, if you have had training (although they might well have design expertise in another field). To give potential clients confidence in yourself, if you do not yet have examples of new work completed, take along a portfolio of drawings of schemes, even magazine cuttings of gardens that you like, mounted in a scrapbook, and flip through these to get some discussion going about their garden. Many clients are not aware of the possibilities of their site, and are bogged down in its negative aspects. Remember that if a design looks too simple, the client will not feel it necessary to consult a garden designer to achieve it.

Present yourself in the manner in which you want to be taken. If you are acting as a glorified gardener, do not be surprised at being treated as one. If you want acceptance as a designer, present yourself in that light.

The Initial Consultation

The first discussion with the client is a bridge-building operation to establish mutual trust. It is advisable to make up a checklist of points to be covered, for there are many questions to be asked. The designer's job is that of a coordinator, working along the lines of a computer, and at this stage you are formulating your program.

On meeting a client for the first time, remember that should you be commissioned, and this results in the building of a garden, your client is allowing you to advise him on spending a huge amount of money. Therefore, it is as well to realize that while the designer is assessing his client, ultimately to the client's benefit, the client is also carefully sizing up the designer.

One of the most difficult areas to establish with the client in this initial contact is exactly what the scope of the designer's work will entail. It will vary from designer to designer, but a broad discussion can open up new vistas (sometimes literally) for a client, who may think that you are only interested in the design and not the planting or vice versa.

Assessing Each Other

If clients have never used a garden designer before, they will be unaware that you need to know so much about them. Are they formal or informal people, what are the number and ages of their children, and so on. I find that a study of the interior style of a client's house, such as the design of the furniture, the color schemes they have chosen, and the pictures on their walls, tells me a lot about them (curtains are particularly revealing). What might seem to the clients to be an unnecessary interest in the interior can of course be discussed with them. You can always mention the point that certain well-known architects actually stay with their clients before coming up with any basic design ideas!

From the clients' point of view, they want to be assured in this initial briefing that should your relationship come to fruition, you, the designer, are both responsible – they will seek to establish this from previous work – and able to handle their money sensibly in terms of payment to a landscape contractor who might build the garden.

Establishing a Preliminary Estimate for the Work

Part of the initial consultation will be to discuss money, both your fee (unless you have established this over the phone and confirmed it in writing) and the potential cost of the work. Pricing the work often disturbs the new designer. Ask local landscape contractors for the costs of laying a square yard of brickwork, as opposed to a square yard of stone; then the price for preparing a tree hole, planting a tree, and staking it. Get a square yard rate for ground preparation and another for planting. Get a rate for seeding a lawn, and for turfing, or sodding. From these figures you can build up a preliminary estimate. At an early stage always state that pricing "will be in the region of," keeping the subject very broad both at the initial consultation and until you at least have some form of schematic design on paper and can estimate costs more accurately. Remember that a local garden contractor or garden center is there to help you as a designer – seek their advice and tell them why. Clients will come and go for both of you, but a working relationship with a contractor can be permanent.

Personal Differences

At this stage, I would say to the designer that should you not feel happy with your prospective client for whatever reason, do not proceed. Suddenly you have a huge workload, are taken ill – invent any excuse. On the bread line you might be, but nothing is worse than doing a job you do not like for people with whom you are not in sympathy.

Another aspect of this is if you are asked to produce a design to surround a house, or an addition to a previous designer's work, which you do not like. Providing you like the client, I would take the work on and do what is asked of you in the new idiom, merely seeing it as an exercise in that idiom. It is all good experience.

Do not work for friends if you want to keep them, and avoid getting on too friendly terms with your clients until the bills are paid. The nicest potential client may become a monster when later asked to part with money. Those with wealth have not usually amassed it by giving it away!

Conversely for a client, if you do not like a designer whom you have interviewed, tell him nicely that unfortunately his style is not yours, and all will be well. You can spare yourself this embarrassment by checking out different designers' work through illustrations, personal inquiry, and asking to see their previous jobs. A new designer will have to rely on presentation drawings.

When to Charge

The following list details the occasions and drawings for which you might charge. There is really no reason why you should do anything for anyone else without charging – your practice is not a charitable institution.

The consultation. Visits of advice should be charged for on an hourly basis. Travelling time and any expenses incurred should also be included: gas, parking, tolls, and so on. However, there are times when it might be good public relations not to charge directly for the first consultation. The cost can be spread over the subsequent work that arises from it, and you can inform your client at the outset that this is your practice.

Schematic plan. This is a drawing which sets out your broad proposals for the site and situation. It is a plan to be argued over with the client and changed if necessary. The proposal might include sketches and a projection; this will depend upon the site. Ideally, if you cannot present the plan in person to your client, it should be accompanied by a typed report.

Structural plan. Based on the decisions arising from your schematic plan, this constructional drawing tells whoever is to build the garden how to do so. It too may need greater explanation on a larger scale with a three-dimensional projection, and with sections or elevations.

Other construction plans. A separate plan showing landscaping may be included if you are altering the site topography with contours and elevations. There may also need to be an irrigation plan and a plan for the electrical wiring, perhaps produced by subcontractors. Add to this the swimming pool and the tennis court detail where necessary.

Planting plan. This should be separate from the structural plan. For a start, it might need to be on a different scale, but usually the work is completed by quite a different team, one that is not interested in such things as drainage fields.

Your planting plan should either have on it, or be accompanied by, a plant list. Plants should be designated with their full Latin names and any cultivar name. State the size and number of plants you require and, with trees, specify whether they are standard, dwarf, of feathered form, and so on.

I prefer to write plants' names by the plants on the plan. I find a cross-reference to a number in the margin irritating. Try checking someone else's planting plan rendered this way to understand their intention. Worse still, try to plant from it one wet November day. Drawings are intended to be read on site by an individual who only has your drawing to tell him exactly what to do.

Written specifications. To obtain a price from a landscape contractor for the detailed construction work on the site, you will need to accompany the working drawings with written specifications. This typed document lists each component of the job in chronological order, and might be specific on items that your plan cannot cover, such as clearing the site, dumping topsoil, and the type of tree supports, although it also substantiates and expands what you have on plan, for example, the type of paving and the depth of the foundations. Standard works on landscape specifications are available.

Detailed specifications to a standard format are particularly important when you are involved in any public work, and is preferable for all jobs for which you are bidding. Since the specifications are itemized, it can also be costed along the same lines for easier assimilation by your client.

While this procedure might seem weighty, it ensures that you get exactly what you want on site with no gray areas. You may well be working in association with an architect, a builder, and a site engineer, as well as a landscape contractor. They are all used to operating in this specific way.

Charging the Client

I have no intention of advising on fees, for what is feasible changes so. At the end of the day, ask yourself: "If I received that drawing, would I be happy to pay what I am asking for it?" Remember that clients only see what is on paper – they do not know the hours that you have spent to get it there. Many clients will be professional or business people who make a living from offering a service, so ensure that the service *you* offer appears to be on a par with what they do; better still, let that be the case.

It is up to you to decide how you will charge. The preparation of drawings

might be on a similar hourly scale to that of consultation, or you may agree upon a lump sum at the outset. Where you are generally running a job, preparing working details, certifying the bills, and so on, secure a fee that represents a percentage of the completed price of constructing the job.

When you need to call in a specialist, such as a landscape contractor, a surveyor, or an irrigation expert, always confirm their fee with your client in writing, and let the client sign the contract with them. Never sign it yourself.

For those approaching garden design, but with a commercial foot in either horticulture or landscape construction, my advice is to try to run the various aspects of the business side by side, but keep separate accounts.

Since personal recommendation is by far the best way to business success, I believe that you should complete a job with a client saying, "Well, they weren't exactly cheap, but we got a wonderful garden," rather than, "Well, we got a nice garden, but, lord, could they charge!"

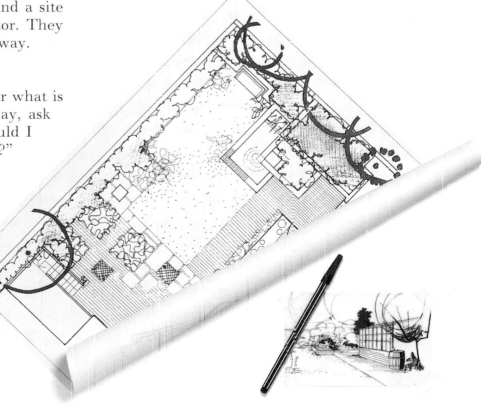

INDEX

ACKNOWLEDGMENTS

Author's acknowledgments
My own personal journey into garden design has been punctuated and conditioned by many to whom I am lastingly grateful.

My professor was Peter Youngman P.P.I.L.A.; as a fledgling I worked for Sylvia Crowe, now Dame Sylvia Crowe, in whose office I learned much, particularly her fluidity of line and thought when evolving a design. When I then chose a somewhat unorthodox path through journalism, Geoffrey Jellicoe, now Sir Geoffrey Jellicoe, was unfailingly supportive. It is perhaps only in retrospect that one appreciates these great influences.

More current acknowledgments must go to all my students, from whom I learn just as much as I ever impart – they might think on that! And of course to all the others who currently work with me. Friends in contracting have been enormously supportive in making my gardens, without my having to cross every t and dot every i. I would acknowledge also my associate, Michael Neve, and my assistant, Michael Zinn.

We would all join in thanking Carole Dickens, my secretary, for her untiring skills.

Lastly I thank the staff at Dorling Kindersley – my editor, Sarah Pearce, and art editor, Carole Ash, who have remained cool and calm throughout the often frenetic time schedule that was imposed upon them in the preparation of such a book.

Publisher's acknowledgments
Macmillan would like to thank Jeff and Liz Ball for their assistance on lawns, John Elsley for his horticultural expertise, Gene and Katie Hamilton for their help on matters constructional, Peter Loewer for his lighting knowledge, and James van Sweden and Perry Guillot for their inestimable landscaping and design expertise.

We extend special thanks to Kathryn Bradley-Hole for the Plant Catalogue and Susan Berry for Planting Solutions.

DTP
Peter Cooling; Sharon Lunn

(T=top, B=bottom, M=middle, L=left, R=right)

Location photography by Steven Wooster
1-3, 6, 7, 8-9, 10, 11, 13, 24-7, 38-9, 41TL, 43L, 43BR, 45B, 46T, 47, 57, 59BR, 62TR, 63, 70-1, 77TR, 77BL, 85TR, 97M, 98-9, 100L, 100ML, 100MR, 101L, 101TR, 101BR, 102L, 104T, 104R, 106-9, 110TL, 110R, 112-22, 124-7, 128, 130-1, 132, 134-43, 146TL, 146TR, 156-79, 184-97, 200-13, 217MT, 217MR, 219BR, 221M, 222L, 225TL, 226TL, 228, 229, 231, 232, 233M, 238, 239B, 243TR, 244-6, 250-1, 253, 258-9, 260M, 260R, 261, 262TL, 262TR, 263, 264L, 265TL, 265TR, 266TL, 266TM, 266TR, 267, 268T, 269TL, 269TM, 269TR, 271R, 272TL, 274T, 274BL, 275TL, 275TR, 277R, 277ML, 278TL, 278BL, 279R, 280TR, 280BL, 282T, 282BL, 282TR, 282MM, 283T, 286BR, 287TM, 287BM, 290TR, 291TR, 292T, 292BMR, 293TL, 293TR, 296BR, 299TR, 300TM, 300TR, 301ML, 302TR, 303TR, 303TML, 304TR, 304BML, 305BR, 305BL, 311BM, 312BL, 313ML, 313MR, 314BR, 315TR, 317TR, 319TL, 320.

Studio photography
Geoff Dann: 5, 103BR, 105BR, 107BR, 109BL, 111BR, 113BR, 167BL, 280, 284, 286L, 291B, 293BR, 297MR, 298TL, 299TL, 300L, 302R, 305TR, 309BR, 310M, 313BL, 314TL, 315TL, 316L, 326TL; Steve Gorton: 223BR; Dave King assisted by Jonathan Buckley: 72, 74-5, 77BR, 78-9, 81BR, 82-3, 85BL, 86-7, 89BR, 90-91, 93BR, 94-5, 93BR, 97BR; Tim Ridley: 40T, 42, 48, 49, 52-5, 58, 59TL, 59TR, 60-61, 62, 63, 152, 153BR, 154T, 156BR, 157TL, 216, 217TL, 217TR, 217M, 217BL, 218, 219TL, 219ML, 219B, 220L, 221TR, 221MR, 221B, 224, 225TR, 225B, 226BR, 227, 229 group BR, 237B, 240BR, 240BML, 240BMR, 241R, 254, 255B, 256, 257B, 294L, 306BL, 310L, 319BR, 324, 325, 326M group; Tim Ridley/Steve Gorton: 234B, 235, 236.

Illustrations
David Ashby: 56, 58, 64L, 66T, 68L, 114, 115, 124BL, 126, 129, 130, 137B; John Brookes: 40-41, 44-47, 48, 49, 64TR, 65TR, 65BL, 66BL, 68M, 116-17, 123, 131, 135, 137T, 158T, 260, 324-31; Val Hill: 42L, 43TR, 64BR, 65TL, 65BR, 66BR, 67, 68R, 69; Sandra Pond: 280, 284, 288; Sarah Ponder: 262, 263, 264, 265, 267, 322-3, and all planting plans in Part 8 excluding those listed above.
All plans supplied by John Brookes, except: Oehme, van Sweden & Associates 198-9; Steve Martino & Associates 220BR; Henk Weijers 184-5, 202-3, 225ML; James Kellogg Wheat 182-3.

Styling
Hilary Guy, Part Three; Victoria Wood, Part Seven.

Props
Construction: Andy Kirkby. Loan: Jamie Andrews (sculptor) for the blue sculpture on p. 79; Blanc de Bierges; British Gates & Timber Ltd; The Chelsea Gardener; Clifton Nurseries; Dulwich Garden Centre; ☘ ECC Building Products Ltd, London (Bradstone, Swindon, Wilts.; Countryside, Swindon, Wilts.); Fired Earth; Highgate Garden Centre; J & B Art Metal; Jacksons Fine Fencing; Knollys Nurseries; Landscape Management Construction; Patio; Redland Bricks Ltd; Townsends Salvage Ltd.

Picture research
Joanne King; Shona Wood.

Photography credits
Dorling Kindersley would like to thank the following for their permission to reproduce material.
ARCAID/Richard Bryant: 81BL, 88, 89L; Kathryn Bradley-Hole, Gardenart Press: 290LM, 294BL, 294BR, 299MM, 301MM, 305TM, 306BR, 307BMR, 314BM, 315MM; Kenneth A. Beckett: 290MR; Brinsley Burbidge: 31R; The Bridgeman Art Library: 22M; John Brookes: 16BL, 32-3, 62B, 63, 93T, 157TR, 234, 240T, 242B, 243L, 247BL, 252T, 255TR; Geoff Dann: 214, 215, 326T; Elizabeth Whiting Associates: 12; ET Archive: 18T; The Garden Picture Library: 276TL; /John Neubauer: 29BR, 30-31M, 44-45M, 46T, 81T, 103R, 105M, 198, 199TR, 199BR, 243TR; /Jerry Pavia: 34-5M, 35R, 133R; 233T; /Joanne Pavia: 123BR, 272BL, 272BM; /Gary Rogers: 62TL, 92, 100R, 249; /Ron Sutherland: 80, 96, 218BR, 222R, 223, 241TL, 247BR, 270T;

/Steven Wooster: 260L; /Kate Zari: 36-7M, 37R; By permission of the Earl of Harewood: 20-21M; Jerry Harpur: 22BR, 24R, 84, 93BL; Michael Holford: 16R, 17; /Janet Chapman: 97T; /Gerry Clyde: 16-17M; Georges Lévêque: 73; The Mansell Collection: 18-19M, 19R; Michael McKinley: 28-29M, 199TL; The National Trust: 20L; Hugh Palmer: 102R, 104BL; Jerry Pavia: 110BL, 129TR, 180-3, 188, 189, 190-91, 220MR, 233T; Philippe Perdereau: 14, 24, 219TR, 230, 237T, 239T, 240BL, 252B, 257TR, 276TR; Photos Horticultural: 76; Photo Lamontagne: 85M, 89TR; George Waters: 15, 23.
Plant portraits in Part 8 except those listed above are by Eric Crichton, John Glover, Jerry Harpur, Andrew Lawson, Andrew de Lory, with Neil Holmes, Jacqui Hurst.

Steven Wooster would like to thank:
Mr and Mrs P. Aldington; Mr and Mrs T. W. Bigge; Mr and Mrs M. B. Caröe; Lord and Lady Carrington; Mr and Mrs N. Coote; Mrs J.E.M. Cowley and Mr D. Bracey; Jackie Douglas; Mr and Mrs Dresher; Mrs du Boulay; The Lady Fitzwalter; Mr and Mrs Foulsham; Mr and Mrs Gourlay; Mr and Mrs Hampton; Mr and Mrs Hobart; Mr and Mrs P. Holland; The Edward James Foundation; Hugh and Judy Johnson; Mr and Mrs King; Nick Lawrence at Landscape Management Construction; Peter and Pam Lewis; Mr and Mrs J. R. McCutchan; Mrs Maverty; Mr and Mrs Milward; The National Trust; Mr and Mrs Newmark; Mr and Mrs D. B. Nicholson; Mr and Mrs O'Hea; Mrs Overy; Michael Polhill; Werner Seehof; Mr and Mrs Slocock; Dolph Sweerts; Mr and Mrs Van Os; Mr and Mrs Wates; Mr and Mrs Watts; Wisley Gardens. He would especially like to thank the following: Mylles Challis; Beth Chatto; Anthony Paul; The Hannah Peschar Sculpture Gallery (100MR, 250, 251R); Martin Puddle of Bodnant Gardens; Mien Ruys; Rosemary Verey; Henk Weijers.

Garden designers (where known)
John Brookes: 1, 6, 7, 10, 13, 24, 43, 57, 59BR, 77TR, 98-9, 100L, 100ML, 101BR, 104T, 106L, 106R, 108L, 108R, 115, 118-9, 120, 121, 122, 124, 127R, 130, 134-5, 136-7, 139, 142-3, 166-79, 186-97, 204-9, 210-11, 212T, 212 group T, 217MR, 219BR, 221M, 226TL, 229BR, 231TL, 231TR, 244, 245BL, 246L, 258-9, 260R, 262TR, 263, 264L, 266TL, 267, 268T, 269TR, 272TL, 274T, 275TR; Roberto Burle Marx: 15; Beth Chatto: 112L, 113R; G. P. Crowther & Associates: 243TR; Santi Diaz: 37R; Paul Flinton: 96; Brian Huxham: 218BR; Steve Martino & Associates: 30R, 220MR; Oehme, van Sweden & Associates: 12, 28-29M, 29BR, 44-45M, 81T, 198, 199TR, 199BR, 199TL; Anthony Paul: 70-1, 97M, 100MR, 222L, 231BR, 246R, 250, 265TR; Mien Ruys: 41TL, 47TL, 62TR, 63, 126R, 131, 140, 229M, 245BR, 260M; Max Thomas: 222R, 223; Rosemary Verey: 132; Henk Weijers: 25R, 101L, 101TR, 104R, 184-5, 200-3, 225TR, 261.